Welfare in Rural Areas

Brookings Studies in
SOCIAL EXPERIMENTATION

TITLES PUBLISHED

Educational Performance Contracting:
An Evaluation of an Experiment
Edward M. Gramlich and Patricia P. Koshel

Work Incentives and Income Guarantees:
The New Jersey Negative Income Tax Experiment
Joseph A. Pechman and P. Michael Timpane, Editors

Planned Variation in Education: Should We Give Up
or Try Harder?
Alice M. Rivlin and P. Michael Timpane, Editors

Ethical and Legal Issues of Social Experimentation
Alice M. Rivlin and P. Michael Timpane, Editors

Welfare in Rural Areas: The North Carolina–Iowa
Income Maintenance Experiment
John L. Palmer and Joseph A. Pechman, Editors

Editors: JOHN L. PALMER

JOSEPH A. PECHMAN

Welfare in Rural Areas: The North Carolina-Iowa Income Maintenance Experiment

Contributors: Larry L. Orr

D. Lee Bawden and William S. Harrar

Harold W. Watts and D. Lee Bawden

Finis Welch

Orley Ashenfelter

Robert T. Michael

Michael T. Hannan

G. Edward Schuh

Marvin M. Smith

The Brookings Institution
Washington, D.C.

Library of Congress Cataloging in Publication Data:

Main entry under title:
Welfare in rural areas.

   (Brookings studies in social experimentation)
   Papers presented at a conference held at the
   Brookings Institution, Washington, D.C.,
   January 13 and 14, 1977.
   Includes bibliographical references and index.
   1. Income maintenance programs—North Carolina
—Congresses. 2. Income maintenance programs—
Iowa—Congresses. I. Palmer, John Logan.
II. Pechman, Joseph A., 1918– III. Series:
Brookings Institution, Washington, D.C.
Brookings studies in social experimentation.
HC110.I5W44   362.5   77-91826
ISBN 0-8157-6896-6
ISBN 0-8157-6895-8 pbk.

9 8 7 6 5 4 3 2 1

THE BROOKINGS INSTITUTION is an independent organization devoted to nonpartisan research, education, and publication in economics, government, foreign policy, and the social sciences generally. Its principal purposes are to aid in the development of sound public policies and to promote public understanding of issues of national importance.

The Institution was founded on December 8, 1927, to merge the activities of the Institute for Government Research, founded in 1916, the Institute of Economics, founded in 1922, and the Robert Brookings Graduate School of Economics and Government, founded in 1924.

The Board of Trustees is responsible for the general administration of the Institution, while the immediate direction of the policies, program, and staff is vested in the President, assisted by an advisory committee of the officers and staff. The by-laws of the Institution state: "It is the function of the Trustees to make possible the conduct of scientific research, and publication, under the most favorable conditions, and to safeguard the independence of the research staff in the pursuit of their studies and in the publication of the results of such studies. It is not a part of their function to determine, control, or influence the conduct of particular investigations or the conclusions reached."

The President bears final responsibility for the decision to publish a manuscript as a Brookings book. In reaching his judgment on the competence, accuracy, and objectivity of each study, the President is advised by the director of the appropriate research program and weighs the views of a panel of expert outside readers who report to him in confidence on the quality of the work. Publication of a work signifies that it is deemed a competent treatment worthy of public consideration but does not imply endorsement of conclusions or recommendations.

The Institution maintains its position of neutrality on issues of public policy in order to safeguard the intellectual freedom of the staff. Hence interpretations or conclusions in Brookings publications should be understood to be solely those of the authors and should not be attributed to the Institution, to its trustees, officers, or other staff members, or to the organizations that support its research.

Foreword

In the mid-1960s dissatisfaction with the inequities and inefficiencies of public assistance programs became widespread. Benefits varied greatly among the states, and over half the nation's poor received no assistance whatever. The single largest group excluded, then as now, was the so-called working poor—families with two able-bodied parents. Except for the meagerly funded and restrictive AFDC-UP (aid to families with dependent children–unemployed parents) program in about half the states, families of the working poor were ineligible for cash assistance even though more than 40 percent of all poor people lived—and still live—in such households. One result was that social reformers and government officials became interested in the negative income tax—an income maintenance system that would provide income supplements to all poor families, with benefits scaled to need. A universal negative income tax was attractive to many because it would provide comprehensive coverage, uniform benefits among states, administrative simplicity, and efficient targeting on the poor.

President Richard M. Nixon proposed a negative income tax scheme in 1970. Congress approved the portion of it applicable to the aged, blind, and disabled, but disapproved the portion applicable to families. One of the principal objections to the adoption of a negative income tax for families—and, indeed, one of the principal reasons for the long-standing exclusion of the working poor from the welfare system—was the belief that extension of cash assistance to the working poor would greatly discourage work effort and thereby promote continued dependency. Moreover, critics argued that if the working poor did reduce their work effort in response to cash payments, the cost of the program might become excessive; government payments, in effect, would subsidize leisure.

To test the importance of this and other effects of cash assistance on the behavior of low-income families, the Office of Economic Opportunity and

vii

the Department of Health, Education, and Welfare began a series of controlled experiments in 1967. In each experiment, sample low-income families were randomly assigned either to one of the several different income-conditioned transfer programs or to a control group, and the behavior of all families in the sample was carefully monitored over several years. Statistical analysis of the data from these experiments allows direct estimation of the labor supply response of families receiving payments in relation to that of the control families.

The results of the first of these experiments, in urban areas of New Jersey and Pennsylvania, were reviewed and evaluated in a 1975 Brookings book, *Work Incentives and Income Guarantees,* edited by Joseph A. Pechman and P. Michael Timpane. The present volume reviews the results of a rural income maintenance experiment conducted in Iowa and North Carolina. Both these experiments were conducted by the Institute for Research on Poverty of the University of Wisconsin. Other organizations are now analyzing the results of experiments in Gary, Seattle, and Denver.

The papers in this volume and the comments on them were originally prepared for a conference of economists, sociologists, political scientists, and research administrators, held at the Brookings Institution on January 13 and 14, 1977. The editors, John L. Palmer and Joseph A. Pechman, are, respectively, senior fellow in and director of the Brookings Economic Studies program.

This is the fifth book in the Brookings series of Studies in Social Experimentation. The series, which was supported by a grant from the Edna McConnell Clark Foundation, assesses the usefulness of experiments as a way of increasing knowledge about the effects of domestic social policies and programs of the federal government. A Ford Foundation grant also supported, in part, the research upon which this book is based.

The editors and contributors acknowledge the assistance of Frances Glennon, who prepared the volume for publication, and of Evelyn P. Fisher, who verified its factual content.

The views expressed here are those of the contributors, and should not be ascribed to the Edna McConnell Clark Foundation, to the Ford Foundation, or to the staff members, officers, or trustees of the Brookings Institution.

BRUCE K. MAC LAURY
President

March 1978
Washington, D.C.

Contents

Larry L. Orr
An Overview   1

Design and Methodology *3*
Validity and Interpretation of Findings *5*
Behavioral Responses to the Experiment *6*
Administration of a Negative Income Tax in
  Rural Areas *20*
Summary *21*

D. Lee Bawden and William S. Harrar
Design and Operation   23

Design of the Experiment *23*
Operation of the Experiment *34*
Lessons for Administration of a National Program *41*
Comment by David N. Kershaw *46*
Comment by Robert G. Spiegelman *52*

Harold W. Watts and D. Lee Bawden
Issues and Lessons of Experimental Design   55

Evaluation of Critical Choices in Design *56*
Surprises and Other Lapses from Omniscience *63*
Additional Afterthoughts *67*
Comment by Irwin Garfinkel *68*
Comment by Charles E. Metcalf *71*

Finis Welch
The Labor Supply Response of Farmers   77

What Does Theory Predict? *78*
How Should Effects Be Estimated? *80*
What the Data Show *83*
Accounting Rules and the Games Farmers Play *87*

ix

What Do the Data Show about Income Flows and
    Reporting? *90*
Conclusion *99*
Comment by Michael J. Boskin *100*
Comment by Luther G. Tweeten *104*

Orley Ashenfelter
The Labor Supply Response of Wage Earners   109
What Is the Theoretical Framework? *110*
What Were the Expected Results? *117*
What Were the Actual Results? *120*
Estimating Tax Rate and Guarantee Effects *125*
Conclusion *129*
Appendix A: Conventional Theory of Labor Supply
    and Its Implications for a Negative Income Tax
    Program *131*
Appendix B: A Simplified Analysis of Tax Evasion
    Possibilities in the Negative Income Tax
    Experiment *137*
Comment by James J. Heckman *138*
Comment by Michael J. Boskin *147*

Robert T. Michael
The Consumption Studies   149
What Might Be Learned? *150*
Channels through Which Income Maintenance
    Might Affect Consumer Behavior *153*
Findings from the Studies *156*
An Assessment *162*
Appendix A: Description and Discussion of the
    Research Papers on Consumption Behavior *165*
Comment by Stanley H. Masters *171*
Comment by Robinson G. Hollister *173*

Michael T. Hannan
Noneconomic Outcomes   183
Rationale for Studying Noneconomic Outcomes *183*
Experimental Impacts: An Overview *186*
Experimental Impacts: A Closer Look *189*
Conclusion *203*
Comment by Robert J. Lampman *206*
Comment by Aaǧe B. Sørensen *208*

G. Edward Schuh
Policy and Research Implications   211

Causes of Poverty in Agriculture *211*
The Policy Issues *213*
Research Suggestions *233*
Some Concluding Thoughts *236*
Comment by James T. Bonnen *236*

Marvin M. Smith
Summary of Conference Discussion   243

Experimental Design: A Retrospective View *243*
Farmers' Labor Supply Response *249*
Wage Earners' Labor Supply Response *255*
Other Behavioral Responses *259*
Overview and Policy Implications *262*

Conference Participants   267

Index   269

Tables

Larry L. Orr

1. Average Annual Income and Payment, Nonaged Husband-Wife Families, by Site, over Course of the Rural Income Maintenance Experiment, 1970–72   4
2. Effect of Rural Income Maintenance Experiment on Income and Work Responses of Nonaged Husband-Wife Wage Earner Families, by Site   8
3. Effect of Rural Income Maintenance Experiment on Farm Operators' and Wives' Labor Supply, by Site   12
4. Long-run Response of Assets and Debts to a Negative Income Tax, by Families of Wage Earners and Farmers   15
5. Effect on School Performance of the Rural Income Maintenance Experiment, by Site   19

D. Lee Bawden and William S. Harrar

1. Regional and Target County Characteristics of the Rural Population in Final Areas Considered for the Rural Income Maintenance Experiment, 1970   27
2. Number of Heads of Households by Change in Marital Status, by Sex of Head and Quarter of Experiment, 1970–72   32

3. Characteristics of Family Units Present in Quarter 13 of the Rural Income Maintenance Experiment 35

Finis Welch

1. Number of Farm Families in the Rural Income Maintenance Experiment, by Group 84
2. Average Hours Worked on and off Farms and Net Farm Income for Experimental and Control Operations, 1970–72 86
3. Average Benefit Payments under Alternative Farm Income Definitions 93
4. Estimates of Contribution of Income Components to Tax Liability 98

Orley Ashenfelter

1. Values of the Ratio of the Income below Which Families Choose to Participate to the Breakeven Income in a Negative Income Tax Program, by Various Elasticities and Tax Rates 112
2. Expected Percentage Decline in Wage Income of Families Initially below the Breakeven Level and Offered a Negative Income Tax Program 118
3. Annual Average Wage Income of the Family, Husbands, and Wives of Control and Experimental Groups in the Year before Enrollment and the Three Years of the Rural Income Maintenance Experiment 121
4. Difference-in-Means Estimates of the Effect of Participation in the Rural Income Maintenance Experiment on Wage Income of the Family, Husbands, and Wives, by Year 122
5. Comparison of Difference-in-Means and Regression Estimates of the Effect of Participation in the Rural Income Maintenance Experiment on Income of the Family, Husbands, and Wives, Three-Year Average 123
6. Alternative Schemes for Estimating Tax and Guarantee Level Effects on Wage Earnings in an Income Maintenance Program 127

Robert T. Michael

1. Additional Clothing Expenditures from a $500 Increase in Each of Three Sources of Income, by Wage and Nonwage Earners 159
2. Mean Values of Selected Durables, Debts, and Assets Held by Households in the Rural Income Maintenance Experiment, 1970–72 160
3. Long-run Effects of $1.00 of Additional Income on Holdings of Durables, Assets, and Debts of Wage-working Households, by Source of Income 161

4. Estimates of Marginal Propensities to Consume, Families in the New Jersey and Rural Experiments, by Race, Selected Consumption Items   181

Michael T. Hannan

1. Impact of the Rural Income Maintenance Experiment on Marital Dissolution, by Tax and Guarantee Levels   191

Figure

Finis Welch

1. Labor Supply as a Function of the Net Wage Rate   103

LARRY L. ORR

An Overview

The rural income maintenance experiment is the second of four major experiments to test the consequences of a universal income-conditioned cash transfer program. Its uniqueness lies in its focus on the rural sector. The New Jersey experiment yielded a great deal of information about the effect of various negative income tax plans on behavioral and attitudinal characteristics of urban wage earners.[1] But these results were not expected to be directly applicable to the rural sector, in which over one-third of the nation's poor reside. Differences in the work responses of rural and urban residents to such a program were expected because of differences in alternative employment opportunities and in the proportion of self-employed people. An accurate estimate of the size of any work disincentive, both rural and urban, was necessary to estimate the cost of a nationwide program.

Also, it seemed likely that there would be some features in a program designed for addressing urban poverty problems that were not suited for rural poverty. For example, a large number of rural residents with low incomes are operators of farms or businesses in small towns. Determination of annual income as well as the appropriate timing of payments are

The author is heavily indebted to the principal authors of the Health, Education, and Welfare Summary Report on the rural income maintenance experiment, D. Lee Bawden, William S. Harrar, and Stuart H. Kerachsky, and Florence Setzer, as well as to the authors of the other papers prepared for this volume, and to the researchers of the rural experiment staff. The author is solely responsible for the characterizations and interpretations of the studies discussed here.

1. The results of this experiment were reviewed and evaluated in Joseph A. Pechman and P. Michael Timpane, eds., *Work Incentives and Income Guarantees: The New Jersey Negative Income Tax Experiment* (Brookings Institution, 1975). Results from the remaining two experiments in Gary, Indiana, and Seattle-Denver are not yet available.

1

different for the self-employed than for wage earners. This is especially true for those farmers who receive their entire annual income at harvest time. The provisions for self-employed individuals in the New Jersey experiment were admittedly simple and probably inadequate for a nationwide comprehensive negative income tax program.

The New Jersey experiment restricted eligibility to families of two or more members, with an able-bodied male head between the ages of eighteen and fifty-eight. Since a large number of poor households are headed by females of working age, a study of their work behavior was considered desirable by the Office of Economic Opportunity (which funded the project). The second major category excluded from the New Jersey experiment was composed of those of retirement age. Men and women sixty-five years of age and over made up 16 percent of the poor people, and headed about one-third of the poor households, in the United States. While the work incentive issue was less significant for this group, it was nevertheless considered important.[2]

The need for experimentation in a rural setting in conjunction with the urban experiment in New Jersey led to a planning grant from the Ford Foundation to the Institute for Research on Poverty at the University of Wisconsin. Under the grant Poverty Institute staff members representing the disciplines of economics, agricultural economics, sociology, political science, law, and social work joined in an interdisciplinary effort to design the rural experiment. The experiment was patterned after the one in New Jersey: it had the same basic objectives, a similar experimental design, and identical duration. It differed from the urban experiment in that it extended eligibility to single households as well as to those headed by females and the aged. Minor variations also existed in the definition of earned income and in the accounting period for determining income and payments due.

Subsequent papers in this volume provide a detailed review and critique of the design, operation, and findings of the experiment. In this paper the purpose is to present a broad overview.

2. The female-headed portion of the sample, numbering 108 (less than fifty-eight years of age) added breadth to such studies as those of nutrition, health, and children's school performance, but by itself was too small to provide a comprehensive answer to the question of the negative income tax effect on the labor supply of female heads. The same may be said of the older heads (114 at enrollment) and the impact of the negative income tax on retirement decisions. Policymakers must await the results of other experiments to gain meaningful insight into these issues.

Design and Methodology

The rural experiment was conducted over the three-year period 1970–72 in rural counties of Iowa and North Carolina. The experimental sites were purposively selected to be representative of five states in the South and three in the Midwest that contain about one-third of the U.S. rural poverty population. All participating families in the Iowa sample were white; in North Carolina the sample was about evenly divided between black and white families.

The experimental treatments included five different negative income tax plans, each characterized by a basic benefit, or guarantee, and a benefit reduction, or tax, rate.[3] Guarantees ranged from 50 to 100 percent of the poverty line, and tax rates ranged from 30 to 70 percent. In addition, a control group that received no payments, but was interviewed periodically along with the treatment groups, was also enrolled.

A total of 809 families was initially enrolled; of that number, 729 remained enrolled for the entire three years of the experiment. Families were selected randomly within the experimental sites and eligible families were randomly assigned to treatment plans and the control group. To be eligible for selection, families were required to have incomes in the year prior to the experiment that were less than 150 percent of the official poverty line. Selections were stratified by family type to obtain subsamples of 587 intact nonaged husband-wife families, 108 families with female heads, and 114 families with an aged head. The results reported here are primarily for the husband-wife subsample. The initial allocation of the 269 families in the experimental group among the five treatment plans is shown in the following tabulation:

Guarantee (percent of poverty line)	Tax rate (percent)		
	30	50	70
50	. . .	37	. . .
75	67	75	30
100	. . .	60	. . .

There were 318 families in the control group.

3. The guarantee is the benefit that would be received by a family with no other income; the tax rate is the rate at which benefits are reduced as other income rises.

Table 1. Average Annual Income and Payment, Nonaged Husband-Wife Families, by Site, over Course of the Rural Income Maintenance Experiment, 1970–72
Dollars

| Type of income | Wage earners | | | Farmers | |
| | North Carolina | | | North Carolina | Iowa |
	Black	White	Iowa		
Total income[a]	5,692	5,544	7,364	5,649	5,676
Wage income[a]	5,460	5,280	6,568	3,260	931
Net farm income[a]	...	...	...	2,615	4,882
Negative income tax payments	1,574	1,560	1,343	1,723	1,534

Sources: Wage earner income data are from U.S. Department of Health, Education, and Welfare, "The Rural Income Maintenance Experiment: Summary Report" (HEW, November 1976; processed), p. 18; wage earner negative income tax payments are from the files of the Institute for Research on Poverty; other data are from Wendell E. Primus, "Farm Work Response of Farm Operators," in D. Lee Bawden and William S. Harrar, eds., *Rural Income Maintenance Experiment: Final Report* (University of Wisconsin–Madison, Institute for Research on Poverty, 1976), vol. 4, chap. 1, pp. 63, 66.
a. Control group mean.

Payments were made biweekly on the basis of monthly reports of income and family size filed by the families. For the self-employed, income was defined net of business expenses. Average family income and experimental payments over the course of the experiment for various subgroups of the nonaged husband-wife sample are shown in table 1.

In addition to the income reports, interviews were conducted quarterly with household members fifteen years of age and over to gather attitudinal and behavioral data. Information was also gathered from schools and other public organizations.

The effects of the experimental treatments were estimated through regression analysis.[4] A number of different outcome variables (as measured by the quarterly interviews) were analyzed as dependent variables. In each case, a set of control variables, such as age, education, and family size, was entered to standardize for any nonexperimental differences among the treatment groups. In most cases, the preexperimental value of the dependent variable was also included as a control variable, both to account for any preexperimental differences among treatment groups in the level of response and to improve the precision of the estimates of experimental effects.

4. The estimation technique was an error components pooling method. Quarterly observations were pooled for wage earners, and annual observations pooled for farmers.

The experimental treatments themselves were characterized with a set of three independent variables denoting whether the family was in a treatment or control group and the levels of the guarantee and tax rate of the plan to which it was assigned. In addition, in some analyses the treatment variables were interacted with various measures of family and individual characteristics to test whether the response to the experiment varied systematically across families.

The measures of experimental response presented in this overview are, in most cases, differences between treatment and control families obtained by evaluating the response function for treatment families for a plan with a 45 percent tax rate and a guarantee at 80 percent of the poverty level of income.[5] These values were chosen to represent the weighted average of the five experimental treatments.

Validity and Interpretation of Findings

Several factors bearing on the validity, interpretation, and generalizability of the findings of the rural experiment should be noted.

When the experiment began in 1970, about 35 percent of the U.S. poverty population lived in rural areas (on farms and in towns of 2,500 or less). It was administratively infeasible, however, to draw a sample that represented the entire U.S. low-income rural population. Instead, two sites were selected that appeared to be typical of two major areas of concentration of the rural poor—the South and the Midwest. While the samples in these sites are not a strict statistical probability sample of even those areas, they are probably reasonably representative of the five southern states (Alabama, Georgia, Mississippi, North Carolina, and South Carolina) and three midwestern states (Illinois, Iowa, and Wisconsin) from which they were selected. These states included about one-third of the U.S. rural poverty population in 1970. The results of the experiment cannot be generalized with the same confidence to other rural areas, or to ethnic groups not included in the experimental sample.

A second significant feature of the experiment was that, like that in New Jersey, it lasted only three years. The response of participants in a permanent program might be somewhat different. There are theoretical reasons for believing that the observed work response to the guarantee may be

5. In some of the analyses where tax and guarantee effects were insignificant, the reported differentials are based on a simple treatment/control dummy variable.

understated and the observed response to the tax rate may be overstated compared to that in a permanent program. While these biases tend to be offsetting, they are of concern. More information on the extent of the bias, if any, should come from the Seattle-Denver experiment, where variation in the duration of the experiment was explicitly introduced as an experimental variable.

Third, no work requirement was imposed; participants did not have to register for work or accept offered employment to receive payments. Observed reductions in work and income may therefore be greater than those under an income maintenance program with a work requirement.

Fourth, relatively few families were assigned to plans at the 50 percent guarantee and at the 70 percent tax rate. Consequently, generalizations about the effects of low guarantees, or about high tax rates, should be made with considerable caution.

Fifth, sample attrition was remarkably low for a three-year panel study: only 9.9 percent of the families dropped out (voluntarily or involuntarily) during the entire period. According to an analysis of those who dropped out, attrition should not have led to any appreciable bias in estimates of work response to the experiment.[6]

Finally, it should be noted that neither Iowa nor North Carolina has an aid to families with dependent children–unemployed parents (AFDC-UP) program, so that there was no confounding of treatment effects due to a cash welfare program for the same population, as there was in the earlier New Jersey experiment.[7] Sample families were eligible to receive unemployment compensation benefits and food stamps but participation in these programs was quite low.

Behavioral Responses to the Experiment

In this section, the major behavioral responses, as estimated by the rural experiment analysts, are presented. Income and work responses were estimated separately for wage earners and farmers. In addition, a number

6. See Glen G. Cain and Steven G. Garber, "Attrition," in D. Lee Bawden and William S. Harrar, eds., *Rural Income Maintenance Experiment: Final Report* (University of Wisconsin–Madison, Institute for Research on Poverty, 1976), vol. 2, chap. 1 (hereafter *Rural Income Maintenance Experiment*).

7. For a discussion see Henry J. Aaron, "Cautionary Notes on the Experiment," in Pechman and Timpane, eds., *Work Incentives and Income Guarantees,* pp. 88–110.

of other types of response were analyzed, including several forms of expenditure and consumption, job change and job search, geographic mobility, psychological well-being, marital stability, political participation, and the attitudes, behavior, and school performance of children.

Income and Work Responses of Wage Earners

Separate analyses of income and work responses were performed for families of wage earners and those of farm operators in North Carolina and Iowa. The wage earner sample was limited to husband-wife families of constant marital status, where the husband was less than sixty-three years old and not disabled, and where the primary source of income was not from self-employment activities. A total of 264 families met these criteria, 146 in the control group and 118 in the treatment groups. The allocation of the 118 treatment families among plans is shown below:[8]

Guarantee (percent of poverty line)	Tax rate (percent)		
	30	50	70
50	. . .	5	. . .
75	36	40	7
100	. . .	30	. . .

Approximately one-half of the wage earner sample was composed of North Carolina blacks, about one-fourth were North Carolina whites, and one-fourth Iowa whites.

Within the wage earner sample, separate analyses were performed for husbands, wives, and dependents as well as for the family as a whole.[9] Measures of income and work responses that were analyzed as dependent variables included total income (excluding public assistance and experimental transfers), wage income, hours worked for wages, and employment status (or number of earners).

The experimental effects on these measures, as estimated by regression

8. The analysis was performed on pooled quarterly observations so that there were approximately twelve times the number of observations as the number of families shown.

9. See the four papers by D. Lee Bawden in *Rural Income Maintenance Experiment:* "The Analytical Approach to Measuring Work and Income Response of Wage Earners"; "Income and Work Response of the Family"; "Income and Work Response of Husbands"; and "Income and Work Response of Wives and Dependents," vol. 3, pt. 1, chaps. 1–4, respectively.

Table 2. Effect of Rural Income Maintenance Experiment on Income and Work Responses of Nonaged Husband-Wife Wage Earner Families, by Site[a]

Percent of control mean

Wage earner and variable	North Carolina		Iowa[b]	Eight-state aggregate[c]
	Black[b]	White[b]		
Husband				
Wage income	−7**	0**	−10**	−4
Wage hours	−8	+3***	−1	−1
Employment rate	−1	−1	0	−1
Wife				
Wage income	−41***	−3	−32	−25
Wage hours	−31***	−23	−22	−27
Employment rate	−25*	−28**	−38**	−28
Dependent				
Wage income	−19	−57**	−8	−39
Wage hours	−16	−66**	−27	−46
Family as a whole				
Total income	−14***	−9***	−18***	−13
Wage income	−14***	−8**	−17***	−12
Wage hours	−10**	−18**	−5	−13
Number of earners	−6***	−16***	−8**	−11

Sources: U.S. Department of Health, Education, and Welfare, "The Rural Income Maintenance Experiment: Summary Report" (HEW, November 1976; processed), p. 38, and computer printout in the files of the Institute for Research on Poverty.

a. Significance levels, based on joint F-test on coefficients of treatment dummy and tax and guarantee variables, are indicated as follows:
* Significant at the 0.10 level.
** Significant at the 0.05 level.
*** Significant at the 0.01 level.

b. Responses are standardized to a 45 percent tax and 80 percent guarantee plan.

c. Weighted averages of the basic data from which the subsample percentages were derived, using the following weights: North Carolina blacks, 0.31788; North Carolina whites, 0.48943; Iowa, 0.19269. No tests of significance can be computed for these differentials. The eight states from which the experimental sites were selected are Alabama, Georgia, Illinois, Iowa, Mississippi, North Carolina, South Carolina, and Wisconsin.

analysis, are shown in table 2.[10] The first three columns of this table show responses by race/site subgroup. The fourth column gives the combined weighted-average response, with weights chosen to reflect the racial and regional composition of the rural, nonfarm, low-income population in the eight states from which the experimental sites were selected.

10. The tests of significance shown in table 2 are joint F-tests on the three treatment parameters in the regression, *not* tests of the significance of the treatment/ control differential at the point at which the response surface is being evaluated. For a more direct test of the significance of the treatment/control differential, see Department of Health, Education, and Welfare, "The Rural Income Maintenance Experiment: Summary Report" (November 1976; processed), tables 3–6, where a simple treatment dummy specification is employed.

The experimental responses of wage earners varied substantially among family members, and, to a lesser extent, among measures of response and among sample subgroups. In general, the responses of husbands were much less significant than those of wives and dependents. However, the relatively large percentage reductions in income and work of wives and dependents were measured against a small base. The wage income of wives accounted for only 5–21 percent of total family wage income in the three subgroups, while wage income of dependents was less than 10 percent of total family wages. Husbands showed reductions in wages or hours in only two of the three subgroups, and in none of the three groups did any noticeable withdrawal from employment occur.

When the income and work responses of all family members are combined, a somewhat more consistent pattern emerges. In two of the three groups, wages and total family income (excluding experimental payments) fell by 14 to 18 percent, while hours and employment were reduced by 5 to 10 percent. Among the third group, the pattern is reversed, with a reduction in hours and employment of 16 to 18 percent and a reduction in wages and total income of 8 to 9 percent.

The combined weighted responses for the three groups show a much more uniform response across the various measures. As shown in the last column of table 2, the weighted income and work reductions of husbands ranged from 1 to 4 percent; for wives, 25 to 28 percent; and for dependents, 39 to 46 percent. For the family as a whole, all weighted response measures fell by 11 to 13 percent.

While the detailed responses of the three subgroups give a useful indication of the variability and statistical significance of the various responses, the weighted responses give a better summary of the overall pattern of response. On the basis of these estimates, we can conclude that for rural wage earners a negative income tax of the type and level considered here will have little or no impact on the employment rate and earnings of husbands, but that it will cause about a one-fourth reduction in the employment rate of wives and a decline of nearly one-half in the employment rate of dependents, with concomitant reductions in their hours and earnings. Overall family income—which determines the level of benefit payments and net cost to the government—would fall by about 13 percent.

Analysis of the variation of response relative to the levels of the guarantee and tax rate yielded mixed results. In general, the level of the guarantee had no effect on the size of the response. About half of the response measures for the three subgroups, however, did appear to be sensitive to the tax rate in the expected direction. The most statistically significant tax rate effects were found for family and husband income measures for the two North Carolina groups, where an increase in the tax rate of 10 percentage points resulted in increases in the treatment/control differences of 8 to 21 percent of the control mean.

Various analyses of interaction variables were performed to test whether the experimental response varied with family or individual characteristics. Among black husbands in North Carolina, for example, the response declined significantly with age. In general, none of these differences in response proved to be statistically significant although there was some evidence of a greater response among North Carolina husbands working as hired farm workers, wives either with school-age children or whose families engaged in some farm work, and dependents eighteen to twenty years of age. The response of wives also varied seasonally, with the largest response during the winter months when employment rates were lowest in both treatment and control groups.

Income and Work Responses of Farmers

In the first year of the experiment, 262 families reported some hours of work devoted to operating or managing a farm. After exclusions for such factors as negligible or discontinuous farming activities, extreme age, and changed marital status, about 220 families remained in the sample.[11] The allocation of the 117 farm operators of the experimental group among treatment plans is shown below:[12]

Guarantee (percent of poverty line)	Tax rate (percent)		
	30	50	70
50	...	24	...
75	17	28	14
100	...	24	...

The farm operators were about evenly divided between the two sites.

The principal measure of income analyzed for farm families was farm profit, defined as gross revenue less current operating expenses.[13] This

11. The exact sample size varied among analyses, as different criteria were applied to define the appropriate sample.

12. Lynne Fender, William S. Harrar, and Brian Kastman, "Sample Selection and Description," in *Rural Income Maintenance Experiment,* vol. 1, chap. 4, table 3. There were 110 families in the control group.

13. See Lewis T. Evans, "Relative Economic Efficiency of Farms," in *Rural Income Maintenance Experiment,* vol. 4, chap. 4.

definition of profit includes gross returns to fixed factors of production (land and capital), as well as to the operator's own labor. Average farm profits in the control group were substantially higher in Iowa ($11,895 a year) than in North Carolina ($4,758 a year). In both sites, the experimental treatments appeared to reduce farm profits—by 25 percent in North Carolina and by 8 percent in Iowa—although these reductions had low statistical significance (20 percent and 15 percent, respectively). Changes in the tax rate or income guarantee level had no significant experimental effect, and there was no distinct time trend over the three years of the experiment.

The observed reduction in farm profits may be partly the result of underreporting of farm income in the experimental group. Farm income was seriously underreported on the income report forms used to calculate payments and while the interview data showed considerably higher farm income, it too may reflect some systematic underreporting.

Several measures of labor supply were analyzed for farm families. Since 78 percent of farm families in North Carolina, and 50 percent of those in Iowa, had one or more members who worked for wages, effects on both farm work and wage work were estimated. The labor supply results for farm operators and their wives are shown in table 3.[14] In both sites, operators and their wives considerably reduced their hours of wage work under the plan although in Iowa both spouses showed an increased probability of employment in wage work.[15] Hours of farm work by farm operators, on the other hand, increased by about 11 percent in both sites; however, only the increase in North Carolina is statistically significant. The net result—in total hours of work, for both farm operators alone and for operators and wives—was a decline in North Carolina, and an increase in Iowa. These results, particularly those for wage work, must be viewed with some caution because of the small number of operators and wives who actually worked for wages, and the generally low statistical significance of the estimates.

It may seem surprising to find a positive experimental effect on hours of farm work, but the effect of a negative income tax on the labor supply of farm operators is not theoretically unambiguous as it is for wage earners. Farm operators have the opportunity to change the mix of land and capi-

---

14. See Stuart H. Kerachsky, "On Farm-Off Farm Work Decisions," in ibid., chap. 2.

15. It should be borne in mind that these estimates are based on annual data, so that the employment variable measures the probability of working for wages at any time during the year, rather than at a given point in time.

**Table 3. Effect of Rural Income Maintenance Experiment on Farm Operators'
and Wives' Labor Supply, by Site**

Percent of control mean

Worker and labor supply measure	North Carolina	Iowa
Farm operators		
Hours of farm work	10.7*	10.9
Hours of wage work	−31.3[a]	−10.0[a]
Employment in wage work	−6.0	25.6
Total hours of work	−2.7	9.5
Wives		
Hours of wage work	−62.7[a]	−53.5[a]
Employment in wage work	−8.2	7.0
Farm operators and wives		
Total hours of work	−16.4[a]	7.3[a]

Source: Stuart H. Kerachsky, "On Farm-Off Farm Work Decisions," in *Rural Income Maintenance Experiment*, vol. 4, chap. 2, table 12.
* Significant at the 0.10 level.
a. This differential is derived from other estimates; therefore no significance levels can be computed.

tal they employ as well as the amount of their own labor; they can easily shift from wage work to farm work. This might account for part of the observed increase in farm hours except that the increase was not significantly larger for farmers who worked for wages than for those who did not.

It is also possible, of course, that the observed increase in farm hours merely reflects systematic overreporting of hours by farmers in the experimental group. Hours devoted to farm work are not as easily defined or measured as wage hours, and may therefore be subject to serious reporting errors. However, the only obvious reason for experimental families consistently to report more farm hours than control families is that the reduction in their wage work resulted in more nonmarket time that could be attributed to farming activities. Reporting bias is therefore difficult to distinguish from a real shift from wage work to farm work; moreover, overreporting should not account for the increase in farm hours of those who did not work for wages.

Furthermore, direct analysis of production activities showed no substantial shifts in the composition of farm output toward labor-intensive goods.[16] The same analysis did indicate an experimentally induced drop in production, consistent with the finding of lower profits.

16. See William E. Saupe, "Farm Business Decisions," and Wendell E. Primus, "Farm Work Response of Farm Operators," both in *Rural Income Maintenance Experiment,* vol. 4, chaps. 5 and 1, respectively.

The experimental effect on farm hours did not differ significantly with variations in the levels of the tax rate or the guarantee. There was, however, a marked time trend, especially in North Carolina, with the size of the response growing over the course of the experiment. Analyses of interaction variables indicated that the increase in farm hours was largest for younger operators with smaller families and a smaller proportion of rented land.

The simultaneous findings of decreased profits and output, and increased hours of farm work among operators, imply that efficiency of farm operations declined among treatment families and direct analysis confirms this fact.[17] Both price efficiency—use of the optimal combinations of inputs—and technical efficiency—the amount of output produced from a given combination of inputs—were analyzed. Farmers in the treatment groups were found to be less technically efficient than those in the control group, while price efficiency appeared to be unaffected. The differences in technical efficiency were most pronounced in North Carolina, where the differential increased over the three years of the experiment. Furthermore, the decrease in technical efficiency was significantly greater at higher tax rates.

Effects on Consumption, Assets, and Debt

During the periodic interviews a variety of data were collected on patterns of expenditure and holdings of assets and debt. Analyses were performed on the experimental effect on nutrition, homeownership and housing expenditures, clothing purchases, use of medical care, ownership of consumer durables and liquid assets, and levels of loan and store debt. The major findings of these studies are briefly described below.

NUTRITION.[18] Dietary intake data for a 24-hour period were collected from 612 families in the third quarterly interview, and from 710 families in the eleventh quarterly interview. From these data, indexes of consumption of ten basic nutrients, expressed as a percentage of the recommended daily allowance, were formed. A combined index, the mean adequacy ratio (MAR), was defined as the arithmetic average of the ten individual indexes. In North Carolina, where control families scored 79 on the MAR scale, significant positive treatment effects of 3.0 and 3.6 percentage points were found in the two quarters, as well as positive effects for nine of the

17. See Evans, "Relative Economic Efficiency of Farms."
18. See J. Frank O'Connor, J. Patrick Madden, and Allen M. Prindle, "Nutrition," in *Rural Income Maintenance Experiment,* vol. 5, chap. 6.

ten individual nutrients.[19] In Iowa, where nutritional adequacy was higher initially (a MAR of 89 for the control group), no significant effects on nutrition were found.

HOUSING.[20] Among the 321 families who had not purchased a home prior to the experiment, the probability of buying a home during the three years of the experiment was about 0.06 higher among families in the treatment group than the control group, with most of the differential effect attributable to North Carolina families. Among the 55 families who bought a home during the experiment, treatment families appeared to make the purchase two or three years earlier in their life cycle, with the differential being significant for farmers but not, in general, for other families. No significant difference in purchase price was detected, nor was there any significant experimental effect on rents paid by families who moved during the experiment.

CLOTHING.[21] Clothing expenditures in the winter months of each year were analyzed separately for two-parent families, both those in which the husband had wage income in every year and those in which the husband did not. Families of wage earners spent $0.025 out of every additional dollar of experimental payments on clothing, as compared with $0.05 from an added dollar of wives' income and $0.007 from other income earned by the family (including the husband's). Total clothing expenditures of nonwage earners' families were not significantly affected by the experimental payments.

MEDICAL CARE.[22] No significant experimental effects were found on the use of medical care, as measured by expenditures, medical visits, and possession of health insurance, or on the state of health, as measured by bed-days, work-loss days, and presence and severity of chronic conditions.

CONSUMER DURABLES AND CARS, LIQUID ASSETS, AND DEBT.[23] Increases in family income in the form of income maintenance payments

19. A score of 67 on the MAR scale is deemed nutritionally inadequate or dangerous to health. The individual scales were truncated at 100.

20. See Aaron C. Johnson, Jr., "Housing Consumption," in *Rural Income Maintenance Experiment*, vol. 5, chap. 1.

21. See Christine J. Hager and W. Keith Bryant, "Clothing Expenditures," in ibid., chap. 4.

22. See Stuart H. Kerachsky, "State of Health and the Utilization of Medical Care," in ibid., chap. 5.

23. See W. Keith Bryant and Christine J. Hager, "Consumer Durables, Cars, Liquid Assets, and Debts of Wage-Working Families," in ibid., chap. 2; and Bryant, "Consumer Durables, Cars, Liquid Assets, Short-term Farm Capital and Nonreal Estate Debts of Farm Families," in ibid., chap. 3.

Table 4. Long-run Response of Assets and Debts to a Negative Income Tax, by Families of Wage Earners and Farmers
Dollars

Type of family and race	Consumer durables	Cars	Store debt	Loan debt	Liquid assets
Wage earner					
Black	168	167	−12	658	42
White	170	130	57	−1,245	187
Farmer	122	−87	−60	−268	19

Sources: W. Keith Bryant and Christine J. Hager, "Consumer Durables, Cars, Liquid Assets, and Debts of Wage-Working Families," in *Rural Income Maintenance Experiment*, vol. 5, chap. 2, tables 4II.1, and 4II.5 through 4II.8; and Bryant, "Consumer Durables, Cars, Liquid Assets, Short-term Farm Capital and Nonreal Estate Debts of Farm Families," in ibid., chap. 3, p. 22.

may cause the family to alter the level of its holdings of assets and debts. Because these adjustments may require several years to complete, estimates were made of both the short-run—that is, current year—and complete long-run adjustment of assets to transfer payments. Separate analyses were performed for black and white families in which the husband had wage earnings, and for farmers. The estimated long-run effects on holdings of various types of assets as well as debts for wage earners and farmers are shown in table 4. The estimation technique does not allow confident calculation of statistical significance for these figures. In general, however, it appears that the effects for black wage earners were more statistically significant than those for white; the estimates for the farm sample were generally not significant.

The total experimental effects for wage earners shown in table 4 are based on regression equations that included a binary treatment variable, denoting eligibility for experimental payments, and a measure of the amount of payments a family would receive at its "normal" income level. In some cases these two effects were offsetting. For example, for black anu white wage earners, simple eligibility for payments appeared to reduce loan debt by $2,638 and $1,540, respectively, while increases in the size of payments increased loan debt. Unfortunately, the estimation technique did not allow the analysts to distinguish between the effect of eligibility and initial differences in stocks held by the treatment and control groups. Thus, in those cases where the overall effect is dominated by a large eligibility effect—particularly the large decline in loan debt for white wage earners—considerable caution should be used as they may partly reflect initial differences in holdings rather than treatment effects.

Other Effects

Analyses were also performed on the experimental effects on job change and search, geographic mobility, psychological well-being, family structure, political participation, and various aspects of behavior of youth. Their results are briefly summarized below.

JOB CHANGE AND JOB SEARCH.[24] Job turnover, duration of unemployment, and job selection were analyzed for male wage earners who were employed at the beginning of the experiment. The experimental payments appeared to have no overall effect on the probability of leaving a job, though significant effects were found for some subgroups of workers. For instance, those in experimental groups who initially had more desirable positions were less likely to leave their employers than similar people in control groups, while those in experimental groups with less desirable positions were more likely to leave their employers. These tendencies appeared to increase with plan generosity.

Individuals in experimental groups who left their initial employer were unemployed about three weeks more than those in control groups over a two-year period. Unemployment duration for members of experimental groups compared to control groups was greater for those who had low wage earnings prior to the experiment, faced high implicit tax rates, or had incomes from another worker in the family. Younger and better educated experimental members were also unemployed longer.

Experimental individuals who changed jobs tended to obtain jobs with more desirable nonwage characteristics than similar people in control groups if they had relatively desirable jobs to begin with, and to do worse than those in control groups if they initially had relatively undesirable jobs. Experimental heads with secondary earners in their families were able to obtain jobs with better earnings prospects and higher status, particularly if they were on high guarantee plans and the secondary earner had relatively high earnings.

A standard experimental plan (50 percent tax rate, basic benefit level of 75 percent of the poverty line) led to increased wages in subsequent jobs, presumably due to a longer job search. But the increases were not statistically significant, and the gain in earnings in one year was more than offset by the earnings lost while unemployed. Higher tax rates and guar-

24. See Luther Tweeten, "Job Search Behavior and Its Impact on Earnings," in ibid., vol. 3, pt. 2, chap. 7; and Richard E. Miller, "Job Change Behavior," in ibid., chap. 8.

antee levels, however, significantly reduced wage gains, increased unemployment, and reduced earnings.

An analysis of job search methods showed the U.S. Employment Service to be most effective, far exceeding all other approaches. The infrequency of its use suggests that rural families in the selected areas had inadequate access to it.

GEOGRAPHIC MOBILITY.[25] Families in the treatment groups had a 17 percent higher incidence of residential change than similar control families. This differential was statistically significant at the 0.05 level for families with a wage earner at the beginning of the experiment. Essentially all of this movement occurred among families in North Carolina.

PSYCHOLOGICAL WELL-BEING.[26] Scales were constructed to measure a variety of aspects of mental health and psychological well-being—for example, self-esteem, psychosomatic and nervous symptoms, positive and negative emotional states, life satisfaction, a sense of powerlessness, and a sense of being cast adrift in a chaotic world (anomie). A number of single-item questions were asked each participant—what were his or her worries over money, health, jobs, and other problems; feelings about the quality of life; hopes and aspirations for the future; subjective sense of general health; and so forth.

There was no consistent pattern in these individual measures of well-being. While some statistically significant effects were found, they were scattered and unstable over time. An overall index of psychological well-being formed from a number of individual scores showed a more consistent pattern, however. For both adults and teenagers, the three most generous plans tended to produce higher scores on this index than those of comparable control families, with the differentials statistically significant for three of the six plan/age groups. The least generous plans tended to have a negative differential in the well-being index—significantly so for adults on the least generous plan—so that the overall experimental/control differential was small. Similarly, the level of the guarantee had a significant positive effect on the overall index of well-being for both adults and teenagers.

MARITAL DISSOLUTION AND FAMILY INTERACTION.[27] Income maintenance payments have an ambiguous effect on marital stability: they

25. See Aaron C. Johnson, Jr., "Geographic Mobility," in ibid., vol. 6, pt. 1, chap. 9.

26. See Russell Middleton, "Psychological Well-Being," in ibid., chap. 7.

27. See Russell Middleton and Linda Haas, "Marital Dissolution and Family Interaction," in ibid., chap. 8.

might strengthen the relationship by raising family income or, alternatively, they might facilitate marital dissolution by providing an alternative source of income to wives. Overall the treatment group appeared to have a higher incidence of divorce, separation, and desertion than similar control families, with families in the least generous plans showing the highest rates of dissolution and those in the most generous plan showing lower rates than control families. These differentials were generally not significant; however, the level of the guarantee was found to have a significant negative effect on the rate of dissolution.

No significant treatment effects were found for a variety of measures of family interaction, including marital happiness, satisfaction in marriage, marital disagreements, parent-child relations, and the division of household tasks within the family.

ASPIRATIONS, SCHOOL ATTITUDES, SCHOOL BEHAVIOR, AND DELINQUENCY AMONG TEENAGE YOUTH.[28] Self-administered questionnaires dealing with a variety of attitudes and behaviors were completed by 445 youths fourteen through eighteen years of age at the end of the experiment. In general, no systematic significant overall differences were found between youths in treatment families and those in controls. Areas analyzed included educational and occupational aspirations and expectations, self-rating of school ability, self-reports of grades and school behavior, interest in grades, hours of homework, participation in extracurricular activities, and general attitudes toward school and teachers. Moreover, although a relatively high incidence of delinquent behavior was reported, no significant overall differences were found between treatment and control groups under any of several measures of delinquency analyzed. The level of the guarantee did, however, have a significant negative effect on delinquent behavior; this effect was offset by an equally significant positive effect common to all plans, so that only in the plan with the highest guarantee was the delinquency rate lower than that of youths in control families.

SCHOOL PERFORMANCE.[29] Four measures of school performance—attendance, comportment, academic grades, and standardized achievement test scores—were analyzed for 847 children who were in school at

28. See Russell Middleton, Linda Haas, and Ain Haas, "Aspirations, School Attitudes and School Behavior of Teen-age Youth," and Middleton and Ain Haas, "Delinquency of Teen-age Youth," both in ibid., vol. 6, pt. 2, chaps. 10 and 11, respectively.
29. See Rebecca Maynard and David L. Crawford, "School Performance," in ibid., chap. 12.

Table 5. Effect on School Performance of the Rural Income Maintenance Experiment, by Site

Difference between experimental and control means as percent of control mean

Performance measure	Grades 2–8		Grades 9–12	
	North Carolina	Iowa	North Carolina	Iowa
Days absent	−30**	−20	3	−17
Comportment	7**	0	n.e.	n.e.
Academic grades	6*	−5	4	−5
Achievement tests (deviation from norm)	19**	−18.8	n.e.	n.e.

Source: Rebecca Maynard and David L. Crawford, "School Performance," in *Rural Income Maintenance Experiment*, vol. 6, pt. 2, chap. 12, p. 38.
* Significant at the 0.10 level.
** Significant at the 0.05 level.
n.e. Not estimated, due to lack of data.

the beginning of the experiment and had completed at least one year of school after that. The treatment effects for the four age/site groups analyzed are shown in table 5. The experiment significantly improved performance by elementary students in North Carolina by all four measures, although there were no statistically significant effects among the other three groups.

The differential strength of the treatment effect in North Carolina, as compared to Iowa, may reflect the lower socioeconomic status of families and the lower educational achievement of children in North Carolina at the beginning of the experiment. For example, about 62 percent of the North Carolina families were below the poverty line initially, as compared with 37 percent in Iowa, and the mean ranking of North Carolina children on nationally standardized tests was in the 25th percentile, as compared with the 50th percentile for Iowa children.

POLITICAL PARTICIPATION.[30] Two measures of political participation, voting and an index of interest and involvement in political campaigns, were analyzed for the 1970 and 1972 elections. Separate analyses were performed for husbands and wives in two-parent families and for female heads of families. The treatment effect was positive in all twelve cases, although only significantly so for wives, whose voting probabilities in the two elections were increased by 6 to 10 percentage points.

30. See Joseph Heffernan, "Political Behavior," in ibid., chap. 13.

Administration of a Negative Income Tax in Rural Areas

Self-employed farmers present unique difficulties in the administration
of a negative income tax because their income flows are much more complex and irregular than those of wage earners. Although administrative
rules and procedures were not varied experimentally, the experiment provided a good deal of practical experience in the design and implementation
of rules governing the treatment of income, expenses, and assets of self-
employed farmers as well as information about participant understanding
of, and compliance with, these rules. The rural experiment represents the
only systematic attempt to date to deal with these issues, even though
farmers may comprise as much as 18 percent of all male heads eligible for
assistance under a universal income maintenance program.[31]

The experiment established rules for the definition of self-employment
and developed a method of calculating income for the purposes of a cash
transfer program. This accounting method differed from the Internal
Revenue Service rules in disallowing accelerated depreciation and the investment tax credit, adding the value of rent-free housing to income, and
imputing to income a percentage of assets above a given level. A one-
month accounting period with a twelve-month carry-over provision was
developed to deal with the seasonal variability of farm income. Experience in administering the program led to additional recommendations
requiring the accrual method of accounting rather than the cash method,
and treating both realized and unrealized capital gains as income.

Participants' understanding of the experimental rules was very poor.[32]
Only about one-half of the families understood the guarantee, tax rate,
and breakeven level they faced, and understanding of these program characteristics did not improve despite the careful instruction of participants.
Nevertheless, as we have seen, there were definite changes in labor supply
as a result of the experiment.

Data on family size, wage income, and transfer income were reported
with acceptable accuracy, but assets were underreported on the monthly
report forms by 14 to 27 percent, and farm income by 39 percent, as compared with the edited interview data.[33] On the basis of these results, under-

31. *Social Security Amendments of 1971*, Report of the House Committee on
Ways and Means on H.R. 1, H. Rept. 92-231, 92:1 (GPO, 1971), p. 230.
32. See William S. Harrar, "Participants' Understanding of the Experimental
Program," in *Rural Income Maintenance Experiment*, vol. 2, chap. 5.
33. See William S. Harrar, "Quality of Wage Income and Hours Data," and
Harrar, "Accuracy of Self-Administered Reporting," both in ibid., chaps. 2 and 4.

reporting by farmers could be expected to affect program costs far more than any likely change in their labor supply.

Summary

Many of the results of the rural income maintenance experiment closely resemble the results of the New Jersey experiment. In families of wage earners in the rural experiment there was a somewhat larger decline in income relative to that of control families, than there had been in New Jersey, but the decline was still modest. In the rural experiment husbands' hours did not show a consistent decline, and those declines that were found tended to be even smaller, on the average, than in New Jersey. As in New Jersey, husbands did not withdraw from the labor force, but the percentage of working wives fell considerably. One new outcome in the rural experiment was that wage work of dependents also fell. But since wives and dependents had worked only a small number of hours before the start of the experiment, the effect on total family work for wages was small.

Among farm families, there was a marked reduction in hours of work for wages, with a reduction for husbands of 10 percent in Iowa and 31 percent in North Carolina, and wives working 50 to 60 percent fewer hours than those in the control group. Hours of farm work reported by farm operators rose by about 11 percent in both sites, however, so that total hours of work by farm operators and their wives actually rose in Iowa. When combined with the observed decline in net farm profits in the treatment group, this increase in farm labor supply implies a reduction in the efficiency of farm operations.

As in the New Jersey experiment, there was a negligible overall effect in terms of various psychological variables, but there were some nonlabor market consequences of note. Of particular interest were the relative improvements in nutrition and in school performance of grade school children among North Carolina experimental families. A positive experimental effect also occurred for several forms of consumption, including purchase of cars, durable goods, and houses.

The experiment also indicates the need for special care in defining administrative and reporting procedures for self-employed farmers in order to avoid serious problems of underreporting and misreporting of income and assets. An accurate measurement of farm income and assets may be of greater importance among this population than any likely labor supply response.

D. LEE BAWDEN AND
WILLIAM S. HARRAR

Design and Operation

Interpreting results of the rural income maintenance experiment will be helped by an understanding of the experiment's design and operation. A review of these aspects should also clarify many of the issues that would have to be addressed if a comprehensive income-tested cash assistance program were implemented in the rural areas of the United States. This paper first provides information on the process of site selection as well as the design and characteristics of the sample of households enrolled in the experiment. Next, it discusses the operations of the experiment and explores the participants' understanding of the rules of the program and the accuracy of the self-reported data. It concludes with comments on some important lessons learned about the administration of a comprehensive income-tested cash assistance program for rural populations.

Design of the Experiment

The principal purpose of the rural experiment was to measure the effect of a negative income tax on the work effort of low-income families in small towns and on farms. The response of these poor families was expected to contrast with that of the urban poor because of differences in labor markets and the proportion that were self-employed. The design had many of the same features as that of the New Jersey urban experiment: the program was to last three years and provide a variety of guarantee and tax treatments among a dispersed sample. Other design features (the choice of two regional sites, the inclusion of two other groups of family heads in the sample) were distinctly different, bringing new problems along with the benefits of the added research knowledge.

23

Site Selection

A random sample of the entire U.S. rural population would have allowed the greatest generalization of results, but it would also have entailed enormous administrative and research costs in sample selection, interviewing, and program operation. With an upper constraint on the total budget, there was a trade-off between geographic concentration of the sample and administrative and research costs—the more concentrated the sample, the lower the attendant costs and therefore the larger the sample that could be bought with a limited budget. But greater geographic concentration of the sample, while leading to gains in sample size, results in losses in the generalizability of the sample to the total U.S. rural population (assuming certain socioeconomic-demographic [SED] factors are likely to condition response to the experiment and assuming those factors are not evenly distributed over geographic areas).

The decrease in administrative and research costs resulting from greater geographic concentration of the sample was relatively straightforward to calculate (though the related gains in uniformity of administrative and research procedures were, at best, subjective). But assessing the consequent losses in generalizability was a more difficult task. It was hypothesized that there were four factors that might be important in conditioning response to the experiment and that might be unequally distributed over geographic areas. (1) Race or ethnicity. Of the rural population, whites make up 93 percent of the total and 79 percent of the rural poor; blacks, 6 percent of the total and 19 percent of the poor; families of Spanish heritage, 2 percent of the total and 3 percent of the poor.[1] (2) Pervasiveness of poverty. The SED characteristics of both poor and nonpoor families may well differ between areas in which poverty is widespread, as in the South, and in areas in which poverty is limited to a relatively few scattered pockets amid a relatively prosperous area, such as in the East and Midwest. (3) Density of population. In low-population-density regions such as the Great Plains, work opportunities outside one's own community are not often within commuting distance. (4) Type and diversity of agricultural production (for the farm subsample). To the degree that rural nonfarm economic activity is agriculturally related, this can affect the employment patterns of rural nonfarm residents but it is of primary importance to the farm subsample of the experiment. Both the

---

1. According to the 1970 Census of Population of the U.S. Bureau of the Census. The percentages do not add to 100 because of rounding.

ability and incentive to adjust to negative income tax payments is conditioned by the type of agricultural production and the degree of diversity; the more diverse the activity, the greater the opportunity to change enterprise mix or eliminate secondary activities.

After evaluating data pertaining to the four regional criteria mentioned above, the decision was made to have two sites, one in the South (in Alabama, Georgia, Mississippi, North Carolina, or South Carolina), the other in the Midwest (Iowa, Illinois, or southern Wisconsin). More than one-half of all rural poverty is found in the South, and a southern site allows the measurement of differences in response to the experiment between blacks and whites in that region. The southern and midwestern sites also provide a sharp difference in the pervasiveness-of-poverty criteria, with the South representing area poverty conditions and the Midwest representing the condition of scattered poverty in a prosperous agricultural region. The two regions also offered a range of agricultural operations and, to a lesser extent, a range of population densities (these ranges, of course, are further narrowed with the selection of specific sites). On the other hand, the selection of these two regions necessarily limited the generalizability of the sample. Excluded by this selection were: (1) Chicano and American Indian populations, (2) sparsely settled areas such as found in the Great Plains, and (3) the fruit-growing agricultural sector.

The selection of sites within the two regions was a three-step process. The first involved selecting acceptable *areas* within each region; the second step identified acceptable *counties* within these areas; and the third step was the actual selection of *sites* among these acceptable counties. The selection of acceptable economic areas was based upon four considerations: (1) the area must have a reasonable degree of agricultural diversity rather than specialization in the production of just one commodity; (2) specific counties within the area should not be located within 25 miles of a city with over 50,000 persons, so that there would be no confusion between truly rural people and those currently referred to as "exurbanites"; (3) areas containing a few counties with a moderately sized city between them (10,000–50,000), being more typical, were given preference over isolated areas with no nearby city at all; and (4) mountainous and swampy areas were avoided since the consequent low population density might render the prospective sample population too inaccessible.

The second step involved selecting candidate counties from each of the previously determined acceptable areas. The judgment was made that each candidate county must typify the entire *region* (the five states in the South or the three states in the Midwest). Seven social, economic, and demographic characteristics were selected as important in representing the respective region for this particular experiment: (1) racial mix, (2) incidence of poverty among families, (3) unemployment rate, (4) level of education, (5) median income of families, (6) age distribution (with particular attention to dependency ratios), and (7) population density. "Ranges of acceptability" were then established for these seven characteristics, and counties were eliminated if they did not fall within these ranges. The remaining counties were then rated for their eligibility as an experimental site according to how closely they matched the average profile, that is, the midpoint of each range (which represented the average of all counties of the entire region).

An additional eligibility criterion was imposed that concerned the number and size of rural towns within the county limits. Ideally, an experimental county would have a wide distribution of rural town sizes, with at least one town of 2,000 to 2,500 people.

Approximately six counties in each region were designated the most acceptable, and on-site visits were made to narrow the choices to those finally selected[2]—Duplin County in North Carolina, and Pocahontas and Calhoun Counties in Iowa.[3] Table 1 shows the characteristics of these counties compared with the averages for their respective regions.

Sample Design and Selection

The sample size of the rural experiment was small relative to the three urban income maintenance experiments. There were about 1,350 sample households in the New Jersey experiment, 1,800 in the Gary experiment,

2. The purpose of these visits was two-fold: (1) to determine if any major changes had occurred between 1960 (the year of the census data used to establish the ranges and midpoints of the above criteria) and 1969, which might render the county less desirable as a sample site; and (2) to learn first-hand about other conditions in the county that were not found in published data sources but were thought to be important characteristics for potential sites, for example, type of tenure arrangements of farm renters, intra-county variations in the above-mentioned characteristics, whether the local welfare officer may be hostile to conducting such an experiment in the county. Personal interviews were held with the county agricultural extension agent, the head of the county welfare department, and people in the local office of the State Industrial Commission.

3. Permission to conduct the experiment in these sites was subsequently sought and obtained from the governor of the respective states, from the congressman of the two districts, and from local county commissioners.

Table 1. Regional and Target County Characteristics of the Rural Population in Final Areas Considered for the Rural Income Maintenance Experiment, 1970

Characteristic	Five southern states[a]	Duplin County, North Carolina	Three midwestern states[a]	Calhoun County, Iowa	Poca- hontas County, Iowa
Median income (dollars)	5,783	5,710	7,704	7,741	7,686
Percent of households below poverty line	25.5	28.9	15.8	11.4	9.9
Unemployed as percent of labor force	4.0	3.6	3.4	3.9	1.8
Households per square mile	6.2	13.7	4.7	8.4	7.0
Percent black	26.2	34.1	0.5	0.1	0.0
Distribution of persons 25 years and over, by schooling (percent)					
Less than 5 years	13.4	12.6	2.9	1.6	2.3
Less than 1 year of high school	44.7	41.1	34.3	29.6	26.5
College degree or more	4.7	4.5	5.7	7.3	6.6
Median school years completed	9.6	10.4	11.8	12.2	12.2
Distribution by age (percent)					
Under 18 years	37.8	38.5	37.0	34.5	37.5
21 and over	57.1	61.4	59.1	65.5	62.5
65 and over	7.2	8.7	11.5	17.2	15.7
Households with children under 6 years (percent)	26.8	20.1	26.5	16.6	18.8

Source: Lynne Fender and William S. Harrar, "Site Selection," in D. Lee Bawden and William S. Harrar, eds., *Rural Income Maintenance Experiment: Final Report* (University of Wisconsin–Madison, Institute for Research on Poverty, 1976), vol. 1, chap. 2, table 1. The basic data are from the 1970 Census of Population of the U.S. Bureau of the Census.

a. The five southern states are Alabama, Georgia, Mississippi, North Carolina, and South Carolina. The three midwestern states are Illinois, Iowa, and Wisconsin.

and 4,900 in the Seattle-Denver experiment. All samples were drawn from cities of over 50,000; there was, therefore, a total sample of about 8,000 to represent the 31.4 percent of the U.S. poverty population residing in cities of over 50,000. In contrast, there were only 809 sample households in the rural experiment to represent the 35.5 percent of the U.S. poverty population residing in rural areas.

The small sample size of the rural experiment was a conscious, though in retrospect perhaps an unwise, decision by the Office of Economic Opportunity (OEO). The justification was that the urban poverty problem was more important than the rural poverty problem, therefore less money was allotted to the rural experiment than to the New Jersey experiment (the other two experiments were funded later by the Department of Health, Education, and Welfare [HEW]).

This relatively small sample was further compromised by the fact that the target population was spread over two geographic regions with disparate racial compositions, and by the insistence of the OEO, which was funding the project, that a small part of the sample be composed of female heads and of aged heads (of either sex). As a result, 108 sample households were headed by a nonaged (fifty-eight years or under) female and 114 were households with older heads (more than fifty-eight years of age). This left a sample of 587 to represent the rural, two-parent working poor families—the prime population target of the experiment.

Finally, the usefulness of this remaining sample was weakened even more for certain types of analysis because the sample included both farm and rural nonfarm residents. These two subsamples could not be pooled for some kinds of analysis, including that of work response; for example, the behavioral models for self-employed farmers are substantially different from those for rural nonfarm wage earners. For some areas of analysis, this effectively cut the sample size in half, since roughly half of the sample were farmers and the other half were wage earners.[4]

Given these exogenously imposed constraints on the total budget and on stratification by age and sex of heads of families, the Conlisk-Watts allocation model was separately applied to each of the three groups of family heads—nonaged males, nonaged females, and older heads of both sexes.[5] Within each group, the sample was allocated across a design space consisting of 36 cells—five treatments and a control group, each stratified by three preexperimental income categories (0–50 percent, 50–100 percent, 110–150 percent of the poverty level), and two locations (North Carolina and Iowa). The objective function for the model incorporated a weighted sum of ten subobjectives, and involved obtaining a minimum variance estimate of the differential labor force response between a single program in a particular location and a corresponding con-

---

4. In reality, these two groups are not mutually exclusive since many farmers hold part-time wage jobs. Of the 587 sample households, approximately one-quarter were full-time farmers, one-half full-time wage earners, and the remainder were some combination of the two.

5. Both the technical features of this model and methodological issues associated with its use are discussed in John Conlisk and Harold Watts, "A Model for Optimizing Experimental Designs for Estimating Response Surfaces," in American Statistical Association, *Proceedings of the Social Statistics Section* (1969), pp. 150–56, and Charles E. Metcalf, "Sample Design and the Use of Experimental Data," in Harold W. Watts and Albert Rees, eds., *Final Report of the New Jersey Graduated Work Incentive Experiment* (University of Wisconsin–Madison, Institute for Research on Poverty and Mathematica, 1974), vol. 2, pt. C, chap. 5.

trol group.[6] Two alternative sets of policy weights were used for each of the five treatments in solving the model:

Treatments		Policy weights	
Guarantee (percent of poverty level)	Tax rate (percent)	Early runs	Later runs
50	50	10	4
75	30	6	6
75	50	10	10
75	70	6	3
100	50	6	10

These policy weights were then combined with the estimated population densities in the two target regions to form final weights that varied by region and welfare level. These final composite weights led to an allocation of 62 percent of the sample to North Carolina and 38 percent to Iowa.

The regression functional form used for the rural model runs was very similar to the one adopted for the New Jersey experiment. It had sixteen parameters, and permitted a substantial degree of nonlinearity in the three underlying exogenous variables of the model—the guarantee, the tax rate, and the income level of participants. The cost per cell reflected interviewing costs, payment costs, and the same specific assumptions about the anticipated labor force response of participants as were used for the New Jersey experiment.

There were 587 households headed by a nonaged male, 54 percent of which were assigned to the control group and 46 percent to the experimental group; this division was the same for both North Carolina and Iowa. The percentage distribution of the 269 experimental families among the five experimental treatments are shown below (figures are rounded):

Guarantee (percent of poverty level)	Tax rate (percent)		
	30	50	70
50	. . .	14	. . .
75	25	28	11
100	. . .	22	. . .

6. The objective function used for the New Jersey experiment was slightly different—it focused on the budgetary cost associated with the labor force response rather than the labor force response directly.

For the household sample headed by nonaged females, there were 108 sample families, 53 percent of which were assigned to the control group and 47 percent to the experimental group. Because the aid to families with dependent children–unemployed parents (AFDC-UP) program in Iowa had higher payments than all but the most generous treatment plan— 50 percent tax rate, 100 percent of poverty level guarantee (50T/100G) —no female-headed families in Iowa were assigned to the four less generous plans. Instead, three new plans were established for Iowa only— 30T/100G, 50T/125G, and 70T/125G. The total experimental sample of fifty-one female-headed families was distributed among the eight plans as shown below (in rounded figures), with the 50T/100G cell the only one representing families from both regions:

Guarantee	Tax rate (percent)		
(percent of poverty level)	30	50	70
50	. . .	12	. . .
75	10	18	8
100	10	20	. . .
125	. . .	14	10

The third subsample was of older family heads of either sex. There were 114 such families (and single individuals), with 53 percent assigned to a control group and 47 percent distributed among the five experimental plans, approximately the same as for the nonaged, male-headed subsample.

Data from the 1960 Census were used to estimate the total number of dwelling units to be contacted in each county to obtain the desired sample size. The first step in each county was to locate, map, and number every dwelling unit (resident institutions were excluded). Over 11,000 units were so listed at each of the two sites. From these, 3,000 North Carolina and 3,800 Iowa dwelling units were randomly selected to receive the screening interview. From the interviews, total income and family size were used to compute eligibility for enrollment, with a family required to have income less than 150 percent of its 1968–69 poverty level to be eligible. Early yield calculations revealed the need for additional dwelling units to be added to the screening sample because there were fewer low-income families than the official data indicated. In North Carolina an additional 959 sample points were contacted, and in Iowa, 4,496.

A second preenrollment interview was given to those families passing the income test in the screening interview. The purpose was two-fold: to obtain a more accurate estimate of family income, assets (for calculating the asset imputation), and rent estimates for homeowners and those living rent-free (for making rent imputations), as well as other important preexperimental (baseline) information on the families. From these families a final sample was drawn, excluding: (1) those who, when a better measure of income was made in this preenrollment questionnaire, were found to have incomes more than 150 percent of the poverty level, (2) refusals, (3) vacancies, and (4) a few disabled male heads denied eligibility because they could not respond to the experimental plan in terms of work effort. The final sample for enrolling consisted of 335 families in Iowa and 512 in North Carolina.

Sample Description

A series of tests were performed on important demographic variables for the sample of male heads less than sixty-three years of age, to test for differences between the control and experimental groups. Sample selection appeared to have the desired randomness with regard to race, age, marital status, education, home ownership, family size, and number of other adults in the household besides the head and spouse. There was a slight bias in occupation: 34 percent of the control group were farmers in 1970 compared with 39 percent of the experimental group. Such a distribution could occur by chance about 30 percent of the time. The control group also had a slightly higher average wage income.

The largest experimental/control differences related to the presence of young children and to the spouse's initial (1969) earned income. Children under six were found in 48 percent of the control families but in only 41 percent of the experimental families, a distribution occurring randomly only one time in eleven. In 1969, 25 percent of the spouses in control families earned at least $200, while only 18 percent of experimental spouses earned this income, a difference that would occur randomly one in three times. This difference was present only in the North Carolina portion of the sample.

While the differences between control and experimental groups were generally small, there was an enormous difference between the Iowa and the North Carolina samples, reflecting the contrasts in characteristics of low-income families in the South and Midwest. While blacks comprised 56 percent of the North Carolina sample, there were no blacks in the Iowa

Table 2. Number of Heads of Households by Change in Marital Status, by Sex of Head and Quarter of Experiment, 1970–72

Description	0[a]	Quarter of experiment, 1970–72												Post-experiment quarter[b]	
		1	2	3	4	5	6	7	8	9	10	11	12	13	14
Original male-headed families															
Constant marital status	647	602	589	575	565	552	545	541	536	524	517	514	510	497	486
Attritions or no longer heads (cumulated)	…	8	17	25	29	38	43	47	49	54	57	60	62	68	82
Remaining, with a change in marital status (cumulated)	…	37	42	47	53	57	59	59	62	69	73	73	75	82	79
Original female-headed families															
Constant marital status	162	162	160	159	158	154	152	151	151	150	148	143	141	139	134
Attritions or no longer heads (cumulated)	…	0	2	3	3	4	6	7	7	7	7	10	12	15	19
Remaining female heads who married (cumulated)	…	0	0	0	1	4	4	4	4	5	7	9	9	9	9
New two-parent families formed (cumulated)	…	50	57	86	132	138	145	146	194	200	212	216	230	240	216

Source: Lynne Fender, William S. Harrar, and Brian Kastman, "Sample Selection and Description," in Bawden and Harrar, eds., *Rural Income Maintenance Experiment*, vol. 1, chap. 4, table 6.

a. December 1969 enrollment.
b. The experimental income payments stopped at the end of quarter 12 (December 1972), but two more interviews were administered—the 13th quarterly in April 1973 to get annual information on taxes, asset changes, and so forth, for 1972, and a 14th quarterly in September 1973 to get data on postexperimental adjustment.

sample. Of the Iowa male family heads less than sixty-three years of age, fully one-half were less than forty years of age. Only 35 percent of the North Carolina heads were less than forty years of age, suggesting a lower trajectory for earnings over a lifetime. Perhaps the greatest difference was in education—63 percent of the Iowa male heads had graduated from high school, while less than 9 percent of the North Carolina heads had done so.

Another important difference was in the occupational mix. Just over half of the Iowa family heads were self-employed, primarily as farmers; only 30 percent of those from North Carolina were in this category. The Iowa farmers had more net equity in farm assets, even though more North Carolina farmers owned their own farms. Nearly all of the farmers in Iowa had a net equity in farm assets of at least $10,000; no more than a third of the North Carolina farmers had so much.

Initial eligibility in the plan was determined from income estimates made in the fall of 1969. However, interviews early the following year revealed that some of these estimates were faulty: among families with a male head less than sixty-three years of age, 38 percent of Iowa families and 20 percent of those in North Carolina turned out to have 1969 incomes over 150 percent of their poverty level. None were supposed to have incomes this high. Eight percent of the entire sample actually had 1969 incomes over two times the poverty level.

Finally, there were important regional differences in income earned by spouses: 30 percent of the North Carolina wives earned at least $200 from wages in 1969, while only 7 percent of the Iowa wives earned this much.

Thus the North Carolina sample was characterized by a poorly educated, older mix of small farmers and unskilled wage earners, who were less likely to rise out of poverty on their own. In Iowa the families seemed to be more middle class, such as reasonably well-educated farmers who for one reason or another had a bad year in 1969, and younger hired hands waiting to get a farm of their own.

Much of the research for the experiment analyzed only families that remained in the experiment for the entire three years. Furthermore, it often focused on families whose heads had no change in marital status during the period. Table 2 shows the number of heads with constant marital status over the 14 quarters of interviews. At enrollment there were 647 families headed by males of all ages; by quarter 13—the last regular interview—there were only 497 male heads with constant marital status. Sixty-eight of the original group were attritions—about ten and a half percent of the original number. Of those remaining in the sample, 82 either had separated or their spouse had died, or they were originally single and had remarried. At quarter 13 there were 139 of the original 162 female heads who had neither married nor been lost through attrition.

The last row of table 2 also shows the formation of new families in accordance with the rules of operations for changes in family composition. There were 240 new families formed as of quarter 13. The large initial jump at quarter 1, as well as the jumps at quarters 4 and 8, was largely due to the rule that defined as a new head any dependent between eighteen and twenty-one years of age who had left home to attend college full time.

Table 3 describes the salient characteristics of the sample with a focus on families with constant marital status. There were 262 male heads in this category in the control group and 235 in the experimental group for 13 quarters. Female heads numbered 69 and 70, respectively. Of the 497 male heads with constant marital status, 190 (38 percent) were in Iowa, 136 (27 percent) were North Carolina whites, and 171 (34 percent) were North Carolina blacks. In the analyses of the results of the experiment, the number of observations varied considerably in accordance with the population definition that the researcher found most congenial to his particular task.

In conclusion, the sample selected for the rural income maintenance experiment was representative of the rural poor of the South and Midwest, except for the deliberate selection of a low percentage of female heads, retired heads, and disabled heads of households. The subsample randomly assigned to the experimental group appeared to be quite similar to the subsample assigned to the control group with respect to common demographic variables. As expected, there were large demographic differences between the North Carolina and Iowa portions of the sample. During the three years (1970–72) of payments, the sample's income, exclusive of payments, increased by roughly 20 percent. Of the 809 households initially enrolled in the experiment, 636 (79 percent) finished intact, 11 percent underwent a change in the marital status of the family head and 10 percent were lost through attrition.

Operation of the Experiment

Rules and regulations for the administration of payments were developed prior to the experiment and then were continually refined, with a large number of changes occurring during the first six months of the ex-

Table 3. Characteristics of Family Units Present at Quarter 13 of the Rural Income Maintenance Experiment

Number of units

Characteristic	Original families with male heads			Original families with female heads		
	Constant marital status	Nonconstant marital status	Total	Constant marital status	Nonconstant marital status	Total
Program status						
In control group	262	43	305	69	5	74
In experimental group	235	39	274	70	4	74
Total	497	82	579	139	9	148
Region and race						
Iowa, white and black	190	22	212	53	8	61
North Carolina						
White	136	18	154	28	0	28
Black	171	42	213	58	1	59
Age (years)						
18–58	458	71	529	94	9	103
59–64	3	14	17	11	0	11
65 and over	8	25	33	34	0	34

Source: Same as table 2.

periment. Those rules applied principally to the definition of income (upon which payments were based), the income accounting period (the period over which income was considered in calculating payments), and the definition of the filing units (those units jointly filing monthly reports and receiving transfer payments).

Definition of Income

Income was defined as the total gross income in cash or kind received by the household from all sources, less business expenses for the self-employed. The definition of farm and business income generally followed that of the Internal Revenue Service. For some groups, imputed income was added to reported income for purposes of calculating program payments. Homeowners had an imputed rental value added to their income. For those with assets, 10 percent of net capital wealth was added annually to income to represent potential capital consumption. However, the first $20,000 of business assets, the first $10,000 of equity in owner-occupied homes, $1,000 in cash or savings, and all personal effects were excluded from net capital wealth for purposes of this imputation.

A portion of out-of-pocket medical expenses was deducted from income. Federal and state income taxes were reimbursed on a dollar-for-dollar basis.

Payment Interval and Income Accounting

Payments were based on income and family size, as reported on returns filed by the participants every four weeks (or monthly, at the recipient's option). All households were paid biweekly (or semi-monthly, if they filed monthly), with married heads receiving one check made payable to the husband and wife jointly. The accounting period for computing income was treated as an experimental variable. The basic accounting plan for both the rural and urban experiments was a three-period moving average, each period representing four weeks (or one month). In addition, seventy-five families in the rural experiment received payments based solely on income earned in the preceding period.

The income accounting procedure also embodied a carry-over provision. Income in excess of the breakeven level (where payments become zero) was carried forward for a maximum of one year and was added to income in any period in which such income fell below the breakeven level. Payments were based on income earned during the previous three periods (or one period) plus any amount assigned to that period from the carry-over. This was a major innovation from the accounting procedure of the New Jersey experiment, necessitated by the uneven flow of income of the self-employed.

Family Composition

Each family unit in a household was eligible to receive its own separate income maintenance payment. A family unit was defined as any single person twenty-one years of age or older, or a married person eighteen years of age or older, his spouse, and their dependents. The family unit containing the "head of household," who was the person responsible for the household's shelter, received a slightly higher guarantee level than did other family units. If one of these other family units left the original household, that person became eligible for the full "head of household" guarantee level. A family head or spouse who left the original unit was eligible for a payment of one-half the amount that a head and spouse together were entitled to when living together. After one year of separation, each was entitled to a full head-of-household payment.

Reporting and Payment Procedures

Families eligible for payments were required to file an Income Report Form within five days after the end of the month (or four-week period).[7] They were asked to report address changes, family size changes, wage income of every family member over fifteen years of age, transfer and property income by source, certain deductible expenses (income taxes, child care, support paid to former wives or absent children, medical expenditures), and self-employed income and expenses, item by item. Once a year filers reported their asset holdings (and indebtedness) by category. At the same time, farmers reported their depreciation and capital gains (all taken as ordinary income). Bimonthly payments were promptly made to the families two and four weeks following the end of the monthly reporting period.

Families were requested (but not required) to mail in paystubs with their monthly income reports. About half of the wage earners regularly complied with this request. Every incoming monthly report was manually checked for completeness, reasonableness, and consistency with the previous month's report. Payments processors quickly became familiar with acceptable orders of magnitude for wage earnings and other items of income and expenses, although no formal standards were established. During the latter half of the experiment payments administrators instituted a random audit, in which a small percentage of the families were asked to document their monthly reports. This same request was made of a few families with suspicious income reports. There were no audit procedures using sources other than the testimony of the target family itself.

Despite the low literacy level in North Carolina and the prevalence of large and complicated farm income flows in Iowa, this reporting procedure was workable; 90 percent of the forms were received on time each month, and less than 3 percent were more than two weeks late. Twenty percent of the forms had some minor error, such as forgetting to check an

7. Each site had its own payments office. In North Carolina the office was located in Duplin County in the same building as the field interviewing operations. In Iowa payments were handled from the data processing office in Ames, using the computer facilities of Iowa State University. The payments staff consisted of one payments manager and a part-time clerical assistant at each site, plus the equivalent of a one-quarter-time programmer. On average, payments were processed for 325 filers in North Carolina and 200 in Iowa. Administrative costs were approximately $100 per filer per year. Uniformity of procedure was promoted by coordination through the office of the assistant project director in Madison, Wisconsin.

answer "yes" or "no," and 5 percent had an error serious enough (illegibility, income omission, unusual amount) to require a contact with the filer before the payment could be computed and mailed.

Individual Interviews

Questionnaires were administered to the enrolled sample four times a year, with each wave about 90 percent completed within a three-week period. Interviewers worked in pairs to minimize the total time spent at the respondent's home. Typically, one interviewer administered an individual questionnaire to the husband, while the other interviewer administered individual questionnaires to the wife and other adults. Each adult in the family was paid $5.00 upon completion of the interview.

Dependents sixteen to twenty-one years of age were administered a brief questionnaire concerned with their work behavior. Teenagers in the sample were asked to complete a self-administered sociopsychological questionnaire. Finally, data on school performance were obtained from records at the county schools.

In a study of data collection biases it was found that experimental families were slightly more cooperative than control families in the opinion of the interviewers. But no significant differences between these groups were found with respect to their ability to recall their employment status three months prior to the interview or their willingness to provide documented tax information about their wage income. However, farmers receiving payments were more willing than farmers in the control group to report their quarterly income and expenses using farm account books or other written evidence (as opposed to reliance on memory alone). A major longitudinal data editing process, which adjusted the initial interview data in the light of other physical production, inventory, and annual tax information, was directed at mitigating this bias.

Participant Understanding and Accuracy
of Self-Administered Reporting

A central question in the implementation of any program similar to this experiment is how well the beneficiaries understand the rules of operation. An understanding of the effects of earnings on benefits is essential, not only for the observation of an experimental labor supply response, but ultimately for the success of a program which attempts to build in work incentives. In the rural experiment education and literacy levels were low: the average educational attainment of household heads was eight years in North Carolina and eleven years in Iowa. Enrollers estimated that one-half of the North Carolina family heads either had difficulty in reading or could not read at all, and that one-quarter could write only their names.

Conscientious efforts were made to instruct the participants. The average family received nearly two hours of instruction in the rules of operation, had immediate access to written summaries of those rules, received with each benefit check a statement detailing the calculations that produced the monthly payment, and was contacted on the average once a year concerning a particular problem on his monthly report form.

Families were asked a short series of questions about the program's rules at seven months and again at seventeen months after enrollment. In these surveys 66 and 78 percent of the families, respectively, understood the rules regarding freedom of action (to quit work, to move, to spend the payments), and those relating the size of the monthly payment to family size. But the rules concerning the program parameters—the basic benefit (guarantee) level, implicit tax rate, and breakeven level—were understood by only about one-half of the famlies, and their understanding did not improve during the experiment. More than one-quarter of the families thought that the program's tax on their income (which in fact ranged from 30 to 70 percent) was either zero or 100 percent. The large number of recipients who did not understand how their payments were computed suggests that recipients of income maintenance payments have to be given careful, and in some cases repeated, instruction in the program's rules of operation.

Accuracy of reporting is extremely important because underreporting of income and assets could result in an unequitable distribution of payments and excessively high program costs. Program costs are, of course, just as sensitive to misreporting of income as to a real reduction in labor supply or income. To estimate the accuracy of reporting, data on family size, assets, and income reported to the Payments Office were compared to the extent possible with information from the quarterly interviews, W-2 earnings statements or Internal Revenue Service tax forms voluntarily furnished, and social security statements. The quarterly personal interviews may have inhibited the intentional misreporting of large amounts of income on the income report forms, and may have taught the sample members to remember and report their income better than would participants in a national program. On the other hand, the absence of government-enforced penalties may have encouraged misreporting.

Family-size changes reported to the Payments Office were nearly identical to those reported to interviewers during the regular quarterly interviews, in spite of frequent family composition changes. But since information on initial family size and age composition was obtained before the families knew they were to become recipients of income maintenance payments that were linked to family size, one cannot be confident that a national program would enjoy comparable reporting accuracy.

Self-reported asset data gathered annually were also compared with information obtained in the quarterly interviews. In Iowa about 27 percent less equity was reported to the Payments Office than to interviewers; in North Carolina the amount was 14 percent less.

A similar comparison was made for data on income from social security, veterans' benefits, food stamps, unemployment compensation, and pensions. Such income is usually received in unvarying amounts each month, and was taxed at the same implicit tax rate as earned income. Families reported to the Payments Office about 95 percent of their income from transfer payments as recorded by in-person interviewers. Small amounts irregularly received were seldom reported to Payments.

To construct a standard of wage income, against which to compare the monthly reported wage income, a reconciliation was made of quarterly in-person interview information with W-2 withholding statements and social security statements, which were obtained for nearly all wage earners and farmers. Compared to this standard, about 91 percent of the wages of male heads were reported to the Payments Office. The percentage was slightly higher in Iowa than in North Carolina. About 80 percent of the wage income of wives was reported, as compared to this standard.

Net farm income (defined to exclude interest, depreciation, capital gains and losses, and cash rental income) was estimated from in-person interview income and expense tabulations, annual acreage, yield and inventory reports, and federal income tax statements. Only 61 percent of this income was reported to the Payments Office. The underreporting of net farm income arose largely from the underreporting of gross farm sales, rather than from overreporting farm expenses.

In summary, monthly self-reported data on family composition and transfer and wage income appeared to be acceptably accurate, but farm assets and farm income were considerably underreported. Underreporting of these items, in fact, was of such a magnitude as to increase program costs much more than any likely labor supply response among farmers.

Regression analysis found that families with low, unsteady incomes reported a lower percentage of their incomes than higher-income families. Single heads reported less of their income than married couples. But there were no large and consistent differences in accuracy among families of different ages, verbal ability, residence, or race. However, underreporting of wage income was found to be more pronounced among families on experimental plans with either low guarantee levels or high tax rates.

Lessons for Administration of a National Program

The rural income maintenance experiment provided experience with several of the administrative problems that would arise in an income-tested cash assistance program covering the working poor. Let us first consider the implications for rural nonfarm families (who comprise over three-fourths of the rural poor) and then turn our attention to the more difficult problem of administering such a program for the self-employed.

A major finding of the rural experiment was that self-reporting of income and family size by rural wage earners was both feasible and acceptably accurate. The reporting forms were not simple, and there was initial concern that the poorly educated could not fulfill the reporting requirements. This concern proved to be ill-founded. The large numbers of families with heads who were functionally illiterate proved to have wives, teenage children, other relatives, or friends who normally handled written communications for them. As a result, virtually all families were able to comply with the reporting requirements and to report information with a high degree of accuracy, lending strong support to the cost-saving administrative procedure of self-reporting by participants in welfare-type programs.

The self-employed farmers did not perform as well as wage earners. They too were able to file the monthly reports but with far less accuracy than wage earners. Moreover, the experiment had to deal with a number of conceptual and administrative problems peculiar to self-employment activities, and to devise equitable operational rules for handling them. Lessons from the experiment in four areas regarding treatment of the self-employed are discussed below. They are the definition of self-employment income, measurement of farm income and expenses, treatment of assets, and an appropriate accounting period to deal with seasonal fluctuations in farm income.

Definition of Self-Employment Income

The distinction between property and self-employment income for owners, and between wage and self-employment income for tenants, presented a difficult problem in the rural experiment. Various common renting or sharing arrangements appeared to possess characteristics of each type of income for either landlords or tenants. The distinction is important since work expenses were deductible from income for the self-employed but not for wage earners.

For the purposes of the experiment a person was considered self-employed if some or all business assets were owned or rented and were complementary to his labor input; or if income was based solely on output rather than on labor input, and the person had control over his labor input. To be considered self-employed, an owner of resources had to make a managerial input that required time and influenced the amount of income derived from those resources. If an owner rented out his property on a share basis, income from that property fell in the self-employment category because an owner was considered unlikely to rent on a percentage basis without any say in the operation of the business. In most share-rental arrangements, income derived from the resources was defined as self-employment income for both the landlord and tenant. If resources were rented on a fixed-fee basis, only income to the tenant was self-employment income. Farm laborers working solely for a share of the output and having no control over either the resources or their own labor were not considered self-employed.

While the above concept and definitions were not without difficulties in their operational application, they were satisfactory and workable, and their use in any similar nationwide program should be strongly considered.

Measurement of Farm Income and Expenses

Since most of the self-employed are familiar with Internal Revenue Service measures of income, IRS guidelines provide the most convenient method of measuring self-employment income. For income maintenance purposes, however, IRS rules create several major problems. The first is created by the option of using either the cash or the accrual method of accounting. Under the cash method, income is counted only when it is actually received and expenses are counted only when actually paid. The accrual method takes into account changes in inventories and reflects sales and purchases regardless of when payment is received or made.

The cash method of accounting is the easier of the two, and most farmers and small businessmen use it. But it permits the manipulation of stocks of nonperishable commodities, such as grains, so that a farmer could delay sales of his crop in order to maximize income maintenance payments. Though adjustments in reported income and expenses could be made to insure reasonable consistency from year to year, assignment of income to a period other than that in which it was received would be highly discretionary, and several years' history would have to be acquired for each farmer.[8]

Under the cash method of accounting, a livestock farmer could add to his herd by keeping the offspring, and the increase in herd value would not be reported as income, though the cost of raising the offspring would be a deductible expense. For income tax purposes, higher future income would compensate for the understatement of current income, though it would be counted as capital gains and taxed at only one-half the regular rate. But under an income maintenance program, overpayments in one period could not be recouped later if the farmer were no longer receiving benefits. These problems suggest that an accrual method of accounting, in which increases in inventories are considered as increases in income, should be required for income maintenance purposes.

A second problem in following IRS rules results from the treatment of capital gains, which are not counted as income unless assets are sold. Under these rules, a self-employed person could continue to receive income maintenance payments while at the same time markedly increasing his net worth. Since farmland has tripled in value in the last ten years, farmers are likely to enjoy considerable capital gains. For the purposes of an income maintenance program it may be preferable to treat the full amount of both realized and unrealized capital gains as income, and to treat both realized and unrealized capital losses as expenses.[9]

A third problem occurs in the treatment of depreciation. Two provisions of the tax laws, accelerated depreciation and the investment tax credit, result in distorted measures of true self-employment income dur-

8. The secretary of the U.S. Department of Health, Education, and Welfare was authorized to make such adjustments in determining eligibility for benefits under the revised version of the proposed family assistance program (commonly known as H.R. 1).

9. The rural experiment counted all realized capital gains as income, but ignored unrealized capital gains.

ing the current period. These depreciation methods should probably be disallowed for the purpose of calculating income maintenance payments.

A fourth problem results from the practice of allowing tenant farmers to receive the free use of a dwelling in addition to a share of the crop. The value of this rent-free housing is not included in IRS definitions of farm income. In the rural experiment the value of rent-free housing, based on the family's own estimate of the current rental value of the dwelling, was added to the family's regularly reported income before determining the benefit payment.

Treatment of Assets

Because a self-employed person's capital investment is complementary to his labor, income maintenance program rules should not deny eligibility to the self-employed merely because they possess more assets than the average wage earner. But an upper limit on assets that a self-employed person could hold without losing eligibility would prevent horror cases in which an obviously wealthy person qualified for payments, and even a middle-income farmer or businessman with substantial net worth should be expected to divest or borrow against his assets during low-income years.

A simple limit on the amount of net assets to be excluded creates a "notch" that could cause a recipient to lose all his benefits if he went one dollar over the asset limit. A more satisfactory approach would be to impute to income some percentage of assets above a specified level. This approach reduces benefits smoothly as assets increase while still treating those with large amounts of assets less generously than those with fewer assets. As mentioned previously, this procedure was followed in the rural experiment: 10 percent of business net worth in excess of $20,000 was imputed to income. Thus, those with a negative tax rate of 50 percent and a guarantee of $4,000 would have been ineligible for payments if business net worth exceeded $100,000.

In retrospect, this appears too generous; a farmer with $100,000 equity would rank high among all farmers in terms of net worth, and might well control over a quarter of a million dollars in assets. A higher imputation rate on net worth in excess of the exclusion rate, and perhaps a slightly higher exclusion rate, would be more appropriate. A 20 percent imputation rate and an exclusion of $25,000, or a 25 percent rate and an exclusion of $30,000, would render a farmer ineligible for payments if his net worth was $62,000–$65,000 and he was on a 50 percent negative tax rate and a guarantee of $4,000.

Income Accounting Period

The uneven flow of self-employment farm income necessitated a close look at the accounting period for measuring income, as this has a direct bearing on eligibility and benefit levels. Current transfer programs have eligibility periods that range from one week (unemployment compensation) to a full year (Veterans Administration pensions). Short accounting periods permit the income supplement program to respond rapidly to changes in the beneficiary's income level. But a short accounting period can be unfair to a steady wage earner relative to a farmer. Under a one-month accounting period, for example, a wage earner making $15,000 a year would not qualify for income maintenance payments, while a farmer who cleared $15,000 but received it all from the sale of crops during a three-month period could be eligible for maximum benefits during the other nine months.

To permit short-term responsiveness to income changes while still ensuring equal treatment of wage earners and farmers, the rural experiment developed a one-month accounting period with a twelve-month carry-over procedure. Income received in excess of the breakeven level (the level of income at which benefits are reduced to zero) was carried forward and added to income in any subsequent month (up to twelve months in the future) in which the family's income fell below its breakeven level. Similarly, negative net income was carried forward and used to offset positive income in subsequent months.

In light of the early experience of the experiment that was reported to both the administration and Congress, the twelve-month carry-over was incorporated into the family assistance program. Such a carry-over provision should be considered for any future legislation but it seems preferable to extend it for fifteen to eighteen months for those with any substantial portion of their income derived from self-employment.

In general, the administrative lessons from the rural experiment were an unexpected but valuable byproduct, and should help to improve the effectiveness and efficiency of the operation of any nationwide income-tested cash assistance program for the working poor.

Comment by David N. Kershaw

My remarks are concentrated on the administrative, or operational, aspects of the experiment that interact with and change the experimental treatments. I think it is proper to focus on the more formal technical treatments such as the guarantee levels and tax rates, and to stress hypothesis-testing in the economic and noneconomic areas of behavior. However, the authors of almost all the papers presented at the conference recognize both implicitly and explicitly that the way in which the treatments are provided to recipients—that is, the mechanisms, rules, regulations, and structure involved in the delivery of the treatments—has an important impact on the treatments themselves. As Welch put it, there was a "real world" thing in place that frustrated his attempts to equate—or even compare—what was happening in the experiment with the theoretical treatments he was accustomed to describing to his students. Ashenfelter faced the same problem. Attempting to compare results from the urban and rural experiments, he found that these two experiments employed different eligibility standards, which made pooling of data virtually impossible. Robert Lampman, in a series of comments presented during the conference, suggested that a number of additional administrative parameters actually should have been varied experimentally.

My thesis is that these administrative parameters are indeed critical, both to the interpretation of experimental results and to predictions of the effects of any national cash assistance program we might introduce. In fact, the magnitude of the impact of these administrative parameters on behavior often exceeds that of other features of the experimental treatments that have received more attention. While the magnitude of such effects is difficult to measure since these administrative parameters were not varied systematically in any of the experiments, a considerable amount has been learned about them during the last five years through the use of microsimulation.[10]

The three most important administrative parameters that have been identified to date—important in the sense that they have the greatest

10. See, in particular, Jodie T. Allen, "Designing Income Maintenance Systems: The Income Accounting Problem," in *Studies in Public Welfare,* paper 5 (part 3): *Issues in Welfare Administration: Implications of the Income Maintenance Experiments* (Government Printing Office, 1973); and Harold Beebout, "Microsimulation as a Policy Tool: The MATH Model," Policy Analysis Series, no. 14 (Mathematica Policy Research, 1977).

potential for influencing recipient behavior in ways that may change program costs—are the accounting period, the family unit rules, and the definition of income. In the brief space allowed to me, I would like to describe these administrative parameters, and then indicate how they may be expected to influence both the ability to measure the treatments used in the experiment and their potential influence on the costs, coverage, and equity of an operating program.

The Accounting Period

A great deal has been written about the accounting period since it was first recognized as an important administrative aspect of the New Jersey experiment.[11] Briefly, I am referring both to the frequency with which income and other information is reported by recipients and to the length of time during which recipients can be taxed on what they have reported. Short accounting periods make the payments highly responsive to the immediate needs of recipients, yet they may permit individuals who are only temporarily poor to receive large payments. A longer accounting period, say annual as employed in the positive income tax system, ensures horizontal equity on an annual basis (and would not reward seasonal workers and others with irregular income patterns), but would fail to respond to sudden decreases in income resulting, for example, from the loss of a job. There is virtually an infinite number of combinations of reporting frequencies and length of accountable period, each with different behavioral implications.

While the designers of the income maintenance experiments recognized the importance of the accounting period issue, the fact is that *the accounting period was defined differently in each of the experiments*. This is an extremely important point since it raises very serious problems for pooling information, making inferences across the experiments, and, indeed, generalizing to a national program from even one experiment.

THE INTERACTION OF THE ACCOUNTING PERIOD AND TAX RATES. One of the most critical research issues in the experiment involved the response of individuals to the marginal tax rate. The selection of a given tax rate is expected to influence labor supply by changing the opportunity

11. See Allen, "Designing Income Maintenance Systems," and D. Lee Bawden and David Kershaw, "Problems in Income Reporting and Accounting," in Larry L. Orr, Robinson G. Hollister, and Myron J. Lefcowitz, eds., *Income Maintenance: Interdisciplinary Approaches to Research* (Markham, 1971), pp. 258–67.

cost of leisure (the substitution effect). Since labor supply is the major determinant of program costs (the cost of transfer payments varying inversely with hours worked and earnings), it is crucial to obtain a good estimate of behavioral responses to a range of tax rates. In addition, the lower the tax rate, the higher the breakeven level and thus the more individuals who will be covered by the program (and thus the higher both the transfer and administrative costs). The experiments must therefore yield guidance on the issue of costs resulting from various tax rates in a national program.

The problem is that the accounting period significantly influences the tax rate by changing the marginal effect of a change in income. That is, if an experiment employs a carry-over system of accounting that makes individuals liable for some portion of past earnings above a certain level before they can begin to receive payments, then individuals with such past earnings face a different marginal tax rate from that of individuals with lower past earnings, even though they are both in the same experiment and both have been assigned to the same nominal tax rate treatment. Essentially, since the accounting period has the effect of smoothing the payments stream that results from changes in income, it changes the tax rate for some individuals. Thus a researcher may not be measuring what he thinks he is measuring unless he understands and corrects for the tax rate/accounting period interaction. More important, he may be generalizing his results to a national program that will select an entirely different accounting period from the one used in the experiment. This may mean that the effective program tax rate may be quite different from the nominal rate.

As Welch points out, he gets different results for individuals over and under the breakeven level, as he calls it those "off" and "on" the experiment. Since those over the breakeven are not, in a practical sense, being "treated," one can understand that ceteris paribus they could respond differently. However, almost as important as the guarantee level and the tax rate in determining whether a person is on or off the experiment is the accounting period. A carry-over system of accounting will have the effect of keeping some individuals off the experiment for much longer periods than they would otherwise. To take an extreme example, a seasonal worker whose six months' earnings are at an annual rate that is over the breakeven point would be on the experiment half of the time under a monthly accounting system and never on the experiment under an annual system. Other accounting variations would shift the duration of his exposure to the treatment. To the extent that Welch's findings are correct, the treatment has been importantly influenced by the accounting period.

THE OVERALL IMPORTANCE OF THE ACCOUNTING PERIOD. It is possible that the accounting period may in fact be a more important behavioral parameter than any of those actually measured in the experiments. With the use of simulation models, it has been estimated that holding the guarantee and tax rate constant, with reasonable variations in the accounting period, would affect program costs by at least a factor or two, indeed, the costs of the family assistance plan varied by billions of dollars depending on the choice of accounting periods. In addition, current research in Denver indicates that having welfare recipients report income and family size every month rather than every three or six months, as required in the current system, reduces transfer costs by as much as 10 percent.[12] Both of these cost consequences are more powerful than any of those predicted from changes in labor supply through income or substitution effects.

Family Unit Rules

Family unit rules and the definition of income appear likely to have similarly powerful effects on the experimental results—and on a national program. In the extreme, family unit rules have the effect of excluding large numbers of poor people from existing welfare programs because they are intact families, or they have no disabled member, or they have no aged head. This categorization of individuals and families is hardly a trivial administrative parameter. However, other regulations that appeared initially to both experimenters and welfare reformers as incidental to the research and planning process may be expected to have very important effects on the program. For example:

1. The extent to which individuals in a household are required to pool income was shown by a study for the Department of Health, Education, and Welfare to have cost effects on welfare reform options amounting to billions of dollars.[13]

12. Results from the study are still preliminary. They may be found in Alan M. Hershey, J. Jeffrey Morris, and Robert G. Williams, *Colorado Monthly Reporting Experiment and Pre-test: Preliminary Research Results* (Mathematica Policy Research, February 1977).

13. "Task Force Report on the Administrative Feasibility of an Income Maintenance Program" (report to Secretary George P. Shultz from Donald C. Alexander, Commissioner of Internal Revenue Service, April 1974; processed), section entitled "Definition of Filing Unit," p. 3.

2. The way payments are divided when a family breaks up may significantly influence the decision of a spouse to leave the household. This has considerable cost implications.

3. Marginal payment increases based on additional children may have an effect on birth rates, which in turn will have considerable cost and caseload effects.

4. Treatment of young adults and the aged (counting them in the unit both for purposes of payment calculation and for income pooling) may result in a significant increase in individual households if there are economic gains to the family of removing them from (or forcing them to leave) the household.

Unfortunately, all of the experiments had as their mandate the measurement of the impact of income maintenance, that is, the tax rate and guarantee levels, on family formation and breakup. Since they all had complex and different family unit rules, it is difficult to see how results can be compared across experiments and how inferences can be made to new national programs that will have yet another set of regulations.[14]

DEFINITION OF INCOME. Similarly, since payments are based on reported income, seemingly simple shifts in income definitions may have vast effects on the issues of who is covered by a new program and how much it costs. The most important ways in which income definition affects behavior appear to be: the method used, if any, to impute a return to assets (or the existence of a strict asset level cutoff); the way in which the income of various other members of the family (such as children with earnings, aged relatives, and unrelated members of the household) is treated; the existence of differing tax rates applied to such items as other transfer payments, alimony and child support, dividend income, and medical and life insurance premiums and benefits; and the existence of a substantial number of deductions from income for such things as work-related expenses, capital losses, and so forth.

Each of the above, again different in each of the experiments and likely to be different in some respects in a national program, has various behavioral implications that influence or modify the other treatments being

14. Considerable effort was made to relate the differences in rules in the New Jersey, rural, Gary, and Seattle-Denver experiments, and the probable effects this would have on behavioral outcomes, in David Kershaw and Jerilyn Fair, *The New Jersey Income-Maintenance Experiment*, vol. 1: *Operations, Surveys, and Administration* (Academic Press, 1976), chap. 5.

measured. A cursory comparison of four of the experiments on the above parameters showed that families in similar economic circumstances and assigned to similar nominal treatments could, because of differences in income definition rules, face very different actual tax rate and guarantee treatments.[15]

As in the case of the accounting period, one can pool experimental data and generalize to a national program only if the interaction of both family unit rules and income definitions with the experimental treatments are understood.

Conclusion

Those involved in both the design of the experiments and in the planning for national welfare reform have realized that there are a considerable number of other administrative parameters with important behavioral implications. These include such things as the frequency and method of contacting recipients; how much recipients know about program regulations and payments changes; the length and complexity of the forms used to report income, assets, family size, and change in composition; and the extent and nature of audits of recipient reports.

The effects of many of these parameters can be estimated using microsimulation and other techniques that do not require elaborate controlled field tests like the experiments. It is to the credit of those planning the more recent welfare reforms that they have become increasingly sophisticated about the importance of these administrative elements and have attempted to take them into account when formulating new program options and estimating their costs and effects. However, too much attention has been given to what might be considered the more theoretically traditional treatments, and too little to a systematic test of administrative issues. Indeed, it is becoming clear that the latter may prove to be far more important, both in interpreting the results of the experiments and in estimating the ultimate impact of new programs, than was ever imagined when the current set of experiments was planned. It is time to test them—and with the same care that has been given to the tax rate and guarantee variables.

15. Ibid., pp. 86–94.

Comment by Robert G. Spiegelman

I will address three issues raised by the final reports of the rural negative income tax experiment that are relevant to overall design issues of social experiments. These are: determination of the appropriate assignment model and sample size; appropriate procedures for dealing with population heterogeneity; and methods for extrapolating and comparing the results of site-specific experiments.

The Assignment Model and Sample Size Determination

The Conlisk-Watts model has been used for determination of sample size and the allocation of the sample points to treatments in all the income maintenance experiments. The objective of this model is to minimize a function that is a weighted sum of the error variances for predictions of labor supply for a set of treatment variables, subject to a budget constraint. The underlying assumption is that the experimenters were faced with a fixed budget for the experiment, and that the relevant question was how to obtain the most information from that given budget.

In hindsight, it is clear that the Conlisk-Watts model can produce experimental designs that will meet the budget constraint, but will not provide statistically reliable results. This is distressing, particularly when large response coefficients that are statistically indistinguishable from zero are observed; for example, in the rural experiment, the response coefficient for nonfarm labor of wives suggests a 20 to 30 percent reduction in labor supply, but this coefficient is not significant at the 90 percent level.[16] Even more serious is the point raised by Ashenfelter that response differences by support level or tax rate cannot be inferred from the data. The limited budget was stretched even further by requiring a sample of aged as well as one of unrelated individuals whose labor supply responses cannot be inferred from the data.

I believe that the appropriate assignment model should follow an approach suggested by Ashenfelter and others,[17] in which the objective is to

16. See Larry Orr's paper, this volume, table 2.
17. See Orley Ashenfelter, "The Effect of Manpower Training on Earnings: Preliminary Results," in James L. Stern and Barbara D. Dennis, eds., *Proceedings of the Twenty-seventh Annual Winter Meeting* (Industrial Relations Research Association, 1975), pp. 252–60.

minimize cost, subject to a given variance of the treatment coefficient. The latter is determined on the basis of responses that would trigger policy decisions. The government always has the option of not funding an experiment if the expected benefits do not justify the cost.

Population Heterogeneity

The sample size problem looms especially large when attempting to estimate responses for subpopulations. Even with a sample of 5,000 families, the Seattle-Denver income maintenance experiment cannot provide reliable response measurements for some subgroups of the sample. It is highly desirable to be able to merge samples to the greatest extent possible, and to deal with heterogeneity by the use of a limited number of interaction variables. Merger is especially appropriate if there is no theoretical justification for anticipating differential responses. For example, once demand conditions and socioeconomic backgrounds are controlled, there is no reason to expect different responses for blacks and whites. Obviously, merging the sample across races would greatly increase the chance of finding statistically reliable responses.

Of even greater importance, however, is the apparent need in the rural experiment to estimate separate equations for North Carolina and Iowa whites. This is disturbing because the justification for conducting site-specific experiments rests on the expectation that the results can be extrapolated to larger populations. Inherent in such an expectation is that location, per se, does not affect response. Bawden and Harrar's explanation for the separate analysis of the two sites is that there are essentially two different populations represented; they write, "the North Carolina sample was characterized by a poorly educated, older mix of small farmers and unskilled wage earners, *who were less likely to rise out of poverty on their own*. In Iowa the families seemed to be more middle class."[18] In other words, the poverty level incomes in North Carolina are more likely to be permanent than the same low incomes in Iowa. If this is the reason for differing labor supply response, I believe there is a misspecification. The response differences are not due primarily to regional characteristics, but rather to the fact that in one region the income variables are permanent and in the other region they have a high transitory component. Econometrically, the problem may be solved by having separate regional equa-

---

18. Page 32, this volume. Emphasis added.

tions, but our understanding of the results would be greater if the differences were properly modeled to account for the differences in income measures. In the Seattle-Denver income maintenance experiment, there is strong statistical evidence that the two sites may be merged.[19] Correct specification of the variables in the rural experiment might lead to the same result.

Extrapolation of Results

The reports on the New Jersey experiment did not raise the issue of extrapolation. Although the rural experiment does attempt to address the issue, I believe that the approach presented in the final report is overly simplistic and not likely to produce reliable results. The counties in the rural experiment were selected so that the North Carolina county was representative of a five-state southern region, and the Iowa county representative of a three-state midwestern region. The justification was based on a comparison of a small set of census-like variables, namely, median family income, unemployment rate, population density, racial composition, educational attainment, and age distribution. However, similarity of these variables does not provide an adequate basis for extrapolation of experimental labor supply responses. The dummy variable model estimated in the rural and New Jersey experiments should not be interpreted to imply that the coefficient of the treatment variable measures response to absolute levels of support and taxes, since in fact it represents the responses to differences in these variables from the conditions facing the control group. In other words, the value of the parameter of the treatment coefficient is valid only for a population facing the same set of preexperimental support programs and income taxes. For any other set of supports and taxes, the response parameter would be different, even if the environment in other respects is the same. There is no evidence that these conditions are met even in the states used for extrapolation.

I believe that an entirely different model is needed for extrapolation purposes, one that recognizes the control environment explicitly by having treatment coefficients that directly measure changes in supports and changes in tax rates.

19. Michael C. Keeley and others, "The Labor Supply Effects and Costs of Alternative Negative Income Tax Programs: Evidence from the Seattle and Denver Income Maintenance Experiments, Part I, The Labor Supply Response Function," research memorandum 38 (Stanford Research Institute, Center for the Study of Welfare Policy, May 1977; processed).

HAROLD W. WATTS AND
D. LEE BAWDEN

Issues and Lessons
of Experimental Design

This essay results from an invitation to review and evaluate the consequences of basic decisions and omissions affecting the design of the first two negative income tax experiments. The reader must bear in mind that this self-evaluation has none of the objectivity that might be expected from a disinterested observer.

Two kinds of issues are distinguished here: first are the issues that were considered carefully with the best information available at the time, and second are those that arose as surprises and might have led to different choices if they had been anticipated. Hindsight applied to the former category allows reweighting of arguments made at the time of initial design. The latter category invites speculation both about how foresight might have changed the design and how such surprises could have been avoided.[1]

It is important to recognize the constraints within which the scientific objectives of the experiments were pursued. Financial and political constraints were present and, while not absolutely rigid, they did serve to limit the approaches that could be considered. Many of the features of the experiments cannot be understood without reference to these constraints. Since they were imposed by and negotiated with the Office of Economic Opportunity (OEO), it is clear that the sponsoring agency was an important participant in the final design. Following a retrospective review of the main features of the experiments, and the surprises, the final section will comment briefly on the nature of the sponsor-investigator relationship in social experimentation.

1. We will not explicitly consider the alternative of not doing an experiment. That is a choice which needs to be carefully made, and the following discussion may help to ensure that it will not be made lightly.

Evaluation of Critical Choices in Design

In both the urban and rural experiments a variety of experimental treatments were administered to scattered samples of poor and near-poor households, comparable (via randomization) to parallel control groups. The geographical areas from which the samples were drawn were selected with a view toward representativeness but without randomization. The experimental treatment and collection of information extended over a three-year period. These basic features all represent carefully considered choices relative to plausible alternatives. With the benefit of hindsight, we will ask whether the choices would be the same if we were starting again.

The Variety of Experimental Treatments

A clear alternative to the five (rural) or eight (urban) negative tax treatments would have been to concentrate on one scheme and its contrast with the status quo (as represented by a control sample). A less extreme alternative would have been to limit the variation to one dimension, for example, the tax rate, the guarantee, or some related hybrid (such as keeping the breakeven constant).

Considering the very uncertain results obtained, particularly from variation in the guarantee, should future experiments be less ambitious? We think not, provided there is clear policy relevance and theoretical foundation for the separate dimensions as well as a comparable degree of uncertainty about the magnitude of differential response. If there had been marked or uniform differential response among the various treatments, it would be very important to know about it, and there would be every reason to expect that the experiment as designed would have detected it. As it stands there is evidence against a large response on the part of husbands to guarantee and tax differentials, in the low and moderate ranges, and this evidence would not have been available if a one-plan design had been chosen.

Another alternative would have been to experiment with a larger number of treatment plans. This alternative was also carefully considered, and concern was expressed over the complexity and corresponding increased cost of administration. In retrospect, we may have been overly concerned for it appears this would have added only slightly to the cost. A larger number of treatments would have allowed tax rate response to be estimated in polynomials beyond the quadratic, which could have provided slightly more sophistication to the estimated response surface and hence more refined interpolation of response between any two observed tax rates. Given the sample sizes available, however, it was not possible to distinguish among elaborate functional forms.

Still another alternative considered at the time was to experiment with a broader range of tax rates and guarantee levels. The initial ranges of 30 to 70 percent for tax rates, and 50 to 100 (rural) or 125 (urban) percent of the poverty line for guarantees, appeared then—and still appear —to bracket the policy-relevant parameters for a nationwide program. Given the small tax rate response in the urban experiment and the mixed response in the rural experiment, it would have been of interest to test tax rates on both earned income and nonearned income at or approaching 100 percent.

A final issue regarding the number of treatments is that, ex post, the usable sample was very thin for examining the effects of the 70 percent tax rate. Plans that incorporated the 70 percent tax rate had guarantee levels of 75 percent in the rural experiment and 75 and 100 percent in the urban experiment. These benefit plans were generally dominated in New Jersey by payment schedules under aid to families with dependent children–unemployed parents (AFDC-UP) for those families who became eligible for welfare in 1969.[2] In both experiments the low breakeven levels meant that many families had incomes during the experiment that were too high to qualify them for payments. In the rural experiment lower policy weights assigned to the 70 percent tax rate during the sample allocation process resulted in fewer initial families participating in this plan. It would have been possible to have combined the 70 percent tax rate with higher guarantees, providing a larger final sample of families operating under a 70 percent tax rate. Without an increased budget, such an allocation would have reduced the size of other cells, of course, and hence would have weakened the evidence elsewhere, but such a trade-off would probably have been beneficial on balance.

Saturation versus Scattered Sample Approach

Another feature worth noting is the scattered sample approach. This can be sharply contrasted with what may be termed the "saturation" ap-

2. For a discussion of the problem this created see Henry J. Aaron, "Cautionary Notes on the Experiment," in Joseph A. Pechman and P. Michael Timpane, eds., *Work Incentives and Income Guarantees: The New Jersey Negative Income Tax Experiment* (Brookings Institution, 1975), pp. 88–114.

proach in which all families in one or several areas are eligible for an experimental treatment. We chose the scattered approach for reasons that still seem persuasive. A saturation experiment enables a wider range of questions to be addressed and provides a more holistic evaluation of a prototype public policy. However, an entire local labor market would be needed as the unit of analysis for many of these broader questions, and for these there would only be case-study results unless the budget were increased by a major order of magnitude. Even so, the problem of finding control samples for entire labor markets would be severe.

The approach taken was consistent with limiting the objectives of the studies to aspects of individual and family behavior. Following the classical structure of partial equilibrium analysis, the experiments were designed to examine shifts in labor supply schedules resulting from a specific mix of ad valorem taxes and lump-sum subsidies. These can be studied by introducing such taxes and subsidies for some families and not for others and then observing and contrasting their behavior in identical labor demand situations. Far from counting it a liability that the labor market would not simulate the full equilibrium effect of an income subsidy, it was hoped that the treatment of a scattered sample would have a negligible effect on the level and movement of prices and on employment opportunities.

Why Not a National Sample?

The experimental sites were few in number and selected carefully but nonrandomly. This basic and controversial choice of a "test-bore" strategy meant that households could be studied in specific localities that were thought representative of major and possibly distinct types of labor markets. Further limitation by type of family (age, marital structure) served to narrow the range of generalizability even more. An alternative strategy would have been to use randomization to get a sample that could be readily and routinely generalized to all geographic areas or a wider range of household categories. This would have meant a highly dispersed sample with both interview and program administration in at least fifteen to twenty states and a much larger number of local jurisdictions.

This "national sample" approach was explicitly considered, forcefully argued, and finally rejected. The argument in its favor is obvious. It permits a scientifically respected, widely accepted generalization to populations of direct policy interest. Moreover, there has been a substantial amount of experience with surveys that embody such an approach. Against this was the fact the administration of an actual program—in this case an experimental negative income tax—to a highly dispersed sample was not within the demonstrated competence of survey organizations. A national sample would have made it too expensive to use local offices to answer questions and follow up on problems; part-time agents of some sort would have been necessary. Coordination with welfare and public housing authorities would have been complicated, at least in proportion to the number of jurisdictions entered. Finally, the broad representativeness would have been attained at the cost of reduced homogeneity of the group studied, and the additional sources of variation would have further reduced the precision of response estimates.

In hindsight, we do not believe the "national sample" approach would have been more appropriate for these experiments, or indeed for future experiments with similar objectives. The automatic representativeness is a much weaker advantage when studying a complex behavior pattern than when trying to estimate average ex post income levels or the relative attractiveness of competing political candidates. There is every reason to target important and typical segments of the total array of labor markets and types of families, selected on the basis of prior knowledge and judgment. A more broadly based sample, constrained to the same budget, would probably have yielded less useful information. If spending five or ten times as much were a possibility, we should again carefully examine how a wider range of "test bores" would add to our knowledge rather than assume that a national sample would be superior.

Demographic Characteristics of the Sample

The urban experiment focused on working poor households containing at least one male breadwinner as well as one or more dependents. Female-headed families without adult males and families headed by aged males (eligible for social security retirement during the experiment) were deliberately excluded on grounds related both to the homogeneity of the resulting sample and the priority given to information on the prime-age male categories. The rural experiment made small sample allocations to female-headed and older families at the insistence of OEO, which had encountered criticism for neglect of these groups in the earlier urban income maintenance experiment.

Aside from possible relief from the charge of neglect, the diversion of more than one-fourth of the rural sample (13 percent to the female-headed group and 14 percent to the aged male group) yielded little useful information and weakened the precision available for the primary target group. While the small sample could have detected extremely divergent behavior for these groups, there was little reason to expect it and none in fact appeared. Experience in this case reinforces the need to maintain the primary focus of future experiments on an objective that can be handled within the allowed sample size or budget. Politically based digressions may be unavoidable but they should be regarded as dead weight liabilities.

The sample was limited to families whose recent income experience, corrected for short-term abnormalities, placed them below 150 percent of the official poverty line. This was despite the fact that one of the rural and two of the urban experimental plans provided net benefits up to 250 percent of the poverty line. Besides truncating the sample below the break-even point of the more generous plans, this strategy resulted in a sample with relatively few employed women. The former consequence was fully appreciated at the start of the experiment. The latter, having to do with working wives, might have been anticipated, but in fact became apparent only when preliminary analysis of the data began. This example is a clear case of the conflict between scientific objectives and political imperatives. While a clear and persuasive case for the inclusion of higher income families can be made, based firmly on policy needs for information, the Office of Economic Opportunity found it impossible to expend their research funds to support families that far above nominal poverty.

Two possible alternatives might have been considered. One would have been to allow the inclusion of families with recent income experience up to 250 or 300 percent of the poverty line, allowing the optimal allocation model to assign a large proportion of such families to the more generous plans or to the control group for comparison purposes. This solution would have allowed more complete coverage of the eligible subpopulation for policies resembling those plans. The second alternative would have been to base the sample truncation on the earning experience of the primary breadwinner, perhaps augmented by other nonearned, nonwelfare income. As designed and carried out, the urban experiment included very few wives or mothers with full-year, full-time labor force experience, for the simple reason that few families with two full-time earners could be below 150 percent of the poverty line in the labor markets examined. While this situation also existed in the rural experiment, it was less pronounced because of the low-wage labor market, particularly in

North Carolina. Both common sense and previous findings suggest that women carrying full-time jobs and large family responsibilities might well reconsider their options if a substantial part of the income forgone by quitting their jobs would be replaced by transfer payments. This hypothesis simply did not receive a fair test. Using the low eligibility criterion, much of the labor force activity of women was of the marginal or fractional variety—an important but still incomplete segment of the female labor supply potentially affected by family income subsidies.

However unfortunate, it is not clear that the lessons of the experiment would have outweighed the political imperatives felt by OEO. Future researchers will have to decide, as we did, whether such limitations destroy the scientific or policy usefulness of a project.

The Duration of the Experiment

Finally, an important consideration is the time span of the experiment. Experimental treatment plans were scheduled to extend over a three-year period. Observations of the families were begun immediately prior to the introduction of experimental payments to provide a baseline survey. Twelve quarterly surveys followed that, and two postexperimental surveys followed in April and September 1973 after the end of benefit payments. A number of issues are involved here. The most obvious ones are whether the experiment should have been longer (or shorter), and whether the duration of the experiment should have been an experimental variable in its own right. Permanent income theory indicates the desirability of a longer experiment. For individuals with long time horizons or substantial seniority in a secure job, the response to a short-term experiment will surely be attenuated relative to a long-term experiment or a policy presumed to be permanent. Clearly some sort of compromise must be realized unless the sponsors of the research are willing to wait an indeterminate period for results from an experiment that has demonstrated itself to be permanent. Three years is a relatively long period of time for that part of the low-wage population that has unstable employment. If their jobs have rarely lasted longer than a year, a three-year experiment may be as permanent a situation as anything they have experienced. But there is another important segment of the working poor—those who have stable and substantially secure employment in low-wage markets. For such workers three years may be too short to yield reliable adjustments.

A possible alternative would be to stratify families according to the stability of their employment and to design treatments of varying duration appropriate to each stratum. This might provide a sequence of experimental findings eventually covering the entire population eligible for benefits. Even without the stratification a good argument can be made for using at least two different durations (as was indeed done in the Seattle-Denver experiment) so that a first approximation on the sensitivity to duration can be obtained. While it is possible to explore this issue in a single-duration experiment by examining collateral consumption behavior, two or more durations are more direct and powerful. The main conflicting considerations are that extended durations delay the availability of final results, and that the longer duration adds to costs of payments and surveys (which would reduce sample sizes if a fixed budget were maintained). In retrospect, it seems doubtful that multiple durations would have been beneficial under the budgetary constraints for each experiment, although the alternative of stratifying workers according to job stability should be further examined as a strategy for future experiments.

It has been suggested that valuable additional information could have been obtained by observing families for a substantial period prior to the initiation of experimental payments with similar observations for some time after the end of payments.[3] This strategy focuses on intertemporal comparisons of identical families or individuals rather than on interfamily or interpersonal comparisons during the same periods. Clearly a longer observation period, both before and after the experiment, would either compress the duration of experimental treatment plans or extend the overall length and cost of the project. There are, of course, sound reasons for evaluating preexperimental behavior, and this was recognized in the design. But it might be useful in the future to consider more than a simple baseline survey. The evidence from this and other experiments should be helpful in evaluating the marginal contribution of increments of such additional information.

The issues discussed above cover the main features of the experiment that were explicitly chosen when the experiments were designed. In every case there were plausible alternatives, and the constraints of resources, time, and political viability conditioned the choices made. Within these constraints, we do not find any alternative choices that are unambiguously better, with the exception of the need for a more robust sample at the 70

3. See Robert E. Hall, "Effects of the Experimental Negative Income Tax on Labor Supply," in Pechman and Timpane, eds., *Work Incentives and Income Guarantees*, pp. 115–56.

percent tax rate, and possibly a greater variation in the tax rate. At the same time, there is no basis for automatic imitation of those choices in future experiments. Different objectives, different constraints, and added experimental know-how may well call for different solutions, and the issues should be carefully examined in each case.

Surprises and Other Lapses from Omniscience

A review of the experience of designing, executing, and finally analyzing a major social experiment would not be complete without a discussion of unanticipated problems. It is not always clear how specific experience can be generalized, but it is doubtful that the experimental process will ever become so routinized that surprises will be eliminated, and hence aspiring experimenters should allow for events similar to those that follow.

Insufficient or Inaccurate Information about Sample Population

One of the first problems in the urban experiment was the scarcity of very poor families meeting the other criteria for inclusion in the sample. Using the income criterion of 150 percent of poverty, we found a lower density of eligible families in designated poverty areas than census data suggested; more than two-thirds were above the poverty threshold, and virtually none were below 75 percent. The immediate consequences were that larger numbers of households had to be screened in order to find a sufficient pool of eligibles, and that plans to seek some families outside poverty areas were dropped entirely. The same problem was encountered in the Iowa site of the rural experiment. This underscores the need to have up-to-date information on the population of areas to be sampled, and may indicate an overestimate of the numbers of very poor families in the census data, at least for the family types involved here. The absence of families in the lowest stratum meant that the response of families with extremely limited earning capacity was not available for study. Census data indicate that there are substantial numbers of such families in the nation; if those indications are correct, we did not have sample counterparts. It is possible, despite estimates to the contrary, that families including an able-bodied, nonaged male in urban industrial areas are almost never below 75 percent of the poverty line.

A closely related problem was also encountered in the urban experiment as soon as preenrollment field work began. The white component of the eligible families included a majority of Spanish-speaking families, primarily of Puerto Rican origin. This had not been anticipated at the planning stage, partly because the ethnic composition of the area had changed since the 1960 Census. While the response of Puerto Rican families, having both a distinct culture and a pattern of mobility between east-coast labor markets and Puerto Rico, is of considerable interest, that response does not generalize readily to any large segment of the working poor. Hence a source of regular white sample families was needed—families of mixed or nondescript ethnic backgrounds with family or social characteristics primarily related to similar labor markets. A makeshift solution was to add one experimental site in Scranton, Pennsylvania, a virtually all-white area. This produced a severe confounding of site, ethnicity, and timing, which reduced the ability to identify sources of differential response behavior.

A related problem in the rural experiment was the discovery in Iowa of farmers with low incomes and low equity in their business assets, but with large gross incomes, in control of sizable business assets, and living in a style comparable to middle-class families. Calculation of net income, on which experimental payments were based, generally followed Internal Revenue Service (IRS) procedures. Deviations included counting all realized capital gains as income, and adding to income the rental value of owner-occupied homes and a certain percent of net equity in home and business assets above a specified level. However, other features in the IRS guidelines yielded a distorted measure of net income for the purpose of income-conditioned payments. Among such features were accelerated depreciation, investment tax credits, ignoring unrealized capital gains, the sharing of business and personal expenses, and allowing the cash (versus accrual) method of accounting. The close following of IRS guidelines for calculating net income resulted in a few "low-income" farmers with quite comfortable life styles who were eligible for experimental payments.

These problems all have their roots in insufficient or inaccurate information about the population to be sampled. The best suggestion we can make is to improve the information on which the design is based. It may be necessary to carry out some pilot surveys to get an accurate picture of the pool of potential families. The findings may suggest additional or different stratification in order to balance or optimize the experimental design, or different rules in calculating income for eligibility purposes. If such a survey were mounted quickly, there should not be an intolerable delay in the planning and design process and a substantially stronger design might result.

Other Unforeseen Problems

The scarcity of regularly employed women, particularly in the urban sample, has already been mentioned as a consequence of the eligibility criterion. This was unforeseen and might have been discovered by more careful analysis of available cross-section data. An additional relevant fact is that on the average there were four children in these urban families. The large family size in the eligible pool was a surprise since the planning had used the prototype four-person household that is so familiar to everyone. The large family sizes had no strong adverse effect on the design beyond the obvious one of raising the average dollar values of guarantees.

The conjunction of low female labor participation and large family sizes in this urban sample should not be taken as evidence of a causal relation between the two. The apparent relation can be largely explained in terms of the selection criteria; more precisely, by the truncation at 150 percent of the poverty line. Low values of the ratio of income to the poverty standard (the "income-needs ratio") are produced by low income or large needs. Those families with low needs, or high income produced by two regular earners, were deliberately excluded from the sample. It should be remembered, however, that a negative income tax, or any other scheme that bases payments on family income, will be paying benefits to approximately the same sort of truncated subsample. The families in a real program will also tend to be relatively large and have at most one regularly employed member.

Another set of surprises has to do with the heterogeneity of labor supply behavior between major subgroups of the sample. In the urban experiment it was necessary to analyze three ethnic subgroups separately for most purposes—blacks, Spanish-speaking whites, and other whites. Because of the confounding of ethnicity with site and timing, it was not possible to attribute the ethnic differences confidently to ethnicity per se, but the differences were too large to ignore. In the rural experiment the same problem arose between wage earners and farmers, and also between the North Carolina and Iowa sites. These sources of heterogeneity were not adequately foreseen and the consequent separate analysis of subgroups has decreased the precision that might have been achieved.

Advance knowledge of which groups will display distinct behavior patterns would allow the initial design to follow a stratification across such groups, secure adequate sample sizes for each, and the like. But we did not know these things in advance and we are only slightly better off now. Theory and empirical work on microeconomic behavior has not emphasized heterogeneity; moreover some of this heterogeneity may be the result of improper or inadequate specification of behavioral equations. We are not yet prepared to urge that future experiments be designed to analyze separately each ethnic group in each occupational class in each region.

We do urge, however, that further theoretical and empirical work be done on this problem. The possible sources of heterogeneous response need to be sorted out and resolved into more general functional specifications. Econometric models involving random coefficients and composite error terms are coming into general use, and there is now more panel data, including those generated by the experiments discussed here. Both of these developments will be helpful in further study of this problem. As usual, the more that is known about the structure of the response to be estimated, the more efficiently an experiment can be designed to estimate it. It is now possible to learn more about these structures by careful analysis of existing evidence.

In the urban experiment an additional problem arose when the New Jersey welfare program was changed. While this had been anticipated as a possibility, it was excessively discounted in the initial design. When the unemployed-parent provision in AFDC-UP was implemented, a large part of the sample became potentially eligible for public assistance, sometimes at higher benefit levels than the experiment provided. The design had assumed that most of the "working poor" sample would continue to be ineligible for welfare. Again patchwork was applied by adding a more generous plan (with a guarantee at 125 percent of poverty), and by altering the rules on welfare benefits received by families eligible for experimental payments. This change in the status quo for both control and experimental families in New Jersey (combined with subsequent changes in the levels of benefits) severely complicated the interpretation of the evidence.

Finally, aside from the problem of the low-income but comfortably living farmers, the calculation of net income for all self-employed in the rural experiment was considerably more onerous than initially expected. Complicated sharing of expenses and income between tenants and landlords, the evaluation of assets, unusual expenses (for example, the death of a mule), multiple ownership of resources, inadequate records of income and expenses, life estates[4]—all were problems that complicated the calculation of net income. While some of these were foreseen, others were not, and this resulted in a large amount of administrative time related to the complex rules for calculating self-employed income.

Future experimenters will surely encounter unforeseen problems, but some of these may be anticipated as possibilities, and contingent alterations of the original design might be considered from the outset. It would defeat much of the purpose of a social field experiment to try to shield the sample from all contemporary alterations in policy or other influences, but there should be forethought about how the experiment might adapt to changing circumstances.

Additional Afterthoughts

Following this review of recurrent issues and particular surprises, it must seem clear that a foolproof experiment requires only an unlimited budget, lots of time, and prior knowledge of almost everything that might be learned from the experiment. More realistically, future experimenters will have to deal with the complications of resource limitations, great yawning gaps in our knowledge, and political constraints inherent in the nature and timing of the impulse to do an experiment. This last consideration is probably the most difficult to generalize about.

Because social experimentation is expensive it will usually be sponsored by public agencies trying to inform the policy process in some relatively direct and cost-efficient manner. This ensures that political considerations will affect the design, both in framing experimental objectives and in setting constraints. There is nothing improper or unreasonable about such influence in the context of a democratic society. But it is important that potential researchers be aware of the necessity of coming to terms with the political influences that lie behind the search for new experimental evidence. As much as possible, shared and conflicting interests should be explored and negotiated in advance so that the experiment can proceed with mutual trust between the sponsors and those responsible for designing, executing, and analyzing it.

In the two experiments under discussion here there was a broad area

4. A method of delaying inheritance taxes by bequeathing a farm to grandchildren, but allowing the children's parents to make use of the farm until the children reach the age of majority.

of common interest, a joint commitment to the ideal of objective rigor, and enough flexibility and tact to resolve conflicts, however irrational the basis. While we were fortunate, such support is not inevitable, and future experimenters should recognize the dynamic nature of the political process and its relation to the task of designing an experiment intended to serve the policy function.

Comment by Irwin Garfinkel

I plan first to comment on the issues raised by Watts and Bawden and then to say a few words about some issues they did not raise.

Issues Raised by Watts and Bawden

The first substantive issue has to do with the variety of treatments. Watts and Bawden say it could be argued that there should have been more or fewer of them, but that like Goldilocks they had just about the right amount. I see no reason to disagree with that.

Then they discuss the range of treatment plans administered in the program. They believe they might have done better by allocating more people to the 70 percent treatment cell. I agree but wish they had gone into the reasons this was not done. I will return to this important issue below because they do not directly address it.

Watts and Bawden conclude that the "test bore" sample strategy, which was ultimately chosen, is superior to saturation or the national sample strategies. Their argument is persuasive. The major interest was in a partial equilibrium analysis and to try to do more than that would probably have destroyed the possibility of even getting at that.

The argument about the administrative infeasibility of a national sample is powerful, but it would be reassuring to have this confirmed by someone who knows a bit more about administration than I do. However, I am not convinced by their contention that, because the national sample strategy involves a less homogeneous sample, the analyst will have difficulty in making the estimates. Narrowly construed, this is true enough. But at least in the two experiments analyzed so far, it was necessary to disaggregate—by ethnic groups in New Jersey and by ethnic group and location in the rural experiment. Once started on such disaggregation, a substantial amount of explanatory power is directly lost. Moreover, disaggregation is necessary in order to generalize from the sample population to the population as a whole. With a nationally representative sample, there would be no need to disaggregate for the purpose of generalizing the results. So to obtain true population estimates, a national sample strategy may be more efficient than the test bore strategy. Thus the allegedly prohibitive cost of administering an experiment with a national sample is a crucial point.

The next issue is sample selection. While it was appropriate to limit the samples to certain kinds of groups, it was unfortunate that the sample had to be limited to those below 150 percent of the official poverty line. Perhaps political pressures were to blame; if so, researchers should try to combat them. But I do agree with Watts and Bawden that losing on such a point does not merit abandoning the experiment.

I no longer agree with their conclusion that three years was the optimal duration for the experiment.[5] In retrospect, it is apparent that the temporary nature of the experiment has come to be regarded by many as a crucial flaw. Devoting some resources to a longer experiment for a part of the sample would have been a worthwhile investment.

In the second part of the paper, Watts and Bawden raise some additional issues. They note that they had trouble finding poor families with male heads, that many of the whites in the urban experiment turned out to be Puerto Ricans, and that many of the poor farmers in the rural experiment turned out to have a sizable amount of assets. All this leads to Watts' and Bawden's sound suggestion that more demographic survey work should have been done prior to the start of the experiment.

Finally, the authors call for more preexperimental study on both the theoretical and empirical levels to determine the degree to which there will be variations in the responses by the different kinds of groups in the experiment. I can only echo the importance of this problem; it will come up in virtually every experiment because it conditions what the minimally acceptable sample size will be.

Issues Watts and Bawden Did Not Raise

Having agreed with most of what they said, let me raise several significant issues neglected by Watts and Bawden.

5. At the time I first prepared these comments I did agree with their conclusion, but the discussion at the conference led me to change my mind.

The first has to do with the sample allocation model. It would have been appropriate for the authors to go through the model and, with the benefit of hindsight, ask the following questions: What assumptions made in that model now seem inappropriate? And what considerations should have been put into the model that were not? In this context, recall the small number of people allocated to the 70 percent tax rate cell.

Second, no consideration is given to any parameters of the experiment other than guarantees and tax rates—especially the structure of the payments and, in particular, the accounting period. While it is plausible that the response would not have been terribly different had the payments been structured in another way and had the accounting period been different, some hard evidence would be reassuring. My guess is that the response of the self-employed farm population probably would have been different if the accounting period and other parameters had been different.

Third, an issue that comes up again and again is the nonlinearity of the budget constraint around the breakeven level of income. This is related to both the purpose and the design of the income maintenance experiments.

If the purpose is to estimate the effect of an income maintenance program on work behavior, or to determine the costs of such a program, then including in the sample people who are above the breakeven level of income is all right; in any real income maintenance program there will also be people above the breakeven level. The only problem is that the proportions above and below the breakeven level in the sample are not necessarily representative of the true population. The way to handle this is to include in the analysis some measure of permanent income along with the experimental parameters.

However, if the purpose of the experiment is to estimate a labor supply schedule, then including participants above the breakeven point does create a problem, since they obviously do not face the experimental marginal tax rates of the plans to which they are assigned. But whether people are above or below the breakeven point depends upon their labor supply. Marginal tax rates, therefore, are endogenous. The experimental framework begins to break down.

In my view, the purpose of the income maintenance experiments was to estimate the reductions in labor supply and the consequent additional costs that result from such reductions, rather than to estimate labor supply schedules. As a consequence I do not believe that the nonlinearities in the budget constraint around the breakeven level of income create problems. For those who believe that the experiments should be used to estimate labor supply schedules, the existence of an above breakeven level experimental group is troublesome. If the experimental design had ensured that all participants were always below the breakeven level, both purposes could have been served. This would have made the experiment more costly and would in my view have been unjustified. But the issue is worth investigating.

Comment by Charles E. Metcalf

Social experimentation of the type reflected in the New Jersey, the rural, and subsequent income maintenance experiments is now about ten years old. The design of the rural experiment was begun over eight years ago. Harold Watts and Lee Bawden have reflected both upon explicit experimental design decisions, which may or may not have been mistakes, and upon what Edwin Newman might label the "unexpected surprises" that confounded the experimental process.

As one of many individuals who either colluded in or lived with most of the decisions referred to, I am in substantial sympathy with most of the conclusions drawn by the authors. In particular, I agree, even in retrospect, that the following conclusions of the authors were correct.

First, it was a reasonable strategy to apply a variety of guarantee and tax rate treatments rather than to utilize a simpler design with only one or two treatments.

Second, for what designers of the early experiments were trying to accomplish, it was correct to opt for a dispersed sample rather than to concentrate participants in one or two communities. Although saturation is a viable concept in some experiments when used selectively, it involves much larger amounts of resources for implementation in multiple sites. It is not clear that the information gained would have been worth the money.

Third, it is clear that we did not get as much information as we would have liked about the effects of high tax rates. This was not as much the problem of the allocation model as Irwin Garfinkel suggested. Rather, most of the people who were assigned to the 70 percent tax plans—particularly in the urban experiment—were in plans that were dominated by welfare when it came into effect. What were required were treatments not dominated by high tax rates, not just the allocation of more people to existing high tax rate plans.

Fourth, in the early experiments, a great deal of potential information about families with multiple earners was lost because the sample was truncated at low-income levels. To have done something about that, as the authors indicate, would have cost substantially more money and it would have compounded the problems that Garfinkel alluded to in terms of the breakeven problem. However, this feature was a major shortcoming of the early experiments and continued to be a problem in the later experiments as well. I would have stressed the need to correct this deficiency more strongly than did the authors.

The authors did not mention another problem relating to sample truncation. Recent methodological work (for example, by Hausman and Wise[6]) suggests that even for single earner families, sample truncation creates many problems for certain uses of the data.

Beyond these points of basic agreement, I would like to elaborate on the following issues relating to the authors' stated assessment.

Variable Duration Experiments

Watts and Bawden state that a variable duration experiment would have been an interesting feature of the rural experiment, but conclude that it would not have been worth doing unless there was a substantial increase in the budget. I agree that not all experiments should have had variable durations, although it is also quite clear that there are things to be learned from multiple duration experiments which one cannot get otherwise. It was important that at least one experiment did follow that route; it was an extremely good idea, in fact, that it was done in the Denver-Seattle experiment. It does not follow, however, that the technique should be replicated everywhere. Some specialization is needed in designing experiments.

I tend to disagree with Watts and Bawden concerning two points relating to variable duration experiments. First, they indicate that a three-year and a five-year sample would have delayed the analysis until the final results of the five-year sample were available. Similarly, it will take twenty years before the final results of the Denver-Seattle experiment become available. The point to be made here is that it is not necessary to wait that long to get useful results. The methodology underlying a variable duration experiment predicts that during the first three years of the

6. Jerry A. Hausman and David A. Wise, *Social Experimentation, Truncated Distributions, and Efficient Estimation,* Technical Analysis Series 4 (Mathematica Policy Research, n.d.).

experiment (as well as later) people on the five-year and twenty-year plans should be behaving differently. If not, we can pack up and go home anyway.

Second, the authors suggest varying the duration of an experiment by stability of employment. Their motivation is that individuals with long-run stable jobs are not going to quit for a short-run experiment; but those going from job to job anyhow would be more likely to respond normally to a short-duration experiment. The approach is an interesting one, but there are really two issues related to a limited-duration experiment. One is the cost of adjustment: is it worth making a change in the short run? The other is a more explicit time horizon problem, which is not really addressed by tying duration of the plan to the stability of employment. Furthermore, I am concerned that their approach would confound the experimental treatments with types of previous behavior that might be hard to untangle. My reaction is that if one is to have variable duration, it should not be so closely tied to former work behavior.

"Test Bore" versus a National Random Sample

I believe that the decisions in both the New Jersey and the rural experiments to opt for "test bore," nonsaturation samples were correct. In his discussion, Garfinkel reviewed some of the issues involved in the decision not to use a national random sample. One was administrative feasibility. The second was an alleged loss of precision due to the increased heterogeneity of a national sample.

I am not sure I understand the loss of precision argument. There would be a loss of precision in going to a national sample so far as the measured precision of estimates for the sample itself is a concern; but obviously, if there is interest in estimating the effects of a national program, there is a great loss of precision by having the ultimate in a clustered sample—namely, all observations in one or two locations. That is, within-sample precision is gained at the expense of comparability of the experimental population to national population. In such a case, faith has to be placed in other techniques for generalizing to national estimates.

There is a second problem related to sample selection that has bothered me for some time. The problem concerns not the choice of particular test bore locations, but the way in which sample points were chosen within those areas. I refer specifically to the New Jersey experiment, for which I have knowledge of the selection process.

For cost reasons, screening interviewers were sent to well-defined low-income census tracts to find poor households. Otherwise, the yield of eligible sample points per screening interview would have been prohibitively small. The outcome of this process in New Jersey was a sample with a heavy concentration of blacks and Puerto Ricans, and nothing corresponding to the proportion of low-income whites, which a glance at published data would have indicated.

My point is that poor people living in low-income areas are a very specialized group of low-income people. In absolute numbers, there are more poor living dispersed in middle- or low-middle-income areas than there are in the poverty areas. Although the financial cost of a different sampling strategy might have exceeded the budget constraints, it may be that the New Jersey experiments are not even representative of urban New Jersey, let alone of the nation as a whole.

Increasing the Number of Preenrollment Observations

At the 1974 Brookings conference on the New Jersey experiment, Robert Hall suggested that the experiment would have been more efficient if, instead of having one preenrollment interview and twelve observations throughout the benefit period of the experiment, the payments had been delayed until participants were interviewed several times. A fuller set of information about past behavior would have been helpful, but behavior during the "interview only" period might have been influenced by the pending payments. Furthermore, with a continued progression of interviews before the start of the experiment, the subsequent analysis would have been complicated by a higher rate of sample attrition. In principle, instead of delaying the start of the experiment, more retrospective data could have been collected—although such data would have had some obvious weaknesses.

The Definition of Income

There is one issue that is dismissed as an irritation by Bawden and Watts, and elaborated on more fully by Finis Welch. The issue has to do with the fact that the presence of self-employed farmers with business assets caused a lot more time to be spent worrying about the definition of income in the rural experiment than in the urban experiment.

While a great deal of work was done on income definition in the urban experiment, the whole issue of the self-employed individual was ignored. Then in the rural experiment the problem of the self-employed individual had to be faced, with the further confounding presence of income in-kind. Recognition of the problem had a very important demonstration effect for it stressed how much care will be needed in defining income regulations in a national negative income tax. Major difficulties were encountered even though much more thought went into income definition than usually happens in the legislative process. The demonstration of these difficulties was a much more useful result of the rural experiment than it was probably perceived to be.

Sample Size

I think the worst mistake of the rural experiment was to limit the sample size to only 809 people including the control group. Furthermore, 114 of these were allocated to an aged sample and another 108 to a female-headed household sample, neither of which could provide much useful information. This left less than 600 supposedly homogeneous families, some of whom were farmers, some not, some in the rural South, some not. While the heterogeneity of the sample was not fully recognized, the decision was a bad one and it was recognized as such during the experiment. Greater effort should have been made to enlarge the scale.

At the time, those who designed the experiment were swayed by an idea that has not borne fruit. While it was agreed that the rural sample was too small to be analyzed in isolation, there was much talk about having data collection procedures similar to the New Jersey experiment and to others on the horizon. The hope was that the data from the various experiments could be pooled, but the difficulties in doing this were not fully recognized.

"A Foolproof Experiment"

The authors state that "a foolproof experiment requires only an unlimited budget, lots of time, and prior knowledge of almost everything that might be learned from the experiment." They then proceed to talk about the reality of limited budgets, gaps in knowledge, and inherent political constraints.

The deliberate attempt at levity aside, I think the tone may have been misleading. For decades social scientists have bemoaned the lack of controlled experiments in their field; then when social experimentation became a reality, economists seized upon it as the ultimate in policy research methodology. If only there were enough resources, enough ingenuity, and enough foresight, the social experiment was the right way to proceed.

While there are significant advantages to controlled experimentation (at a price), the disadvantages are not just the lack of funds or foresight. I think that the whole concept of social experimentation, implemented in an environment still quite artificial in many important respects, is more flawed in principle than the reputation it developed in the late 1960s and early 1970s. It is one of many alternative research strategies, each with known weaknesses, to be selectively chosen. An experiment is not always the best way to answer a research question; not all questions are worth spending that much money. Some can be handled with reasonable effectiveness at a fraction of the cost by the use of other techniques.

As a general strategy, I believe a social experiment of this sort cannot be justified unless the issue at hand is regarded as critical enough to warrant a much larger sample than was funded for the rural experiment. An effective experiment is an extremely expensive undertaking. Unless society is willing to bear the cost, an alternative research strategy should be used.

FINIS WELCH

The Labor Supply Response
of Farmers

The American farmer has always been overburdened. Not only has he been charged with feeding most of the people all of the time, but his responsibilities have extended to training policymakers in first principles of economics. For example, when price supports were introduced to buffer falling demand, farmers demonstrated what may be a general truth, that supply functions are positively inclined. When acreage controls were introduced, farmers showed that factor substitution exists. More recently, farmers have directed their efforts away from the U.S. Department of Agriculture—which by now should know first principles anyway—to other branches of government. They have tried to show the Internal Revenue Service that even if they are not capable of accrual accounting, they can use cash basis accounting, coupled with simple options of converting ordinary income into capital gains, to excellent advantage. And more recently, they—or at least a few of their representatives in Iowa and North Carolina—have worked hard to show those at the Department of Health, Education, and Welfare (HEW) that textbook theories and real world facts of income maintenance may not even be first cousins.

I have examined the rural income maintenance experiment papers and some of the underlying data and I am convinced that what happened in

I am especially indebted to Iva Maclennan for computational assistance and to Wendell Primus, who supplied the analysis file and was so patient in answering many questions about the content of the file. I am also grateful to my colleagues at UCLA and Rand who served as a sounding board for many of the ideas presented. Any errors are my own responsibility. Computational support was provided through a grant from the Office of the Assistant Secretary for Planning and Evaluation, U.S. Department of Health, Education, and Welfare, to the Rand Corporation.

Iowa and North Carolina was not an income maintenance experiment—at least not as I would describe one to my students. I am afraid, however, that what did happen may be a demonstration of what we might expect from a negative income tax scheme in the real world.

I will not dwell at length on the analytical papers but will describe instead (1) what theory predicts about labor supply for a textbook scheme—and what the data show, and (2) some of the unique administrative-accounting features of the experiment, which generated farmer responses that confound measurement of labor supply effects.

What Does Theory Predict?

Because farmers are people, too, the simple predictions of reduced hours of work for participants, and of reduced probabilities of labor force participation through the reinforcing income and substitution effects of negative income tax programs, appear to hold. But there are wrinkles. The view expressed in the theories sketched by Primus and Kerachsky assumes that the farm income being taxed, that is, the income on which negative income tax payments are calculated, refers to labor income only.[1] If this were true, I would have no quarrel with their presentations. In their view, farm income is simply value added by the labor of the farm family. It is total revenue less costs of nonlabor inputs where (for a specified amount of labor) other inputs are chosen to maximize labor's income. The myopically optimal solution regarding the choice of what these other inputs will be presumably leads to a concave labor budget in which marginal farm wages decline as hours worked rise.

Full-time versus Part-time Farmers

In this case the only distinction of negative income tax effects on hours worked between full-time and part-time farmers is that for those who work for wages (part-time farmers), the market wage is ordinarily presumed to remain unchanged as hours vary; for them, the pretax budget

1. Wendell E. Primus, "Farm Work Response of Farm Operators," in D. Lee Bawden and William S. Harrar, eds., *Rural Income Maintenance Experiment: Final Report* (University of Wisconsin–Madison, Institute for Research on Poverty, 1976), vol. 4, chap. 1; and Stuart H. Kerachsky, "On Farm–Off Farm Work Decisions," in ibid., chap. 2.

is assumed to be linear in relevant ranges. The part-time farmer first determines his farm-labor budget and then switches to off-farm work when the marginal farm wage equals the off-farm wage. Full-time farmers are simply those whose marginal wage at full-time farm work exceeds their off-farm alternative.

Of course, full-time work is itself a decision variable achieved by equating, at the margin, values of work and leisure time. In contrast to a world without welfare, one with a negative income tax affects this choice both through substitution (in lowering the after-tax wage) and through expanded income. All of this is well known. What is interesting is that for part-time farmers, a negative income tax scheme that does not result in a complete cessation of off-farm work will have no effect whatever on farm activities. Neither the amount of farm work nor other input levels are affected.[2] In the relevant range the pretax budget is linear, income and substitution effects of negative income taxes are identical to the standard wage earner case, and all effects are confined to off-farm work.

In contrast, for full-time farmers, a negative income tax will not only reduce hours worked on the farm but will reduce levels of all activities that are positively related to farm hours. In empirical analyses, therefore, it seems reasonable to distinguish between those farmers who work off farms and those who do not.

Taxation and Farm Earnings

I should add that my understanding of negative income tax programs is that income being taxed is not restricted to labor earnings. Taxable income is gross revenue less costs of variable or nondurable inputs and a depreciation allowance for reductions in values of durables associated with their use. Any rise in taxes on net farm income increases taxes on

2. In his paper Kerachsky permits the possibility that farm families do not view farm and off-farm earnings to have a one-for-one substitution rate so that marginal farm wages might be less than the off-farm wages if farm work is preferred. He concludes that by introducing psychic discounting of earnings sources, the stability of farm hours under negative income tax variations is questionable. I would only add that psychic discounting does not change the substitution argument, but if the psychic discount depends on income, then negative income tax budgets will affect farm hours. I would guess that such an effect is minor at best. Activities for part-time farmers can, of course, be affected if, for example, a negative income tax only caused the wife, and not the farmer, to quit an off-farm job. The above argument serves only as an illustration: when considering effects on farm hours, the distinction between those who do and those who do not work off the farm is important.

labor earnings and durable inputs. In farm profits accounting, this amounts to an increased effective price (a reduced return) on owner-used durables. If, on balance, durables are gross-substitues for farm family labor, the secondary effect is to increase the productivity of farm labor. With the gross-substitutes assumption, the theoretical effect of a negative income tax on farm hours is ambiguous for those who do not work off the farm, and for those who do the effect is to increase hours of work on the farm. I do not think that this consideration alters predictions of effects for a three-year experiment since it follows from the aforementioned effect on farm durables. It does point out, however, just how difficult it is to extrapolate experimental information to make predictions of longer-run effects.

In all of this, I assume that farm and off-farm income are viewed as equivalent for purposes of taxation. To the extent that realized taxes on farm income are below those for off-farm income due, for example, to differential costs to the Internal Revenue Service of detecting underreporting, all of the above statements should be qualified. In particular, a higher tax would strengthen incentives for switching from off-farm to farm work.

How Should Effects Be Estimated?

The rural income maintenance regime, as to my knowledge do all negative income tax proposals, implies a discrete break in marginal tax rates at some breakeven income level. The benefit is computed as:[3]

$$(1) \qquad\qquad \text{Max } \{0, G - ty\},$$

where G is the guarantee, $y(\geqslant 0)$ is "income," and t is the negative income tax rate. Earnings are taxed at t to the breakeven level, G/t, and at that point the marginal tax rate falls to zero or the Internal Revenue Service norm. Suppose that income consists of that from nonlabor sources, y_n, and wage income, wh, where w, the market wage, is exogenous and independent of hours worked, h, and assume that in the absence of a negative income tax, the labor supply function is linear in w and y_n:

$$(2) \qquad\qquad h = \alpha_0 + \alpha_1 w + \alpha_2 y_n + u,$$

where u is the unexplained residual.

3. Attention is restricted here to cases of positive income with accounting conventions similar to those of the urban experiments. For farmers whose income flows are frequently negative, the problem is more complicated.

Given experimental data consisting of a control population ($\delta_1 = 0$) and an experimental population ($\delta_1 = 1$) we proceed toward estimation of 2. Some within the experiment receive positive benefits ($\delta_2 = 1$) and their net or after-tax wage is $w(1 - t)$ and their nonwage income is $y_n^* = G + (1 - t)y_n$. Others in the experimental population have income exceeding the breakeven ($\delta_2 = 0$) and their net wage and nonlabor budgets are the same as for control groups. As such, the labor supply function encompassing all those described by the experimental data is:

$$(3) \qquad h = \alpha_0 + \alpha_1 w + \alpha_2 y_n - \beta_1 \delta_1 \delta_2 tw + \beta_2 \delta_1 \delta_2 (G - t y_n) + u,$$

with $\alpha_1 = \beta_1$ and $\alpha_2 = \beta_2$. In most cases that I am familiar with, the estimated relationship has been similar to:

$$(4) \qquad h = \alpha_0 + \alpha_1 w + \alpha_2 y_n - \beta_1^* \delta_1 tw + \beta_2^* \delta_1 (G - t y_n) + u.$$

Problems and Biases

In a forthcoming review of the New Jersey experiment, John Cogan[4] characterizes the estimation problem as I have here, and my remarks simply summarize his critique and revised estimation strategy.

Cogan first points out that equation 3 contains simultaneity between δ_2 and h simply because δ_2 switches from 1 to 0 as income passes the breakeven level. Given the wage and tax rates and the guarantee, breakeven income is determined by hours, h. Cogan recommends an estimation procedure that results in consistent estimates of equation 3. In this, he first computes in an auxiliary relation an instrument for the probability that $\delta_2 = 1$ and substitutes that instrument for δ_2 into regressions estimating 3. The hypothesis $\alpha_1 = \beta_1$ and $\alpha_2 = \beta_2$ is then tested.

With such estimates, it is a simple matter to compute negative income tax effects by first noting that in a program with eligibility extended to everyone, not all would choose to receive payments. The auxiliary relation used to avoid inconsistent estimation of 3, therefore, serves a direct role for participation probabilities, whereas estimates of β_1 and β_2 imply effects conditional on participation. Clearly, the dichotomy between participation and conditional effects is useful for extrapolation to populations with different earnings options from those of the experimental and control populations.

4. "Negative Income Taxation and Labor Supply: New Evidence from the New Jersey, Pennsylvania Experiment" (Rand Corporation, forthcoming).

In comparison to 3, equation 4 errs in deleting δ_2 from the terms involving β_1 and β_2 and ordinary least squares estimates are therefore biased. The nature of the biases is difficult at best. It would be nice if

$$(5) \qquad\qquad (\beta_1^*, \beta_2^*) = Pr(\delta_2 = 1)\ (\beta_1, \beta_2),$$

where $Pr(\delta_2 = 1)$ is the probability of participating. Were this true, we could argue that in dealing with the distribution of characteristics of people in the experimental and control populations, and the distribution of experimental plans, ordinary least squares estimates of β_1^* and β_2^* provide estimates of *average* negative income tax effects. I have not been able to derive easily interpretable forms for comparing these estimates of (β_1^*, β_2^*) to (β_1, β_2), but surely the relation is not as in 5. My guess is that the specification error may either understate or overstate average effects and, indeed, that the sign of the estimated effect need not agree with that implied by 3. In short, I do not know what estimates of the misspecified equation 4 yield, but whatever they are, they are not what I want.

I will add that this problem goes away if $\delta_2 = 1$ always or nearly always. In the rural income maintenance experiment, accounting conventions make it impossible to identify marginal tax rates from analysis files —and I have not had access to payment files. We only know whether a family received a payment during a quarter. If it did, then presumably the rate associated with the plan to which the family is assigned holds. If not, the carry-over accounting provisions lead to a marginal tax rate that is either zero (or the Internal Revenue Service correspondence to being "off" the program) or the assigned rate.

Boundary Benefits

The tabulation below reports the percentage of experimental families who received boundary benefits, indicating either zero benefits when income was temporarily above the breakeven level or maximum benefits when it was temporarily zero or negative.

Length of time benefits were received	*1970*	*1971*	*1972*
For at least one quarter of designated year	57	71	80
For one quarter of designated year when boundary payments persist either for next three quarters or until end of experiment	12	14	63

The rural income maintenance accounting regime computes payments based on current income as well as a carry-over of surpluses from earlier periods (not to exceed twelve months) when income was either negative or exceeded the breakeven level. The complements to the numbers in the first row are understatements. We know that at least 43 percent of the experimental families were "on the experiment" in 1970. Corresponding numbers for 1971 and 1972 are 29 and 20 percent.

The second row shows the proportions of families receiving boundary payments in one quarter of a year who continued to receive boundary payments the ensuing three quarters or until the end of the experiment. The complements to these numbers are neither pure overstatements nor understatements, yet they are better estimates of proportions on the experiment. Since these proportions are not trivial, it is clear that the specification of being "on" and "off" the experiment is an important problem. But as we shall see, the accounting features of the rural income maintenance experiment complicate the interpretation of being "off" much more than indicated in the above illustration.

What the Data Show

The first step is always to define the population to be analyzed, and I have restricted observations to families of constant marital status during the three years of the experiment in which the guarantee did not exceed the poverty income level. Since I am charged with discussing the part of the experiment dealing with farmers, observations are further restricted to families that farmed each year and had at least 400 "budgeted" farm hours for one of the experimental years.[5] Table 1 shows the number of farm households observed, by control and experimental groups, in Iowa and North Carolina. The experimental plans are described by two parameters, a/b, where a refers to the tax rate and b to the guarantee as a proportion of the family's poverty income level.

Identifying Effects

There were 105 experimental families distributed over two states and five plans. Unfortunately, space does not permit a detailed description of

5. Budget hours are constructed from reported output, as in Wendell Primus, "Farm Work Response of Farm Operators."

Table 1. Number of Farm Families in the Rural Income Maintenance Experiment, by Group

Group (experimental by percent tax rate and guarantee)[a]	Iowa	North Carolina
30/75	12	8
50/50	9	11
50/75	12	18
50/100	10	13
70/75	6	6
Experimental, total	49	56
Control, total	57	46

Source: Compiled from raw data files of Institute for Research on Poverty; includes only families of constant marital status during the three years of the rural income maintenance experiment whose guarantee did not exceed the poverty income level, and who farmed each year and had 400 or more budgeted farm hours for one of the experimental years. Budgeted farm hours were constructed from output reported by the families.

a. The guarantee figure refers to percent of the poverty level.

the experience of each family, even for the 70/75 plan that covered only six families each in Iowa and North Carolina.

The analysts apparently felt that farm and off-farm work opportunities were sufficiently different in Iowa and North Carolina to warrant separate analyses for each state. If so, the problem arises of identifying effects in each state from roughly fifty experimental observations. My experience with individual response suggests that it is hopeless to identify partial effects from such a limited number of observations.

If labor supply responds to income and wages, then it must be that responses to the five plans differ since tax rates vary from 30 to 70 percent and the guarantee varies from 50 to 100 percent of the poverty level. But there are so few observations for each plan that I have not tried to distinguish among them. Instead, I have used only the simplest summary statistics for contrasting control families to all families. It should be noted that not all experimental families are "on the experiment" since some have income above the breakeven level and their budgets or opportunity sets are the same as for control families. In principle, effects will be understated because I do not distinguish between those experimental families eligible and ineligible for benefits. In calculations not reported here, I found little apparent difference. In all cases the qualitative results are similar whether comparing all experimental families, or simply those eligible for benefits, with control families.[6]

6. Part of the apparent similarity stems, no doubt, from the fact that the data of the analysis file do not permit exact identification of those on the experiment. As we shall see, the accounting schemes are complex and being off the experiment is always a stochastic event.

Hours Worked on and off the Farm

Table 2 describes average hours on and off farms for experimental and control families, together with net farm income for the experimental years 1970, 1971, and 1972. While it would be reasonable to extend these comparisons to the base year, 1969, as a check of random assignment between experimental and control groups, I have not done so. Nor is there any distinction between Iowa and North Carolina. My intent is not to have these averages viewed as serious estimates of program effects; rather, they are a crude first cut to show some general response patterns.

The first panel includes only those who worked for wages in 1969. Hours worked on the farm are more or less similar for experimental and control farmers except for the anomalous result that in the terminal year of the experiment, average hours worked on farms were 23 percent greater for experimental than for control farmers. Except for 1970, hours worked off farms were less for experimental than control farmers as theory leads us to expect. In each year experimental operators reported fewer hours than control farmers. What theory did not lead us to expect—at least that branch of theory that ignores taxes on owner-operated durables—was that net farm income for experimental farmers would be below that of control farmers. Although gross revenues and expenses were not reported, the data show that reduced net incomes are associated with reductions both in revenues and expenses.

The central panel refers to those who did not work for wages in 1969. There the finding for farm hours is contrary to expectations, since the number of farm hours for experimental farmers was higher than that for control farmers. Similar results were found for total hours, but differences were reduced since control operators worked off the farm more than did experimental operators. As expected, net farm income for experimental farmers was below that of control farmers, but the differentials are small in comparison to the top panel, leading to rather anomalous behavior of farm income.

The bottom panel describes farm and off-farm hours for wives of farm operators. Hours worked on farms were greater for experimental than for control spouses and hours worked off farms were greater for control than for experimental spouses. There was no pattern in total hours and control-experimental differentials were trivial.

Clearly, anyone expecting dramatic experimental effects must be disappointed. Noise, probably only partly attributable to sample size, dominates, and observed patterns are as likely to contradict a priori expecta-

Table 2. Average Hours Worked on and off Farms and Net Farm Income for Experimental and Control Operations, 1970-72

Description	Annual hours worked on farm			Annual hours worked off farm[a]			Net farm income (dollars)			Number of observations
	1970	1971	1972	1970	1971	1972	1970	1971	1972	
Male farm operators who worked off the farm in 1969[b]										
Control	1,697	1,461	1,193	773	948	1,045	5,038	4,090	6,756	27
Experimental	1,468	1,405	1,465	866	713	572	2,993	2,813	4,878	36
Male farm operators who did not work off the farm in 1969										
Control	2,448	2,185	2,001	71	162	195	6,115	5,102	8,575	76
Experimental	2,563	2,305	2,146	39	62	115	5,616	4,768	8,563	69
Female spouses of farm operators										
Control	285	306	227	212	269	295	5,927	4,916	8,171	100
Experimental	331	329	296	171	196	210	4,748	4,137	7,345	104

Source: Same as table 1.
a. Wage and business hours.
b. Wage hours only. (Business hours for 1969 are not available.)

tions as to confirm them. We are immediately confronted with at least two possibilities: either labor supply is only trivially affected by negative income tax parameters within experimental ranges or what happened in Iowa and North Carolina could not reasonably be expected to identify labor supply responses. Those favoring simplified, centralized welfare schemes may be inclined toward the first, but I think the second possibility cannot be ignored.

Accounting Rules and the Games Farmers Play

A quick perusal of the rural experiment's "Rules of Operation" signals two trouble spots.[7] One is that, subject to a three-month moving average, income accounting is cash-basis. Both costs and revenues enter income calculations only when they are realized, not as they accrue. I will not belabor all the implications of this but will mention some problems by way of example. Suppose a farmer produces a commodity (Iowa corn or North Carolina tobacco) that can be stored at moderate cost. Suppose further that his experimental tax rate is 70 percent. Notice that so long as his net income is positive and does not exceed the breakeven level, marginal expenses incurred in raising this crop are reimbursed at a rate of 70 percent. If he sells his 1972 crop in 1972, gross receipts are taxed at a marginal rate of 70 percent. If he sells his 1972 crop in 1973 (after the experiment has ended), sales are taxed at the IRS norm. Why sell in 1972? The same is true of the 1970 and 1971 crops except that storage costs are higher.

Double Taxation

The second feature of the accounting regime is that all owned assets may be double taxed. Let me quote from pertinent passages of "Rules of Operation."[8]

The amount paid to an enrolled family unit depends on the combined "net income." . . . "Net income" is defined as gross income (specified in A below) less deductions allowed (specified in B below) [p. 27].

A. Items included in gross income

3.   Gross income derived from a business. . . . [p. 27]

7. See Jeanette Schreier, "Rules of Operation," in Bawden and Harrar, eds., *Rural Income Maintenance Experiment,* vol. 1, chap. 5.
   8. Ibid.

20. There shall be included in the income of each unit an amount equal to 10% of the "net usable wealth" . . . [p. 31].

Net usable wealth includes

20(a)(1) the amount of equity (as defined below in property used in a trade or business of any member of the unit in excess of $20,000. . . .) [p. 31]. 20(c) The term equity means the market value of the property less the amount of outstanding debt incurred to purchase or carry such property. For businessmen and farmers, property used in a trade or business shall include inventories (merchandise, feed, fertilizer, etc.), equipment, and breeding and feeder animals [p. 32].

B. Items deducted from gross income
2. . . . all operating expenses . . . [p. 32].
7. A deduction shall be allowed for interest paid (a) on a loan the proceeds of which are used in the payor's trade or business . . . [p. 34].

I should point out that most farmers, even poor ones, have producer equities exceeding $20,000. I should also point out that unlike owner-occupied housing, whose rent is excluded from standard (though not the rural income maintenance experiment) income imputations, owner-operated business assets (farmland, buildings, machines, livestock, and grain inventories) produce income that enters revenue flows. To tax the asset directly, and then to tax the revenue it generates, is double taxation pure and simple.[9] Thus, the revenue contractions reported for experimental groups (relative to control groups) may make sense. They would if the long-run is less than three years! The clear intent of the net wealth imputation is to prevent payments to rich farmers. It is usually argued that it is inconceivable that payments would be extended to someone with, say, $100,000 in net assets. Whether this is true or not, the fact remains that assets are taxed twice through rules of the rural experiment, and double taxation could be easily avoided even if payments to rich farmers were precluded.[10]

The Fluctuating Income Problem

Perhaps the most interesting, most subtle, and most important wrinkle of the rural experiment's accounting procedures stems from attempts to

9. With this in mind, I should modify my earlier criticism of cash basis accounting where inventory accruals (and unrealized capital gains) are omitted. For the rural experiment, it seems that 10 percent of accruals are taxed.

10. For example, a simple imputation defining taxable income as

$$y_t = \text{Max } \{rW, y_0\},$$

where y_t is taxable income, y_0 is measured income, and rW is the net wealth imputation, would be sufficient.

adjust for the incongruous timing of expenses and revenues inherent in farming. For those who lead simpler lives, the standard formula of zero benefits for those with income above the breakeven point, and some fraction of the guarantee for those with positive income below breakeven, suffices. But what do you do about someone whose cash basis income is sometimes negative, sometimes above the breakeven, and averages less than breakeven?

The rural experiment's solution—and it is hard to think of a better one other than accrual accounting—is to define the income measure used for computing benefits as current monthly income (usually a three-month moving average[11]) plus accumulated surplus. If this sum, call it adjusted income, is negative, the benefit paid is the full guarantee, and the surplus carried into the next period's calculation is the previous period's adjusted income. If adjusted income lies between zero and the breakeven level, G/t, the benefit paid is $G - t$ (adjusted income) and no surplus is carried forward. If adjusted income exceeds the breakeven level, there is no payment in the current period and the surplus carried forward to the next period is the current period's adjusted income less breakeven income, G/t.

There is a further modification: monthly contributions to surplus are dated and a first-in-first-out accounting convention is used. Under this procedure, if a monthly contribution to surplus is not exhausted in the twelve-month period following its initial entry, it is erased.

Thus the marginal tax rate in the rural experiment is conditioned on the probability of receiving nonboundary benefits within an ensuing twelve months. Today's income is simply taxed at the program's stated rate if at any point in the next year nonboundary benefits are paid.[12]

On the surface this appears to be a superior scheme to one based only on current account. It has the obvious advantage of adjusting for the seasonal nature of income flows that are common in farming. But there are two problems associated with this scheme. First, because timing of sales and payments of expenses are malleable, farmers are given an opportunity to play with the system, to use it to their own advantage. Second, even if income flows could not be manipulated when they are highly uneven,

11. Evidently some farmers had income calculated as current monthly income; for others it was a three-month average, and in some cases 1969 income was used as a basis for setting the machinery in motion. The analysis file contains no information showing how a particular family was treated.

12. When adjusted income is out-of-bounds, the effective marginal tax rate is the stated rate times the probability of receiving benefits in the ensuing twelve months. This obviously complicates estimates of effects via specifications like equation 5.

the process takes time to adjust to an equilibrium. And in a three-year experiment, time is short.

As a simple example, suppose that two families are each placed on identical plans. Their monthly guarantees are each $200 and their tax rate is 50 percent. Each family has an average monthly income of $300 so that its average annual benefit should be $600.

Family A's annual income stream consists of −$300 for each of the first six months of each year and $900 a month for the last six months. Family B's stream is just the opposite. It receives a net flow of $900 for each of the first six months and −$300 for each of the last six months of each year.

We begin in January 1970, and form a three-month running average for each family; we then compute payments as described above, assuming that the running average is the average of the current period and the previous two, and using the first month's income in 1970 as its average, and the average of the first and second months' incomes as the average for the first two months. Annual payment calculations for the experimental years are, in dollars:

	1970	1971	1972
Family A	1,800	1,000	600
Family B	0	450	600

In each case the lagged adjustment mechanism reaches an equilibrium —that is, stabilizes at its average annual equivalence—only in the third year. By that time, family A has realized a $1,600 excess payment that will never be recouped. Family B has incurred a $750 loss that cannot be made up.

With such an accounting scheme, it is difficult to see how any observations of labor supply behavior for any of the years of the experiment would conform to long-run equilibrium behavior. One can easily imagine a sustained run on the system whereby expenses are accelerated and receipts deferred to maintain an initial payment stream near the guarantee. Once deferral of receipts becomes sufficiently costly, cash out. Realize the receipts and leave the experiment.

What Do the Data Show about Income Flows and Reporting?

The rural experiment accounting features have enough twists to warrant attention before even attempting to estimate labor supply effects. If labor supply is presumed to be responsive to something, it would be nice to know what that something is.

Double taxation of owner-operated durables could be directly incorporated in a labor supply formulation. But timing of adjustments has to be considered and it is not clear how much could be learned from a three-year experiment even with a reasonable number of observations. While one might expect to see a farmer defer purchasing a new tractor, it would be surprising if he sold much of his land to avoid taxes for one, two, or three years.

Maintaining accumulated output as inventory that is taxed at a rate of one-tenth of sales and using farm labor and inputs in buildings, fences, and other durables seems attractive. And it may be even more attractive simply to play timing games with the lagged adjustment mechanism.

The Basic Data

As a first and very crude cut, I have played a number of games of my own with the inventory and income data contained in the rural experiment analysis file. This file, obtained from Wendell Primus, contains quarterly income and inventory data, quarterly negative income tax payment histories, and Primus' own calculations of income components, including wages, business income, small enterprise income, net farm income, unearned income, the rental value of owner-occupied housing, and a net asset imputation. The net asset imputation is his best guess at constructing the "net usable wealth" item described in "Rules of Operation" quoted above. I did not form my own definitions, partly because of insufficient information and partly because it is these definitions the analysts used. It seems reasonable in a critique of this sort to consider the analysis as it was performed.

The analysis file contains annual income and inventory measures that are not simply the sum of the four-quarter data reported for the year. The quarterly data run from December 1 to November 30 for each year while the annual data correspond to calendar years. The quarterly data are based on four interviews each year, whereas the annual data stem from only one interview.

In fact, the analysis file is not restricted to interview responses. Instead, interview responses are modified on the basis of a number of consistency checks to provide "best guesses" of income, and so forth.[13] In contrast,

13. Presumably initial interview data are available to analysts wishing to perform their own adjustments. Whether these data can be easily merged with the payments data is an open question.

payments are computed on the basis of written reports prepared by farmers themselves and submitted to a payments office. Other than verbal checks to verify unreasonable income reports, I am aware of no provisions to create incentives to report accurately. Although there probably were attempts to create such incentives, it is clear that there are many inconsistencies between the payments and analysis data.

Alternative Income Definitions

To gain insight into the question of whether farmers used the payment system in the way the incentive structure would suggest, I simply programmed the accounting rules and varied the income definition on which payment calculations are based. As a standard for comparison, I first calculated actual average negative income tax payments received during the three years of the experiment. I then computed payment entitlements from the annual income data, assuming income is evenly distributed throughout the year. I next performed the same calculation substituting the four-quarter sum for annual income. Then I used the quarter-by-quarter data as though the three-month average is the average monthly income for the quarter. The distinction between the "smoothed," or four-quarter sum, and the quarter-by-quarter comparison is intended to give some insight into the income-sequencing phenomenon discussed above, although the possibility of shifting income between years is not explored. Finally, to determine whether inventory options are used, I computed quarterly income inclusive of changes in inventory values as accrual schemes would require. Results are summarized in table 3.

Within the quarterly data, there are no surprises. The lagged adjustment mechanism suggests that timing within the year is important and it is. Average payment entitlements are 35 percent greater under the quarter-by-quarter method than for smoothed income flows. In fact, only two of the 105 families in the experiment would have been eligible for greater benefits under smoothed within-year flows. Thirty-seven would have been eligible for the same benefits in either case and sixty-six had quarterly income flows that under the rural experiment accounting rules would have resulted in larger entitlements than their average monthly equivalence. As anticipated, farmers appear to have used inventories to their advantage. Cash basis, as opposed to inventory-accrual, accounting increased average farmer benefit eligibility by $200 over the three years—a figure that is probably trivial compared to the value of this same option open to farmers under IRS rules.

Table 3. Average Benefit Payments under Alternative Farm Income Definitions[a]
Dollars

Type of benefit	Amount
Actual average benefit	**4,910**
Alternative entitlement imputations[b]	
Annual income	2,026
Four-quarter sum	1,394
Quarter-by-quarter	1,876
Quarter-by-quarter with inventory adjustment	1,660

Source: Calculated from data in the Rural Income Maintenance Experiment analysis file.
a. Three-year total benefit per family.
b. See text discussion for details on the definitions of the plans.

Quarterly data comparisons suggest that farmers do indeed play the kind of games these built-in incentives suggest. This, of course, confounds analysis. It may be that the carry-over features of the rural experiment accounting would simulate accrual accounting if the program were in place for a long time. But for the three-year trial, the advantages of sequencing and inventory manipulation seem important enough at least to raise a question as to whether short-run signals simulate long-run responses. Although I have tried, I have been unable to decipher optimal response patterns for a three-year trial under the rural experiment accounting rules.

Quality of the Income Data

This point is important because the overwhelming evidence of the analysis file is that farmers underreport income. This is no surprise and should be anticipated in any real-world negative income tax program. As long as the degree and pattern of underreporting under the rural experiment and a real-world program are highly correlated,[14] it is possible that stimuli would be sufficiently correlated to make the experimental responses a valid index of what to expect from a negative income tax program. But a three-year trial under the rural income maintenance accounting rules creates incentives that would not exist under a permanent program, even if it were to exactly duplicate these rules.

Inventories offer an example. I have already described short-run in-

14. There really is no reason to suppose that they would be. Both accounting schemes and enforcement mechanisms carry compliance incentives and unless a real-world program directly incorporated these unique features, we should expect different compliance patterns. Even if the experimental scheme were exactly reproduced, long-run and short-run incentives would differ.

centives regarding inventories. They stem from sequencing options both at the program's start and at its termination, when taxes return to IRS norms. For an open-end program, inventory incentives are reversed. First, inventories are taxed while held (via the 10 percent inclusion in net usable wealth), and are taxed again when depleted (revenues from inventory sales are treated as simple income).

In reference to table 3, the four-quarter sum is comparable to the annual income computation and the discrepancy between $2,026 and $1,394 indicates either the importance of the timing of the start of an experimental year or the inconsistency between the quarterly and annual income data.

Of course, discrepancies among the alternative imputations of benefit entitlements pale in comparison to what payments actually are. The annual data imply the largest entitlement and yet actual receipts are roughly two and a half times eligible receipts. From this it is clear that if the annual income data deserve any creditability, then income in the payments data has been systematically underreported.

The rural experiment analysts are aware of this phenomenon. Indeed, cognizance of unreliable reporting led to adjustment of reported income based on the initial interview responses.

The staff had both payment records and interview data and, in some cases, wage stubs were submitted by wage earners along with payment forms. In addition, the interview data contained information of physical production and inventories so that imputations of revenues and expenses could be contrasted to actual reports. Further, farmers were asked to make IRS returns available and over one-half complied. With whatever information was available, the staff attempted to reconcile inconsistencies, usually by increasing imputed income.

What is surprising is not that income was underreported but that the reports were inconsistent because nothing in the experimental procedures would have revealed a pattern of consistent errors (fraud?). There have been a number of papers written describing the imputation process and changes that resulted. These make good reading for anyone wishing to perform social experiments on the self-employed.

In one of these papers, "The Accuracy of Self-Administered Reporting," William Harrar contrasts the self-reported payments data with the edited data (the best guesstimates).[15] He finds that, on average, about 91

15. In Bawden and Harrar, eds., *Rural Income Maintenance Experiment,* vol. 2, chap. 4.

percent of wage income of household heads was reported. For wives, he estimates that 80–90 percent of wage income was reported. In contrast to wages, Harrar estimates that about 61 percent of net farm income was reported to the payments office. From this, I presume that if the edited data were correct, then on average, the tax on farm income was only two-thirds as high as on wages (61/91). Unfortunately, Harrar gives no information on dispersion in this ratio, so I have no idea whether all experimental farmers faced the same farm-nonfarm income tax ratio or whether the distribution was so dispersed that the mean carried no information.[16] But, if the mean ratio (61/91) is to be taken seriously, the pattern of substitution of off-farm for farm work exhibited in table 2 is not surprising. It may continue to be surprising that net farm income fell while hours worked on farms rose, but bear in mind that the editing process only reveals inconsistencies. The way to lower rates of farm taxes relative to nonfarm taxes is to underreport farm income. That edited income of experimental farmers fell short of edited income for control farmers may only point to incomplete editing.

Since the effective tax on an income source is proportionate to the reported-actual income ratio, it would have been helpful if the analysts had incorporated estimates of these ratios when attempting to explain reported labor supply responses. Unfortunately, while actual payments were recorded in the analysis file, the income ingredients used to compute benefits were not.

In another of the papers on data quality ("Impact of Data Errors upon Treatment Estimates of the Farm Population"),[17] Wendell Primus contrasts the original interview data on income and the edited income data separately to IRS income data for the subset of experimental and control farmers who provided IRS returns to the analysts. Bear in mind that there are at least three files: the payments file (for experimental

16. Harrar computes individual reported-edited income ratios for a variety of income sources and attempts to explain variance among families—via regressions on such observables as edited income, year, score on verbal test, age, sex, marital status of household head, and so forth. Computed R^2s range from 0.11 for wages of the household head to 0.375 for transfer income. Only 14 percent of the variance of the reported-edited net farm income is so explained. Even though regression results are reported, neither initial nor residual variances are given. Some patterns emerge. For example, ratios are high in 1970 (the initial year) and are low for blacks. Since the ratio is not so much an index of accuracy as of internal reporting consistency, I infer from this that participants were more consistent in 1970 than in other years, and blacks less consistent than whites.

17. *Rural Income Maintenance Experiment*, vol. 2, chap. 3.

farmers only), which summarizes reports filed to payments offices, the initial data file, which provides unedited interview responses, and the analysis file, which contains the edited data—the analysts' best guesses. Primus compared both the initial and edited data with IRS returns but, unfortunately, did not compare the original and edited data directly. This would have been especially interesting contrasted with those who did not make IRS returns available.

Primus' analysis of original interview data reported net farm income regressed on IRS farm income along with a dummy variable for experimental farmers. An R^2 of 0.57 is reported. The standard error of the estimate is $3,315; a $1 increase in IRS income leads to an 84 cent increase in interview income and, given IRS income, experimental farmers interviewed report to the interviewers $850 less farm income than control farmers. In comparing edited income to IRS income, Primus reports an R^2 of 0.76. The standard error of the estimate is $2,470, the slope coefficient on IRS income is 95 cents, and the experimental-control differential is $37.

Clearly, the editing procedure increased the correlation between the edited income measure used and IRS income, and increased income for experimental farmers relative to control farmers. Since the ratio of interview reported to edited mean farm income is 0.89 for those supplying IRS forms as opposed to 0.85 (described by Harrar) for all farmers, it may be that adjustments for those revealing IRS information are not atypical for income editing. I should note, however, that the major discrepancy in the data is not between interview-reported income and edited income. Rather, it is between the ratio of income reported to the payments office and that reported to field interviewer for the same experiment. For example, Harrar reports that the payment-edited net farm income ratio is 0.61 while the payment-annual interview ratio is 0.70, at the sample mean.

Inferring Behavioral Responses

The data summarized earlier in table 2 suggest that the rural experiment may have generated behavioral responses. Yet if we are to infer that these responses stem from variations in income and tax rates, it would be useful if we knew what the income changes and tax rates were. In what follows, I suggest a simple comparison for (1) inferring average tax rates from experimental data, and (2) inferring whether revealed average rates can meaningfully be assumed to hold at the individual level. Unfortunately, this scheme is better suited to accounting rules that are simpler than that of the rural experiment. Suppose negative income tax benefits are defined by

(6) $$B = G - ty,$$

where B is the benefit, G the guarantee, t the tax rate, and y income tax liability. Clearly, this is the same as

(7) $$y = (G - B)/t$$

and since $G, B,$ and t are observed, y is easily inferred. Now posit,

(8) $$y = a + \sum_i b_i y_i + u,$$

where y_i refers to the ith component of income (farm income, wages and salaries, and so forth). With accurate reporting, $a = 0$ and $b_i = 1$ for all i. If so, the income maintenance scheme is as described. If $a < 0$, income is systematically underreported and if $b_i < 1$, the ith income component is underreported and is therefore taxed at a rate below the stated rate. Further, the residual variance, σ_u^2, should suggest whether the experiment conducted is a tax experiment. If σ_u^2 is small, we can presume that a tax experiment was conducted, and if not, we should be uneasy about attributing behavioral responses to taxes, at least to the average rates implied by estimates of equation 8. It would seem that equation 8 could be easily estimated for most income maintenance experiments and would serve as a simple summary statistic for describing the nature of those experiments.

   Unfortunately, it is not so easy for the rural experiment because observations of boundary benefits need not imply zero marginal taxes. Nonetheless, I have estimated a crude version of this equation: Observations include all families who did not receive boundary benefits in the fourth quarter of the specified year.[18] By retaining only those receiving nonboundary benefits, I have assured that all tax liability accruing during the year in question is taxed at the rate stated. Two dummy variables are added. One signals no payment in the fourth quarter of the preceding year, indicating that a positive surplus had been brought into the current

   18. Also excluded are families whose fourth-quarter payments exceeded one-fourth of their annual guarantee.

Table 4. Estimates of Contribution of Income Components to Tax Liability

Component	Regression coefficient	t ratio
Net farm income	0.089	3.35
All other income[a]	0.269	5.78
Experimental tax rate	−5,940	−4.97
Positive surplus	1,090	1.84
Negative surplus	−801	−1.47
Intercept	4,580	
Addenda		
$R^2 = 0.324$		
Number of observations—164		

Source: Based on text equation 8 and data from the Rural Income Maintenance Experiment.
a. Includes wages and salaries, business and small enterprise income, unearned income, rental value of owner-occupied housing, and net asset imputation.

year. The other signals a fourth-quarter payment in the preceding year greater than or equal to the guarantee, indicating the possibility of a negative carry-over. Regression results are summarized in table 4.

Bear in mind that, aside from carry-over problems, had the payment and analysis files agreed, this expression would be an identity with a zero intercept and tax coefficient and unit slopes on income components. Although I have experimented with several partitions of the "all other income" composite, the pattern is pretty much as summarized here. The overall fit is poor. In no case can income components of the analysis file account for 35 percent of the variance in tax liability. Implied marginal contributions to tax liability are small for nonfarm income and smaller yet for farm income (27 and 9 percent, respectively). Further, an increase in the experimental tax rate appears to reduce tax liability automatically (for example, an increase from a 30 to 70 percent tax plan reduces tax liability by $2,400 annually).

It is hard to take these estimates of average tax rates seriously. The low R^2 signals so much individual diversity that any attempt to transform stated tax rates into individual rates would appear to be best performed at the individual level rather than to resort to an obviously imprecise summary statistic such as the above regression.

This, clearly, is not what I had envisioned an income maintenance experiment to be. The simple fact is that in its present form the data of the analysis file cannot be used even to infer benefits. Why then should we expect the data to reveal underlying truths about labor supply responses to variations in benefits?

Conclusion

I have studiously avoided my assigned task of critiquing the rural experiment estimates of farmer labor supply effects. Instead, I have tried to spell out why we should have little interest in these estimates. All estimates I have seen treat experimental families as though their budget is constrained as in the standard textbook treatment. There is no distinction between those receiving benefits and those not. There is no consideration of the lagged adjustment and associated windfall benefits from carry-over provisions of the accounting system. Neither is there consideration of inventory manipulation options stemming from interactions between cash basis accounting and a limited duration experiment. Further, there is no consideration of differences between stated and actual tax rates, between programs or income sources, even though the evidence is overwhelming that actual tax rates were not programmed rates. It would be nice if all these omissions were mysteriously canceled out, but before arguing that biases might cancel out, I for one would like to have some idea of what the biases are.

Farm operators, like all self-employed, are notorious for underreporting income to the IRS. Yet, based on the Harrar-Primus summaries, it seems that farmers reported 40 percent *more* income to the IRS than to the rural experiment payments office. From this I conclude that when dealing with either social experiments or longer-run welfare programs, it really matters how these programs are administered—more so than many of us would have suspected.

It is possible that one could return to a merged payments analysis file and compute estimates of realized individual tax rates. One might also develop procedures to take account of windfalls at the program's start, which would be analytically similar to guarantees, and of problems of inventory management near the project's end. If so, there may be a basis for proceeding to labor supply estimates. To do so, one would need reasonable assurance that it is possible to control for all those unique features of the rural experiment that would not be imbedded in an actual negative income tax program. In any case, prospects for further analysis of the data would probably be enhanced by the existence in the public domain of a fully documented file. I am not aware that such a file exists.

The rural income maintenance experiment had a total budget of $5.5 million, of which not more than $2 million was transferred as benefit payments to experimental families. If we have learned anything from this investment, it is primarily that a negative income tax program would be difficult to administer. Yet we should have known this in any case. Anyone suspecting that this is not true would be well advised to contrast IRS farm income estimates with those of the U.S. Department of Agriculture.

I have no idea whether there is information here relevant to estimating budgetary costs for a negative income tax program, but I am reasonably confident that there is very little evidence—other than the obvious point that if nonfarm income is taxed and farm income is not, farmers will devote a larger portion of their time to farm work—for determining probable labor supply effects of such a program.

Comment by Michael J. Boskin

I should like to begin by comparing the rural and the urban negative income tax experiments. One of the conclusions I draw is unfavorable to the rural experiment and the other is favorable to it.

First, the analysts of the rural experiment have not greatly improved the methods of evaluation, despite the enormous advantage of being able to draw on the experience of the New Jersey experiment and the recent progress in estimating labor supply functions.

Second, the rural experiment dealt largely with farmers and the self-employed, a group for which it is extremely difficult to estimate a labor supply function. This is not a problem that originated with the administration of a negative income tax. The Internal Revenue Service cannot tax farmers or the self-employed very well either. There is a substantial degree of underreporting of net income on tax returns by the self-employed, who tend to overreport business expenses and also underreport receipts. Some improvements might have been made in the analytical techniques to deal with underreporting in the rural experiment, but this is inherently a much more difficult problem than any faced in the urban experiment.

Finis Welch's paper boils down to the point that there were many more substitution possibilities available to recipients of negative income tax benefits in the rural experiment than in the urban experiment. This makes it very difficult for the analyst to estimate the responses in the rural experiment.

With that in mind, let us turn to page xvii of the rural income maintenance experiment summary report. "The results of the experiment suggest, as did the New Jersey experiment, that a universal income-conditioned cash assistance program would cause only a modest decline in the labor supply of families of wage-workers."[19]

I believe that this conclusion is not entirely warranted. There are so many biases in the data and in the analyses that it is very difficult to conclude much from what has been done.

Problems and Biases in the Experiment

There are four major problems. First, there is the issue of permanent versus transitory effects, which Charles Metcalf analyzed very well for the urban experiment.[20] Any negative income tax experiment lasting only three years will greatly underestimate the true income effect on labor supply and may also overestimate the true substitution effect to some extent.

The degree of error depends on the intertemporal substitution possibilities. According to Orley Ashenfelter's paper, almost all of the reduced labor supply was the result of the wage or substitution effect—the income effect appeared to be small. If the bias in the wage effect is small, the enormous bias in the income effect has not been identified and there could be a large underestimate of the true labor supply response.

Second, in short-duration experiments, effects that might occur after the interval of observation are not observed. It is conceivable, for example, that one of the effects of a permanent negative income tax would be earlier retirement with little or no impact on labor supply earlier in life. The negative income tax would then become a supplement to social security for a few years before the age of eligibility for social security. This may not happen, but it could never be observed from a three-year experiment that was limited to persons under sixty-two years of age.

Third, the sample sizes were very small in the rural experiment, both for farmers and for nonfarm wage earners. As a result, the statistical significance tests were more liberal than usual—hypotheses were rejected at probability levels as low as 80 percent in some cases. Such an attempt to compensate for small sample size is disturbing since it greatly reduces the

19. U.S. Department of Health, Education, and Welfare, "The Rural Income Maintenance Experiment: Summary Report" (HEW, November 1976; processed).

20. Charles E. Metcalf, "Predicting the Effects of Permanent Programs from a Limited Duration Experiment," in Harold W. Watts and Albert Rees, eds., *Final Report of the New Jersey Graduated Work Incentive Experiment* (University of Wisconsin–Madison, Institute for Research on Poverty, and Mathematica, 1974), pt. C, chap. 3.

power of the tests. I believe that it is equally as important to avoid a high probability of accepting a false conjecture as it is to avoid a low probability of rejecting a correct one.

Fourth, results were often reported in terms of averages, and no attempt was made to separate out the income and substitution effects. The problem is that the averages may overestimate or underestimate the effect, depending on the true shape of the labor supply function. This is illustrated by the labor supply function in the accompanying figure. Labor supply is zero up to some reservation wage, $\overline{W}_R$. It rises gradually as the wage increases and then increases sharply until it reaches an upper limit, $\overline{L}$.

Suppose people start off at some point A and there is a 30 percent plan that lowers the net wage to B, a 50 percent plan that lowers it to C, and a 70 percent plan that lowers it to D. The labor supply change is negligible for the 30 percent plan, small for the 50 percent plan, and very large for the 70 percent plan ($\Delta L_1 \approx 0$, ΔL_2 is small, and ΔL_3 is very large, as shown in the figure). Our objective is to calculate a weighted average for the three plans.

The problem is that the elasticity is not uniform. Obviously the accuracy of the weighted average will depend on whether the wage distribution of the experimental data is representative of the wage distribution in the population as a whole. If the high elasticity portion of the curve is not represented, the average from the experimental data will greatly underestimate the true effect of the program.

Substitution Possibilities

I turn now to a specific problem in measuring the labor supply of farmers. It is a special case in the general class of issues raised by Finis Welch about substitution possibilities. The experimental data show that farmers decreased their wage work and increased their farm work, but their farm profits were down. It is not surprising that the farmer would work more on the farm and less on wage work when his earnings are subject to tax. The tax encourages him to reduce the amount of goods sold on the market, hence decreasing his farm profits subject to taxes, and to increase his production (and consumption) of home-produced goods, which are not taxable.

The true labor supply function is a function not just of the net wage and the net income, but of the prices of other commodities. Suppose there are two types of other commodities: the first are goods that are not farm

Figure 1. Labor Supply as a Function of the Net Wage Rate

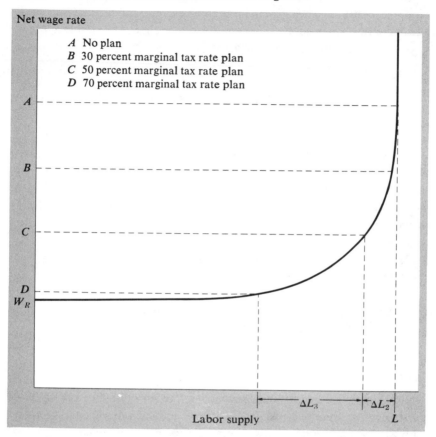

income in-kind and the second are goods that contribute to farm income in-kind, for example, food produced at home. The price of food produced at home is now reduced from P to $P(1 - t)$, where t is the marginal tax rate, because it is not taxable. What happens when an attempt is made to estimate the tax effect of a negative income tax on labor supply?

The observed effect is really a compound of the direct wage elasticity of the labor supply and of its cross elasticity with respect to the price of goods produced and consumed in-kind but not subject to tax. Assuming the utility of income increases as income declines, the marginal value of extra income to low-income families is large. Hence, the measured labor supply response may be capturing the effect mainly of the change in relative prices of taxed and nontaxed commodities rather than of the lower wage. This may be a major reason why the wage elasticities in the labor supply function are large.

All these considerations indicate why the direct estimation of labor supply responses to a negative income tax is extremely difficult. Even complicated models may not be sufficient, let alone reliance on simple average responses of various experimental groups.

Comment by Luther G. Tweeten

Finis Welch's truculent critique of the farm portion of the rural income maintenance experiment is unduly negative. His impatience because the experiment represents a "real world" negative income tax rather than a textbook negative income tax is misplaced. Faced with the choice of a textbook negative income tax that cannot be generalized to the real world and a real world negative income tax that cannot be generalized to the textbook, those who designed the experiment surely made the proper choice by opting for the latter. While citing many real shortcomings of the experiment, Welch's attempt to improve on the analysis is less satisfactory than the analysis he so artfully criticizes. After reviewing several of Welch's points, I shall attempt to summarize what of a positive nature can be said of the experiment.

Interpretation of Empirical Results

Welch makes a major point concerning the processing of data before presenting his empirical results. He perceives that experimental farmers with earnings above the breakeven level or below zero are confronted by different real tax rates than are other experimental farmers assigned to the same plan. Because experimental farmers with earnings above breakeven levels face positive tax rates similar to the control farmers, they may exhibit behavior more like the control group than the experimental group. Welch's estimate of experimental farmers "not on the experiment" is greatly exaggerated because many are aware that income above breakeven levels is carried over to subsequent periods when negative tax rates will apply if income is low.

After raising his point and moving on to test the hypothesis that labor adjustments of persons engaged in both farm and nonfarm work would fall largely on nonfarm work, Welch might be expected to separate experimental farmers above the breakeven income from other experimental farmers. He does not, noting that "not all experimental families [in his analysis] are 'on the experiment' since some have income above the break-even level." Other problems in his analysis are apparent. Experimental effects are aggregated across all plans and across sites. Lumping of experimental farmers across plans and states is done presumably to preserve degrees of freedom. Although recognizing the need to differentiate between responses in Iowa and North Carolina, Welch asserts "the problem of identifying effects in each state from roughly fifty experimental observations" per state renders the situation "hopeless." He seems to ignore (1) that the "observations" are households with several observations of each over time, and (2) opportunities to preserve degrees of freedom using dummy variables in joint analysis of the two states without separate analysis for each state.

Despite these problems and others, including lack of any statistical tests, Welch concludes that farm operators and their spouses on the experimental plans worked less off the farm than did control operators—in accord with his predictions from theory. Reviewing the theory of labor allocation applied to farm people who work both on and off the farm, Welch asserts that "for part-time farmers, a negative income tax scheme that does not result in a complete cessation of off-farm work will have no effect whatever on farm activities." All effects of the negative income tax are confined to off-farm work by this reasoning.

Welch's interpretation of theory did not square with his empirical findings that experimental farmers worked more hours on the farm and received less net farm income than control farmers. These findings accommodate to theory recognizing the consumption value of farming as a way of life. Relieved by the negative income tax of the need to obtain as much earnings from nonfarm employment, experimental farmers are freed to "consume" more of the values farming offers. More hours of labor on the farm are often a complement of this choice. Hundreds of city dwellers holding nonfarm jobs move to the farm each year; most seem aware that their resources will yield low production value but high consumption value.

Welch discounts Kerachsky's assertion that earnings from alternative sources might be given very different utility weights, saying, "I would guess that such an effect is minor at best." Data analyzed by Harper revealed that responses of total and marginal quality of life (that is, utility) to income differed considerably by source of income.[21] In short, failure to

21. Wilmer Harper, "The Role of Income in the Perceived Quality of Life of the Rural Populace" (Ph.D. dissertation, Oklahoma State University, 1977).

reckon with the consumption value of occupations, and institutional impediments (such as rigid work schedules of factory workers) to labor adjustments for farm and nonfarm employment, severely circumscribes Welch's brand of theory as it seeks to explain his empirical results.

Thus far Welch has focused on tractable problems, such as experimental farmers above breakeven income levels behaving like control farmers, small sample size and other venial sins of the experiment that in principle can be corrected either by improved experimental design or analysis. To account for weak and ambivalent responses to negative income tax parameters, Welch offers two other alternatives: (1) labor supply is only trivially affected by negative income tax parameters within experimental ranges, or (2) what happened in Iowa and North Carolina could not reasonably be expected to identify labor supply responses. He clearly leans toward the latter, stating that "I am convinced that what happened in Iowa and North Carolina was not an income maintenance experiment—at least not as I would describe one to my students . . . [but] what did happen may be a demonstration of what we might expect from a negative income tax scheme in the real world."

"What did happen" is underreporting of income, use of smoothed (moving average) payments, double taxation (through an asset consumption imputation), and cash accounting that in all likelihood would characterize a real world negative income tax but which distorts experimental inferences drawn from nominal tax and guarantee parameters. Farmers enjoy the privilege of cash accounting for income taxes, and would press to have the privilege extended in a negative income tax. Although it would be desirable to end this kind of preferential treatment, the reporting problems of monthly accrual accounting are staggering. Society does not favor transfer payments to households that have high income and wealth on the average but that experience short periods of low income—hence income averaging would be likely to attend a real world negative income tax. Society does not favor income transfers to households with large amounts of wealth, even if that wealth was accumulated out of past earnings that were taxed, hence double taxation is likely to continue. And underreporting of receipts and overreporting of production expenses is impossible to stop among the self-employed. The weight of evidence supports the conclusion that experimental farmers were treated to something more like a real world negative income tax than a textbook negative income tax, and those who planned the experiment that way made the appropriate judgment.

The Reliability of Inferences from the Experiment

If the experiment is in fact a demonstration of what we might expect from a negative income tax scheme actually implemented, it is important to examine the results for what they can tell us about the real world. Inferences regarding the behavior of farm people under a national negative income tax, with nominal parameters as specified, can be drawn from the experiment. But it is important to bear in mind that these nominal tax and guarantee parameters are not those actually facing farmers. Farm operators probably faced lower real tax rates and higher real guarantees than did wage earners with the same nominal negative income tax parameters. These two biases have opposite effects on incentives and probably account for the surprisingly comparable labor responses for farmers and wage earners. Farm operators and their wives reduced total hours worked by 16.4 percent in North Carolina compared to wage-earner reductions of 10 percent for blacks and 18 percent for whites in the same state.[22] The situation was somewhat different in Iowa—farm operators and wives increased total hours of work by 7.3 percent and wage earners in the state reduced wage hours by 5 percent. Although data are unavailable to test statistically for differences between these responses, there is clearly no basis to conclude that farm households shift relatively more of their time from labor to leisure than do wage households in response to a negative income tax.

A larger sample and longer duration for the experiment, coupled with greater use of expectation and adjustment models, would have made stronger inferences possible. Because of "noise" in moving toward payments actually consistent with prescribed parameters and because half the experimental farmers apparently did not remember the guarantee, tax rate, and breakeven parameters to which they were assigned, it would appear that considerable time would be required for experimental farmers to gain subjective certainty of the real parameters.[23] Given subjective certainty in their expectations, time is required to overcome inertia and adjust behavior to increase satisfactions in responses to expectations. If experimental farmers can be viewed as moving toward a desired or equi-

22. HEW, "The Rural Income Maintenance Experiment: Summary Report," pp. x and 46.

23. They may not be able to verbalize these, but I am much impressed with the ability of farmers to perceive the likelihood of rain or frost for a particular season from observing past patterns without being formally schooled in such matters.

librium outcome in some predictable form, distributed lag adjustment and expectation models are required to characterize their behavior. Such models seem particularly appropriate for farmers whose actual negative income tax parameters were markedly obscured by the factors mentioned earlier, and I am surprised that greater use was not made of them. It is not necessary that experimental farmers have time during the experiment to make long-term adjustments; it is only necessary that they establish the trajectory of the adjustments as a foundation for computing long-run impacts.

Contributions of the Experiment

To conclude on a positive note, the experiment did reveal useful information about the working of a negative income tax among the self-employed. The farm sector responded somewhat like wage workers—probably withdrawing relatively less labor from the market than wage workers in response to payments. The experiment taught much that we did not know and confirmed some things we thought we knew about behavior of the self-employed. A great deal was learned about administration of a negative income tax to the self-employed, including how payments might be tailored to unstable farm income. The propensity of farmers sometimes to overreport expenses and underreport earnings was confirmed. Accounting practices can deal with some problems, such as memory lapse and failure to keep adequate records that gave rise to such results. These measures will not eliminate reporting bias and it may be necessary to set lower nominal guarantees and higher nominal tax rates for the self-employed than for wage and salary workers.

ORLEY ASHENFELTER

The Labor Supply Response of Wage Earners

An interesting party game for economists is to question whether anyone can think of a behavioral economic response where there is wide agreement about empirical magnitudes. My candidate for such an empirical relationship is always Engel's law, but the fact that the share of a family's income spent on food declines with income probably never drew much controversy and certainly does not do so now. Measuring labor supply behavior, on the other hand, is now big business and I can think of more than one organization whose capital value would shrink if the subject became moribund. Although there is hardly a consensus on the magnitude of the income and substitution effects in the average labor supply function, the results of the rural negative income tax experiment[1] are evidence of the recent scientific progress in the determination of the behavioral responses to the wage and unearned income changes induced by such a program. The difficulty now is to integrate this information into a consistent framework so that conflict and agreement among its various parts can either be reconciled—or, where agreement is genuine, highlighted. Given the diversity of data, the growth in econometric methods to deal with this diversity, and the tendency for different investigators to highlight different results, this is a formidable task.

Since interest in the effects of a negative income tax has provoked

This paper was written during my stay at the London School of Economics and I am indebted to Bettie Jory and Sally Cooper for assistance, and to Richard Layard for helpful conversations. I am also indebted to Lee Bawden and James Heckman for their comments on an earlier draft and to Lee Bawden for his extraordinary help in the analysis of the data contained herein.

1. D. Lee Bawden and William S. Harrar, eds., *Rural Income Maintenance Experiment: Final Report* (University of Wisconsin–Madison, Institute for Research on Poverty, 1976), vols. 1–6. (Hereafter, *Rural Income Maintenance Experiment.*)

much of the research on labor supply behavior, it is natural to proceed with this framework in mind. My own approach has been to examine the data and analysis of the rural experiment with a view to modifying my prior views about what the effects of such a program were likely to be. These views were based primarily on earlier cross-sectional studies and the results of the urban negative income tax experiment in New Jersey and Pennsylvania.[2] Of course, all of this empirical material requires interpretation within some theoretical framework, and I have depended heavily on the classical theory of choice as applied to the family's decisions regarding nonmarket time and consumption goods. Because there may be some confusion about who will choose to accept payments under a negative income tax program, and because this issue ended up being treated differently in the design of the urban and rural experiments, I have spelled out the conventional theory of labor supply and its implications in appendix A to this paper.

What Is the Theoretical Framework?

A negative income tax offers both a harmful and a beneficial change in the opportunity set a family faces. The harmful change is the decrease in the wage rate that each family member faces as a result of the implicit tax (t) the program places on earnings. The beneficial change is the guaranteed income level (G) that the family now has. The family that is offered the opportunity to participate in a negative income tax program presumably will not do so if the harmful effect of participating outweighs the beneficial effect. What this means, of course, is that offering the plan to a family does not necessarily imply that it will participate. It is natural to ask, then, what determines which families will participate?

Determinants of Family Participation

It is easy to see that the answer to this question must depend on the preenrollment earnings level of the family. The higher the preenrollment earnings level, the less likely it is that the family will participate. First, it is clear that all those families with preenrollment earnings below the breakeven earnings level will be better off participating in the program.

2. Joseph A. Pechman and P. Michael Timpane, eds., *Work Incentives and Income Guarantees: The New Jersey Negative Income Tax Experiment* (Brookings Institution, 1975).

Because these families receive a positive subsidy under the plan, they can have both higher consumption of goods and leisure by participating. Second, some families with preenrollment incomes above the breakeven income level may also decide to participate. Although these families will end up with fewer consumption goods by deciding to participate, they will be compensated for this by additional leisure. At a high enough preenrollment income level, however, the sacrifice of consumption goods will eventually become too great. Intuitively, the level of income above which a family will no longer voluntarily reduce its income in order to become eligible for the program depends on the strength of its preference for leisure. Of course, these arguments must be modified when there is a stigma attached to the mere act of participating in the program or when there are burdens of paperwork or other difficulties involved in participation.

ESTIMATING FAMILY PARTICIPATION. In appendix A, I show that as an approximation, and in the absence of stigma or other burdens, it is rational for a family with only one worker to choose participation in a negative income tax program if its preenrollment income[3] is less than the opting-in income level $w_1 h_1^0$, where

$$w_1 h_1^0 \approx (G/t)[1 - 0.5et]^{-1},$$

and e is the income-compensated percentage change in the labor supplied per percentage change in the wage. Where its labor supply is very inelastic and consequently work attachment is great, the opting-in income level is essentially equal to the breakeven income level, and only those families whose preenrollment earnings levels would justify positive subsidies will participate. Where its labor supply is very elastic, however, the opting-in income level may be considerably above the breakeven income level.

This issue is illustrated in table 1, where I have calculated values of the ratio of the opting-in income to the breakeven income for various values of e and t. The top panel takes up the case where only the husband works, while the bottom panel examines the two-earner case under the assumption that the wife's earnings are 20 percent of the total. I have chosen values for the labor supply elasticities that, on the basis of my own prior views, would be considered large in order to explore the upper limits of the likely opting-in income. For a 50 percent tax rate it seems that the

3. I use the term "preenrollment income" here to mean the income that the family would have in the absence of being offered participation in a negative income tax scheme. This would correspond to preenrollment income exactly only at the very outset of the experiment, and would no doubt be greater than actual preenrollment income in the later years of the experiment when wage rates had drifted upward.

Table 1. Values of the Ratio of the Income below Which Families Choose to Participate to the Breakeven Income in a Negative Income Tax Program, by Various Elasticities and Tax Rates

Compensated labor supply elasticity		Tax rate (percent)		
		30	50	70
		Only the husband works		
Husband				
0.15		1.023	1.039	1.055
0.25		1.039	1.067	1.096
0.35		1.055	1.096	1.140
		Both husband and wife work[a]		
Husband	Wife			
0.15	0.6	1.037	1.064	1.092
0.25	0.8	1.057	1.099	1.144
0.35	1.0	1.078	1.136	1.202

Sources: See text discussion and appendix A to this chapter.
a. Assumes that the wife's earnings are 20 percent of the total.

opting-in income level might be as much as 4 to 10 percent above the breakeven income level. Of course, how many additional families would participate in the program depends on the distribution of preenrollment earnings around the breakeven level.

For those families who become participants in the negative income tax program, there are then the conventional income and substitution effects on labor supply. On the usual presumption that leisure is a "normal" good, the subsidy resulting from the program operates to reduce labor supply just as does the substitution effect of the induced wage change. When there is only one worker in the family this is the end of the story, whereas the presence of two workers may lead to a redistribution of these two workers' time between market work and leisure. The upshot of this is that family earnings must decline for participating families although this may be accomplished without a decline in the hours worked by all family members.

Estimating the Costs of a Negative Income Tax Program

Now one way to think about the purpose of a negative income tax experiment is as an effort to estimate the total transfer costs of adopting such a program for a previously uncovered group. Without knowledge of any behavior at all, it is always possible to make a rough first-round estimate of the cost of such a program by simply calculating the subsidy that each family would receive based on the known values of preenrollment income. Let us denote by D^0 the average subsidy per family calculated in this way. If N^0 is the number of families with positive subsidies at preenrollment, then $N^0 D^0$ is the first-round estimate of the transfer cost of the program.

Clearly the quantity $N^0 D^0$ is an underestimate of the eventual total cost of the program for two reasons. First, some families with incomes above the breakeven income level will opt to work less and participate in the program. These families are not counted in N^0. Suppose there are N' of such families and that their average subsidy while participants is X^0. Accounting for this additional participation then adds $N'X^0$ to the total transfer cost of the program. Second, the average subsidy D^0 does not include the decline in the earnings of the participants with preenrollment incomes below the breakeven level that was induced by changes in the opportunity set the family faces. This average decline in earnings multiplied by the tax rate ($t\Delta E$) will also end up as part of the average subsidy. If N families are then offered the option of participation in the program, these two adjustments taken together imply that the ultimate transfer cost of the negative income tax program will be $ND' = N^0(D^0 + t\Delta E) + N'X^0$. In this framework $N - N^0 - N'$ families will have opted against participation in the program and the average cost per eligible family is D'.

DESIGNING THE EXPERIMENT. Next consider designing an experiment to estimate the full transfer costs of a negative income tax plan applied to a previously uncovered group. A natural way to do this would be to draw a random sample of the entire population to be offered the plan and to implement the plan with this group. This would provide an estimate of D', which, when multiplied by the number of eligible participants, would provide an estimate of the total costs of adopting the program. Of course, it would also be possible to estimate the components of D', which include the induced declines in earnings ΔE, the number of actual participants with preenrollment incomes above the breakeven level, N', and the subsidy of this last group, X^0, by the use of data from some form of control group.

As it turns out, the experimental framework I have just described is the basic arrangement that was used in the urban negative income tax experiment. Of course, the population potentially eligible for various plans in that experiment was restricted to those husband-wife families who were below 150 percent of the poverty level. This restriction undoubtedly excluded some families who might have reduced their earnings in order to receive payments from the program, but presumably many still were eligible who had income close enough to the breakeven level for this to be desirable. The design of the experimental group in the rural experiment was slightly different. Primarily because of requirements from the agency sponsoring the experiments, the two plans with the lowest breakeven income levels were dropped from the design of the rural experiment and families were assigned to the experimental group only if, on the basis of their preenrollment income, they were expected to receive a positive subsidy. As we have seen, apart from stigma or other burdens, such families should always opt to participate in a negative income tax program.

In fact, as Lee Bawden[4] notes, in only 13 percent of all the quarterly observations were experimental families above their breakeven income levels during the three experimental years. As a result, the data from the rural experiment are not likely to be of much use in estimating the terms N' or X^0, which represent that part of the cost of a negative income tax plan resulting from participation by families who would otherwise have incomes above the breakeven income level.

Transitory Nature of the Program

To this point I have treated the analysis of a negative income tax experiment just as if it were a permanent negative income tax program and, consequently, I have depended heavily on the conventional static single-period analysis of labor supply behavior. This would perhaps be acceptable in the analysis of a permanent program, but the experiment was clearly designed to last only three years. In a more general model of labor supply, where families plan their work decisions for the current period based on the wage rates and unearned income they expect to receive in current and future periods, the transitory nature of the experiment has important implications for the interpretation of the results.

In particular, the measure of the income subsidy that will determine current period labor supply in an intertemporal model is the discounted present value of all future subsidies received during the planning horizon. Thus, a subsidy promised for only three years will be merely a fraction of the discounted present value of a subsidy promised for *all* future years. It follows that the income effect on labor supply of a transitory program must generally be less than the income effect of a permanent program.

4. D. Lee Bawden, "The Analytical Approach to Measuring Work and Income Response of Wage Earners," in *Rural Income Maintenance Experiment*, vol. 3, pt. 1, chap. 1.

How much less will depend first on the length of the planning horizon. If families consider only the opportunities they will face in the near future in making current decisions, then the income effects of permanent and transitory programs will be very similar. In a similar way, high rates of discount (interest) will reduce the importance of future subsidies for current-period labor supply and also tend to make the income effects of permanent and transitory programs more similar.

At the same time, the tax rate in a permanent program causes non-market time to be less expensive relative to consumption goods in both the current and all future periods. The tax rate in a transitory program, on the other hand, causes nonmarket time in the current period to be less expensive relative to consumption goods in both current and future periods *and* less expensive relative to nonmarket time in all future periods.

If nonmarket time in the current and future periods are substitutes, the transitory program then sets up an additional incentive above that of a permanent program to reduce labor supply during the period of the experiment so as to take advantage of the "fire sale" on leisure the experiment offers. The upshot of this is that it is not possible to determine the effects of a permanent negative income tax program from the results of a transitory experiment without making additional strong assumptions or obtaining additional evidence. Nevertheless, explicit consideration of these issues may be helpful in the interpretation of the actual empirical results of the experiment.

Income Underreporting and Tax Evasion Implications

Finally, it is necessary to qualify the analysis of labor supply to the extent that the stated and actual changes in the family's opportunities differ. For example, there is now considerable evidence that the presumed (and to some extent statutory) tax rates in many actual welfare programs are considerably higher than the effective tax rates actually in existence in many of these programs. Though far from definitive, analyses by Rowlatt for Alberta, Canada, Williams for ten U.S. states, and Barr and Hall for nine U.S. cities suggest that these differences may in some cases be very large.[5] Some difficult issues are raised when analyzing the effects of a

5. J. Donald Rowlatt, "An Estimate of the Tax Rate in a Public Assistance System," *Canadian Journal of Economics,* vol. 5 (February 1972), pp. 84–95; Robert George Williams, *Public Assistance and Work Effort: The Labor Supply of Low-Income Female Heads of Household* (Princeton University, Industrial Relations Section, 1975), chap. 4; N. A. Barr and R. E. Hall, "The Taxation of Earnings Under Public Assistance," *Economica,* vol. 42 (November 1975), pp. 373–84.

negative income tax program on labor supply when there are opportunities for the underreporting of family income. In appendix B, I set out a very simple example of such an analysis and this may provide some guidance, but further analysis would clearly be useful.

Perhaps the most disturbing implication of possible systematic income underreporting is that most of the incentives for such underreporting tend to work in the same direction as purely behavioral responses to changes in unearned income and tax rates that are the result of a fully enforced negative income tax experiment. For example, a tax rate in a negative income tax program raises the subsidy a family receives by t dollars for each dollar of income that is underreported by a participating family. However, the gain from income underreporting is not affected by the guarantee level the participating family faces. It follows that the incentive to underreport income will be greater for participating families and that it will be greater for those families facing high tax rates than for those facing low tax rates. These predictions of the effect of a negative income tax on "reported" income are very similar to the predictions from a conventional analysis of labor supply, and this is particularly the case for the predictions of the effect of a transitory negative income tax program.

Of course, whether income underreporting for the purpose of "tax evasion" is of any quantitative importance in the rural experiment depends on the likelihood of being caught and on what penalties, psychic or otherwise, are imposed for this behavior. So far as I can determine, this issue is not discussed in the report on the experiment. It seems likely that some incidents of underreporting were discovered and it would be useful to have at least a superficial discussion of the experimenters' experience with this issue and the practical efforts that were taken to cope with it. In the absence of any formal evidence, I have simply examined the data on family unearned income that is comparable to the data on family wage income reported in table 3 below.

In a model of tax evasion where labor supply is exogenous, there is an incentive to underreport all forms of income regardless of source, while in a model of labor supply it is expected that only earned income would decline because of reduced hours of work. Moreover, it may be difficult for a family subsequently to underreport unearned income that has been revealed at the time of preenrollment, but it is probably not so difficult simply to "forget" increases in such income during the experimental period. As it turns out, reported unearned income among the experimental group increased by about 62 percent during the experimental years, and declined by only 8 percent relative to the control group over the period. Although this is far from conclusive, there does not seem to be any clear evidence of widespread income underreporting among the wage earners in the rural experiment and I am inclined to view the data from the experiment as primarily a reflection of behavioral labor supply responses. Of course, if the experimental framework is indicative of the way in which an actual program would be enforced, the cost estimates of a universal program, ND', may still be accurate, even if they reflect tax evasion behavior alone or some combination of that behavior and a labor supply response.

What Were the Expected Results?

With the stage set in this way, we may now turn to an examination of previous estimates of income and substitution effects based on cross-sectional data as well as the results from the urban experiment to see what might be expected in results from the rural experiment. In principle, the estimates of behavioral relationships from cross-sectional data could be used to measure the decline in earnings (ΔE) among those families initially below the breakeven level, and the proportion and earnings response of those families initially above the breakeven level that would opt into the program. In practice this rarely seems to have been done.

Income and Substitution Effects

Following the more conventional practice, I have recorded in table 2 some crude estimates of the expected wage income decline (ΔE) as a result of the rural negative income tax experiment. In making these calculations I have assumed a guarantee level of $3,200 a year and a tax rate of 50 percent, which seems to be approximately the average plan used in the rural experiment. I have chosen to present these results as the proportionate decline in earnings that might be expected among the participants with preenrollment incomes below the breakeven point. Assuming that cross-substitution effects in family labor supply are negligible, which I do because of general ignorance about these effects and not because of any good evidence, these proportionate changes are the sum of a substitution effect and an income effect. The substitution effect is the negative of the product of the compensated labor supply elasticity for a family member

Table 2. Expected Percentage Decline in Wage Income of Families Initially below the Breakeven Level and Offered a Negative Income Tax Program

		Change in earnings	
		Based on the New Jersey experimental results for whites	
Earnings affected	Based on cross-sectional evidence	Rees-Watts estimates	Hall estimates
Family	−13.0	−8 to −12	−10.4
Husband	−8.2	−2.4 to −7.0	−7.0
Wife	−45.0	−45.5	−33.3

Sources: The first column is calculated assuming substitution elasticities of 0.1 and 0.8 for the husband and wife, respectively, $w_1(\partial h_1/\partial Y) = w_2(\partial h_2/\partial Y) = -0.1$, where w_1, w_2 and h_1, h_2 are the wage and hours of work, respectively, of the husband and wife, and Y is the unearned income of the family, wife's earnings as 13 percent of total earnings, a guarantee level of $3,200, and a tax rate of 0.5.

In the second column, line 1 is from Albert Rees and Harold W. Watts, "An Overview of the Labor Supply Results," in Joseph A. Pechman and P. Michael Timpane, eds., *Work Incentives and Income Guarantees: The New Jersey Negative Income Tax Experiment* (Brookings Institution, 1975), table 2, results for earnings; line 3 is from their table 1 for hours expressed as a percentage of the control group mean. Line 2 is the implied estimate from lines 1 and 3 assuming the wife's earnings are 13 percent of the total.

In the last column, the last two lines are from Robert E. Hall, "Effects of the Experimental Negative Income Tax on Labor Supply," in ibid. (Hall's most efficient estimator of the average effect of the program for husbands [GLS] and wives [GLST] as a percentage of the average weekly hours of the control group during the experiment). The first line is the implied estimate assuming the wife's earnings are 13 percent of the total.

and the tax rate, while the income effect is the negative of the product of the marginal propensity to consume leisure (or nonmarket time) and the subsidy as a fraction of earnings calculated at preenrollment. Of course, it is not possible for any family member to work a negative number of hours and so I have assumed that the 40 percent of wives that did not work for wages during the preenrollment period would be unaffected by the experiment.

Responses of Husbands and Wives

A crucial component of these calculations is the values assumed for the compensated labor supply elasticities and the marginal propensities to consume leisure from unearned income. In making the calculations I could not help realizing how arbitrary a task it is to assign particular values to behavioral relationships based on the literally dozens of preexisting studies that now exist. The values I have used reflect two general findings that seem to emerge from most studies. First, the estimated compensated labor supply elasticities are considerably larger for wives than for husbands. Second, it seems very likely that the uncompensated labor supply elasticity for husbands is negative or close to zero. Although the cross-section studies play a role in establishing this last finding, I find it more convincing that higher real wages tend to be associated with shorter hours of work both among individuals and over time. The final values selected and listed in table 2 reflect my own crude earlier survey[6] and the later and more complete survey by Cain and Watts.[7] They imply uncompensated labor supply elasticities of zero for husbands and 0.7 for wives.

As can be seen from the table, the application of these cross-sectional results to the preenrollment data suggests a decline in family earnings of 13.0 percent. The decline for husbands is expected to be 8.2 percent, while the decline for wives, averaged over workers and nonworkers, is 45.0 percent. It is important to recognize that conceptually these are estimates of the proportionate decline in earnings for families with preenrollment incomes below the breakeven level, who are therefore expected to receive actual payments. The response of families above the breakeven is not included.

Family Response in the Urban Experiment

The second and third columns of table 2 contain my interpretation of the results for white families from the urban negative income tax experiment in New Jersey and Pennsylvania. As best as I can determine, the average experimental plan in the urban experiment was roughly comparable both to the plan I have used to calculate results based on the cross-section evidence and to the plan used in the rural experiment. However, as should be clear from the earlier discussion, the results of the urban experiment are estimates of the decline in earnings resulting from the labor supply reductions of those families initially both below and above the breakeven income levels. In general, this earnings response will be less than the average response of only those families initially below the breakeven income level. One should not be surprised, therefore, to find that the average response in the urban experiment is less than would be expected based on the cross-sectional evidence.

6. Orley Ashenfelter, "Using Estimates of Income and Substitution Parameters to Predict the Work Incentive Effects of the Negative Income Tax: A Brief Exposition and Partial Survey" (Princeton University, November 1970; processed).

7. Glen G. Cain and Harold W. Watts, eds., *Income Maintenance and Labor Supply: Econometric Studies* (Rand McNally, 1973).

The results of the urban experiment that I have reported in table 2 cover only white families, even though there were both black and white families in the experiment. I have chosen to use only the results for whites for two reasons. First, the results for the groups other than whites are very peculiar and have been criticized by many both for the unreliability of the data and the problem of attrition. Second, I am told that there has been considerable reanalysis of the data for these groups and that the later results for blacks are very much more like those for whites. It is presumably for this reason that many of the reported results of the urban experiment by the original analysts seem very much smaller (in absolute value) than those reported in table 2. Rees and Watts[8] suggest an estimate of an overall reduction in family earnings of 6 percent, while Aaron[9] summarizes his view of the results as a 4 to 5 percent reduction in hours worked by husbands and a 25 to 50 percent reduction in hours worked by wives. Some readers may prefer to accept these estimates as preferable to those recorded in table 2.

As can be seen by comparing the results from the cross-sectional evidence and the urban experiment in table 2, the labor supply effects in the former tend to be larger. Whether this difference can be attributed to the different conceptual bases of the two measures, or to something else, is a topic for future research.

What Were the Actual Results?

In a first reading of the experimental results for wage earners it is easy to get lost in the maze of analysis for the various subgroups and specifications of the experimental effect. In order to see what lay behind the analysis I assembled the data in table 3 on wage income for both the control and experimental groups in the year before and in the three years following the start of the experiment. These are the annual averages of the data that made up the grist for the components-of-variance regression analysis performed by Lee Bawden and his colleagues. Annual averages are useful in this context because they eliminate the very considerable seasonal fluctuations in the quarterly data for these rural families but still provide some idea of how any experimental effects vary over time.

8. Albert Rees and Harold W. Watts, "An Overview of the Labor Supply Results," in Pechman and Timpane, eds., *Work Incentives and Income Guarantees,* p. 86.
9. Henry J. Aaron, "Cautionary Notes on the Experiment," in ibid., p. 109.

Table 3. Annual Average Wage Income of the Family, Husbands, and Wives of Control and Experimental Groups in the Year before Enrollment and the Three Years of the Rural Income Maintenance Experiment
Dollars

		Year of experiment		
Group	Preenrollment	First	Second	Third
		Family		
Control	4,464	5,163	5,694	6,061
Experimental	4,504	4,702	5,048	5,343
		Husbands		
Control	3,668	3,931	4,238	4,451
Experimental	3,884	3,924	4,169	4,412
		Wives		
Control	632	858	954	1,161
Experimental	488	532	501	546

Sources: First column, U.S. Department of Health, Education, and Welfare, "The Rural Income Maintenance Experiment: Summary Report" (HEW, November 1976; processed), p. 93; other data, files of Institute for Research on Poverty.

In table 4, I have computed some very simple estimates averaged over all three sample groups (blacks and whites in North Carolina, and whites in Iowa) of the effect of the experimental treatment on wage income. Wage income seemed the most conceptually appropriate measure of labor supply response, even though from the point of view of the ultimate transfer cost of a negative income tax program, total family income is actually the variable of most interest. In any event, both of these measures gave essentially the same results.

The estimate of experimental response in tables 4 and 5 is just the arithmetic difference between the change from preenrollment to postenrollment in the wage income of the experimental and control groups.[10] Although such an estimator is crude, there are two strong arguments for its use. First, it is simple to explain. After all, the primary purpose of obtaining the experimental effects of the labor supply response to a negative income tax program is the education of a wide variety of people who

10. That is, if R_t^e and R_t^c are the average wage incomes of the experimental and control groups in period t, then the measure of experimental response is merely $\Delta E_t = (R_t^e - R_0^e) - (R_t^c - R_0^c)$, where the preenrollment period is denoted by the subscript 0 and the subscript $t = 1, 2, 3$ refers to postenrollment. Attrition reduces the sample sizes slightly in each consecutive year so that these are 264, 251, and 230, respectively, with about 44 percent of the sample in the experimental group in each year. The overall average response in table 5 is based on a pooled regression with these data that includes a single dummy variable for presence in the treatment group and separate intercepts for each year of the sample.

Table 4. Difference-in-Means Estimates of the Effect of Participation in the Rural Income Maintenance Experiment on Wage Income of the Family, Husbands, and Wives, by Year[a]

	Year of experiment		
Effect	First	Second	Third
	Family		
Monetary (dollars)	−504	−751	−839
	(184)	(253)	(281)
Percentage[b]	−9.8	−13.2	−13.8
	Husbands		
Monetary (dollars)	−220	−387	−404
	(143)	(141)	(223)
Percentage[b]	−5.6	−9.1	−9.1
	Wives		
Monetary (dollars)	−182	−255	−377
	(79)	(109)	(135)
Percentage[b]	−21.2	−26.7	−32.5

Sources: Monetary effect, derived from data in the files of the Institute for Research on Poverty; percentage effect, calculated using control data in table 3.
a. The numbers in parentheses are standard errors.
b. The dollar effect as a percentage of the control mean.

come from many different backgrounds. Designing an experiment so that this information can be easily conveyed is important. Second, there is considerable evidence in the regression results from the experiment that there is some correlation between a number of exogenous variables and observed wage income. In effect, the results reported in tables 4 and 5 are derived from a model that allows for a permanent component for each family, a trend component for each time period, and a transitory component. Moreover, in this framework the permanent component is not assumed to be uncorrelated with experimental status. Hence, the effect of the computation of differences is a simple control for unobservable factors that, because of sample attrition or other reasons, might be correlated with the presence of treatment status and hence bias the estimated treatment effects.[11]

Examining the Simple Estimates

When all is said and done, it is quite remarkable that the effects of the experiment can be seen clearly even in the raw data contained in table 3. For example, the average preenrollment total wage income levels of the

11. Of course, whether this is an efficient estimation scheme is unknown.

Table 5. Comparison of Difference-in-Means and Regression Estimates of the Effect of Participation in the Rural Income Maintenance Experiment on Income of the Family, Husbands, and Wives, Three-Year Average[a]

Effect	Difference in means	Regression[b]
	Family	
Monetary (dollars)	−690	−765
	(138)	
Percentage[c]	−12.3	−13.6
	Husbands	
Monetary (dollars)	−333	−248
	(107)	
Percentage[c]	−7.9	−5.9
	Wives	
Monetary (dollars)	−266	−302
	(62)	
Percentage[c]	−27.1	−30.5

Sources: First column, derived from data used for table 4; last column, derived from regression estimates prepared by D. Lee Bawden.

a. The numbers in parentheses are standard errors.

b. In each case the estimates are weighted averages of separate coefficients for the Iowa, North Carolina–black, and North Carolina–white samples, with weights of 0.261, 0.485, and 0.254, respectively, which are the proportions of the total sample from each location.

c. The dollar effect as a percentage of the control mean. The method of computing the difference-in-means for this table differs from that for table 4, so the percentages are not identical in the two tables.

experimental and control families were nearly identical. In the first year of the experiment, however, the average income of the experimental group was $461 below that of the control group, a 9 percent decrease. More systematic but equally simple estimates are contained in tables 4 and 5. The difference-in-means estimates suggest that, averaged over the three years of the experiment, family wage income declined by 12.3 percent. This was a result primarily of wage income declines for husbands of 7.9 percent and for wives of 27.1 percent. Table 4 reveals that the experimental effect on the wage income of both husbands and wives tended to increase in each year of the experiment. Moreover, the statistical hypothesis that the true experimental effects are zero is firmly rejected by these data.

Comparing Difference-in-Means and Regression Estimates within the Rural Experiment

In table 5 I have compared the average over the three experimental years of the simple estimates contained in table 4 with the more complicated regression estimates contained in the draft report of the results of the experiment. Remarkably enough, for the family as a whole the difference-in-means estimates are very similar to the regression estimates. The decline in wage income for husbands is slightly larger, and for wives it is slightly smaller, in the difference-in-means estimates than in the regression estimates. One difference between the results that is not shown in the table relates to additional earners in the family. The difference-in-means estimate implies a decline in the wage income of these secondary workers as a result of the experiment of $91, or 20.8 percent of the control group mean, while the regression estimates imply a decline of $215, or 49.0 percent of the control group mean. Which of these estimates is to be preferred is not clear at this point. In any case, the differences seem very small and are probably of little consequence compared to the sampling error of the estimates.

Comparing the Rural Experiment Estimates with Other Estimates

Since the design of the rural negative income tax experiment was meant to ensure that members of the treatment group would receive positive subsidies, unlike that of the urban experiment, it should be clear that the rural and urban experiments measure conceptually different parameters. In practice, however, some of the treatment families in the rural experiment were above the breakeven income level for their plans. One might therefore expect that the largest average response to a negative income tax plan would be estimated from the cross-sectional studies, and that the response in the rural experiment would fall between the cross-sectional estimate and the results of the urban experiment.

A comparison of tables 2 and 5 suggests that this is what did happen. However, the extent of the difference between the results of the urban and rural experiments depends somewhat on whose estimates of the urban experiment's effect are considered. Hall's estimates (see table 2) of the effect of the urban experiment on labor supply are nearly identical to the estimates from the rural experiment contained in table 5. On the other hand, the results from the cross-sectional predictions are only slightly larger than those from the rural experiment. Whether this should be taken to imply that the effects of a permanent negative income tax program might differ from those of a transitory program such as the rural experiment, or whether it should be taken to indicate something else, will require further analysis and evidence.

Estimating Tax Rate and Guarantee Effects

It is necessary to examine the effects of variations in the tax rate and guarantee levels of the various experimental plans. The importance of accurate estimates of these effects cannot be overstated. First, they are needed for consideration of the impact of other potential programs. Since tax and guarantee levels in any actual negative income tax program are a subject for public decision, it could be argued that obtaining reliable estimates of the labor supply effect of variations in these parameters is the entire rationale for the experiment and that failure to obtain such estimates would constitute a major failure of the experiment. Second, it is important to verify through variation in the tax and guarantee level whether income and substitution effects were what lay behind the observed response to the experiment. Otherwise, there always remains the possibility that the experimental effect was due to some other causal mechanism altogether.

It is important to have this issue clarified since it has wide implications for the study of labor supply behavior as well as many normative aspects of both taxation and welfare policy. In effect, the experimental data offer an extraordinary opportunity to put some quite basic theoretical structures to a test and this opportunity should not be missed.

As it turns out, this issue does not seem to have received nearly the attention it deserves by the authors of the reports on either the urban or the rural negative income tax experiments. There are many difficulties with the handling of this issue in the report on the rural experiment. First, there is very little discussion of the appropriate functional form for examining the effect of either the tax rate or the guarantee level on labor supply behavior. The tax rate is simply entered linearly into each of the regressions for the various response variables, while the guarantee level as a proportion of the poverty level is entered linearly as well. In some places it seems to be assumed that higher tax rates must lead to lower labor supply, even though there is nothing in the theory of labor supply to suggest this should happen and considerable evidence that for husbands the opposite is likely to occur. Why the guarantee level relative to the poverty income level is the relevant transformation for the guarantee variable is never made clear, and the interaction between the guarantee level and the family's size that this implies for the estimating equation seems never to have been investigated.

Finally, every regression that contains the tax rate and guarantee variables also includes a dummy variable indicating presence in the experimental group. Often this variable's coefficient is large in size and estimated quite precisely, while the tax and guarantee effects are not. Since the experimental effect of the program is supposed to operate *through* the guarantee and tax rate effects, the power of this additional variable should be considered disturbing. Certainly it should have troubled the investigators enough to have caused them to search for specification and other errors that may be present.

Comparisons of Two Estimation Schemes

In order to pursue this issue in more detail, I report the results in table 6 of two very simple regression schemes for the estimation of the tax and guarantee level effects on wage earnings. In the first scheme I have simply used the change in wage earnings as dependent variables, and the tax rate and dollar guarantee as independent variables, in a pooled regression of all 745 observations that allows separate intercepts for each experimental year. This method essentially treats the uncompensated labor supply effects and the marginal propensity to consume nonmarket time as parameters for the purpose of estimation, and forces the experimental response to work through tax and guarantee effects.[12] In the second scheme the independent variables are the tax rate and the estimated subsidy calculated on the basis of the family's preenrollment income. This method essentially treats the compensated labor supply effects and the marginal propensity to consume nonmarket time as parameters for the purpose of estimation, and also forces the experimental response to work through income and substitution effects.[13] The top and bottom panels of

12. In the notation of appendix A the coefficient on the tax rate is an estimate of $-w_i[w_1 \partial h_i/\partial w + w_2 \partial h_i/\partial w_2]$ for the ith individual, and it is $-w'[\partial h_i/\partial w_j]w$ for the family, where $[\partial h_i/\partial w_j]$ is the matrix of uncompensated labor supply derivatives. Elasticities are computed by dividing by the appropriate measure of wage income, and multiplying by -1. The coefficient on the guarantee level is an estimate of $w_i \partial h_i / \partial Y$ for the ith individual and $\Sigma w_i \partial h_i / \partial Y$ for the family.

13. In the notation of appendix A the coefficient on the tax rate is an estimate of $-w_i[s_{i1} w_1 + s_{i2} w_2]$ for the ith individual and $w'S^*w$ for the family. Elasticities are computed by dividing by the appropriate measure of wage income and multiplying by -1. The coefficient on the subsidy calculated on the basis of the family's preenrollment income is an estimate of $w_i \partial h_i / \partial Y$ for the ith individual and $\Sigma w_i \partial h_i / \partial Y$ for the family. This scheme for specifying the model of a negative income tax experiment is related to a suggestion by Ashenfelter and Heckman (Orley Ashenfelter and

Table 6. Alternative Schemes for Estimating Tax and Guarantee Level Effects on Wage Earnings in an Income Maintenance Program

Alternative and effect and elasticity items	Effect on earnings[a]		
	Husbands	Wives	Family
Parameter scheme 1			
Tax effect	−868	−671	−2,634
	(512)	(298)	(658)
Mean uncompensated labor supply elasticity[b]	0.207	0.844	0.494
	(0.122)	(0.393)	(0.123)
Guarantee effect	0.015	0.005	0.144
	(0.067)	(0.039)	(0.086)
Parameter scheme 2			
Tax effect	−708	−714	−2,442
	(478)	(278)	(614)
Mean compensated labor supply elasticity[b]	0.169	0.941	0.458
	(0.114)	(0.366)	(0.115)
Subsidy effect[c]	−0.010	0.013	0.140
	(0.074)	(0.043)	(0.096)

Source: Pooled regressions of 745 observations from the data file of the rural income maintenance program that permit separate intercepts for each of the 1970–72 experimental years. See text for details on the variables, and text notes 12 and 13 for the formulas.

a. The numbers in parentheses are standard errors.

b. Evaluated at the simple average of the control and experimental group earnings levels in the three experimental years.

c. At preenrollment.

table 6 report the results of the first and second estimation schemes, respectively. Both methods have the advantage of simplicity, but they suffer a number of disadvantages. Perhaps the most serious is the failure to account for the fact that many wives in the sample have no earnings and for the obvious possibility that what are treated as fixed parameters in estimation are likely to vary within the sample. Although more sophisticated schemes might be explored, I doubt whether much more can be accomplished for reasons given below.

James Heckman, "Estimating Labor-Supply Functions," in Cain and Watts, eds., *Income Maintenance and Labor Supply,* pp. 265–78), and is a straightforward attempt to fit equation A-4 in appendix A. This method has an interesting interpretation in the context of forecasting the fiscal outlay of adopting a negative income tax program. In effect, the subsidy calculated on the basis of preenrollment income is the estimated cost of such a program if there is no labor supply response, while the regression is a forecasting scheme for determining incremental costs because of a labor supply response as a function of the tax rate and preenrollment subsidy level. Such a regression scheme would thus fit naturally into a model for simulating the total costs of hypothetical negative income tax programs.

RESPONSE OF HUSBANDS. Consider first the results for husbands where the presence of nonzero earnings for all workers might suggest that a linear approximation to labor supply responses would be satisfactory. In the top panel the labor supply elasticity is positive while the guarantee effect is also positive. Although the former is perfectly consistent with the theory of labor supply, the latter is not consistent with the presumption that nonmarket time is a normal good. In the bottom panel both tax and income effects have the expected signs, but in neither the top nor bottom panel can the statistical hypothesis that both effects are zero be rejected. Now in the report of the experiment, these results would be recorded simply as the inability to find "statistically significant" tax and guarantee effects for husbands. Surely this is not the end of the story, however. Recall that a plausible summary of previous cross-sectional estimates of the labor supply functions of husbands would suggest mean compensated labor supply elasticities of 0.1 and mean income effects of -0.1. Suppose, then, that we proceed to test whether the results in table 6 are consistent with these expectations. In the bottom panel of table 6, for example, it is easy to verify that the experimental results suggest a substitution elasticity slightly larger than expected and an income effect one-tenth the size expected.

Nevertheless, it is *not* possible to reject, at any conventional level of confidence, the hypothesis that the parameters estimated from the experimental data are identical with those derived from previous cross-sectional work. It would be just as correct, therefore, to record the results of the experiment as showing the inability to find tax and guarantee effects for husbands that are significantly different from what would have been expected on the basis of previous analyses of nonexperimental data. The basic problem, of course, is that there is simply not enough information in the experimental data to be very confident about the estimates of the tax and guarantee effects for husbands. It seems unlikely that anything but a larger sample size, in one form or another, could surmount this difficulty.

RESPONSE OF WIVES. The experimental results for wives in table 6 do show a tax effect that is statistically different from zero. Moreover, the estimated tax effect is very close to the effect expected on the basis of previous cross-sectional studies. The income effect, on the other hand, is of an unexpected sign, although for both estimation schemes the estimated effect is very close to zero. Moreover, for wives it is just barely possible to reject the hypothesis that the income effects estimated from the experimental data are equal to those expected from previous cross-sectional results. It may be reasonable to conclude, therefore, that the income effects for wives that result from a temporary negative income tax are, in fact, very close to zero.

FAMILY RESPONSE. The experimental effects of the tax rate and guarantee level on family wage earnings not only reflect the responses of husbands and wives. In fact, the estimated tax rate effect on the earnings of other family members that is implicit in table 6 is extremely large. The estimated guarantee effect on the earnings of family members is also very large, and of an unexpected sign. Since the number of other family members was very small, and since their earnings were a small fraction of the total, it is unclear whether the results for other secondary workers should be taken at face value. In particular, both of these problems suggest that the simple estimation schemes used in table 6 might lead to serious problems and further work in this area may be useful.

Implications for Family Behavior

The upshot of this simplified analysis of tax and guarantee effects is that tax effects are larger than might have been expected based on previous evidence while guarantee effects are negligible. As noted at the outset, these findings are consistent with two very different hypotheses. First, they are consistent with the presence of considerable incentives for the underreporting of income by experimental families. Currently available evidence does not suggest, however, that this effect is likely to be the predominant one. These findings are also consistent with the view that the experimental families treated the experiment as only a temporary change in their opportunities, and that they behaved accordingly. If the latter interpretation is correct, it implies that time horizons in family decisions must be fairly long so as to account for the very small income effects observed in the experiment, and also that intertemporal substitution of nonmarket time must not be very great so as to account for the closeness of the actual and expected substitution effects. Only additional analysis and evidence will resolve this issue.

Conclusion

The results of the rural negative income tax experiment show an unambiguous average decline in the work effort of all family members in the experimental group of wage earners. Family wage income declined by an average of 12 percent, while the wage income of husbands declined by 8 percent and the wage income of wives by 27 percent. These results imply that any first-round estimate of the transfer costs of adopting a negative income tax experiment that ignores the behavioral response of family members will underestimate the ultimate transfer cost. For the data in the rural experiment the first-round estimate would have been 78 percent of the ultimate transfer cost. Whether this seems "large" must ultimately depend on one's individual values, but it is considerably larger than some of those writing about the experiment seem to have implied. The estimates of overall labor supply response for wage earners seem to be quite well determined in the rural experiment. They are smaller than would be predicted by a crude application of the results of cross-sectional studies to this problem, but larger than some, but not all, of the estimates of behavioral responses from the urban experiment.

There are already several lessons to be learned from the rural experiment although there remains a considerable agenda for further research. First, it is very important to specify the nature of the behavioral parameters and responses that would be desirable to estimate before designing the experiment. The urban experiment was designed, in principle, to estimate the ultimate transfer cost among a particular sample of the population of adopting various possible negative income tax programs. This transfer cost is composed both of the subsidies received by families initially below the breakeven income level and those who choose to fall below it as a result of the program. In the rural experiment, on the other hand, it is only possible to estimate the ultimate transfer cost resulting from the former behavior alone. It is probably for this reason—and because the rural experiment did not suffer the vagaries of a dramatic change in the welfare laws confronting its participants—that the results of the rural experiment are so clear-cut in comparison with those of the urban experiment. The investigators in the rural experiment also had the benefit of the considerable practical experience that resulted from the operation of the urban experiment.

Second, one of the major reasons for using expensive experimental methods to measure behavioral responses to negative income taxation is to make it possible to apply simple analytical methods to the analysis of the results. The educational value of such simple methods is incomparably greater than the complicated methods invented to overcome the problems of nonexperimental data, which, I might add, are sometimes suspect even to their inventors. The experimental nature of the data should be more fully exploited.

Finally, my own prior views about the likely effects of a *permanent* negative income tax program on labor supply behavior have not been changed very much by the results of the experiment. This results from the failure of the analysts to show that the effects of the experiment are operating *through* the variations in the tax rates and guarantee levels faced by families in the experiment. The simple analysis that I have performed suggests that, to the extent they can be disentangled, the bulk of the labor supply response is a result of the tax effect alone. This suggests that the experimental families may have treated the experiment as merely a temporary change in their opportunities, and that they behaved accordingly. In the absence of further evidence, there must remain serious doubts about the implications of the experimental results for the adoption of any permanent negative income tax program.

Appendix A: Conventional Theory of Labor Supply and Its Implications for a Negative Income Tax Program

The application of the classical theory of consumer demand to the analysis of labor supply is by now a familiar problem. I want here only to spell out a slightly different approach to this analysis that is useful both in the prediction of the effects on earned income or hours of work under a negative income tax plan and in the examination of the issue of which of those families above the breakeven income level will choose to be covered by such a plan. As in the usual framework, the optimal choices of a family of (say) two individuals that acts as if maximizing a conventional utility function may be described by the labor supply functions $h_i = h_i$ (w_1, w_2, Y) $(i = 2)$, where h_i is the hours of work of a family member and w_i is that family member's wage, while Y is the family's unearned income. The actual level of satisfaction obtained by the family is obtained by the substitution of the labor supply and commodity demand functions into the original utility function. Clearly this level of satisfaction depends on the wage rates, price of consumption, and unearned income level the family faces, so that, ignoring consumption prices because they are assumed unchanging, $v = v(w_1, w_2, y)$ is the indirect utility function of the family. The highest satisfaction level that the family can attain for a given set of wage rates and unearned income is v.

Of course, if v is the highest utility level attainable at wage rates w_1 and w_2 with unearned income of Y, then the solution of the equation $v = v$ (w_1, w_2, Y) for the function $Y = E(w_1, w_2, v)$, must give the smallest level of unearned income necessary to reach the utility level v at those same wage rates. The function $E(w_1, w_2, v)$ thus gives the minimum quantity of unearned income necessary to reach the utility level v at the wage rates w_1 and w_2. Since Y is by definition the excess of expenditure over earnings, it is convenient to call $E(w_1, w_2, v)$ the family's excess expenditure function. A very convenient property of this function is the result of the fact that the effect of a change in a wage rate on minimum unearned income is just

$$\partial E(w_1, w_2, v)/\partial w_i \equiv E_i \equiv -h_i \equiv -h_i(w_1, w_2, v).$$

Consequently $- E_{ij}$ $(i, j = 1, 2)$ gives the full set of utility-constant (or income-compensated) labor supply derivatives.

Predicting the Effects

Now the effect of a negative income tax program is to provide a guaranteed income level of G, a tax on income of t, and hence a subsidy of

(A-1) $$D = G - t(w_1h_1 + w_2h_2 + Y)$$

to every family with total income below the breakeven level $B = G/t$, but nothing to those above this level. As it turns out, this kink in the relationship of the subsidy to income raises some special issues that would not be present if, after reaching the breakeven income level, a family then moved on to pay positive taxes at the rate and guarantee in equation A-1. Indeed, the original idea of the negative income tax was perhaps to eliminate such kinks. As it turns out, the implementation of an actual negative income tax would undoubtedly result in an abrupt change in the tax rate at the breakeven income level, and the effect of the presence of this notch on labor supply would have to be analyzed just as it must be analyzed in the context of an experimental negative income tax.

The effect of small changes in the wage rates and utility or unearned income on labor supply are merely

(A-2) $$dh_i = -E_{i_1}dw_1 - E_{i_2}dw_2 - E_{iv}dv$$
$$= S_{i_1}dw_1 + S_{i_2}dw_2 + \partial h_i/\partial Y \cdot$$
$$[h_1dw_1 + h_2dw_2 + dY],$$

where I have used the facts that the $-E_{ij} = S_{ij}$ are the utility-constant derivatives of the labor supply functions, $-E_{iv}\, \partial v/\partial Y = \partial h_i/\partial Y$ [as may be verified by differentiating the identity $-E_i(w_1, w_2, v(w_1, w_2, Y)) = h_i(w_1, w_2, Y)$] and that $dv = \partial v/\partial Y(h_1 dw_1 + h_2 dw_2 + dY)$. For a family that actually receives payments under the negative income tax, wage rates are changed from w_i to $(1 - t)w_i$ and unearned income is increased from Y to $G - tY$. A first order approximation to the change in labor supply resulting from the program is thus

(A-3) $\qquad dh_i = -t[S_{i1}w_1 + S_{i2}w_2] + (\partial h_i/\partial Y)\, D,$

where D is the subsidy evaluated at the preenrollment income level. Of course, $S_{ii} > 0$ and since leisure is taken to be a normal good $\partial h_i/\partial Y < 0$. It is interesting to note, as Killingsworth[14] has pointed out, that so long as the cross-substitution term $S_{ij} = S_{ji}$ is not zero, equation A-3 implies only that at least one family member must reduce its labor supply. Calculating $w_i dh_i$ in A-3 and then adding shows that

(A-4) $\qquad w_1 dh_1 + w_2 dh_2 = -tw'S*w + [w_1(\partial h_1/\partial Y) + w_2(\partial h_2/\partial Y)]D,$

where the vector $w' = [w_1 w_2]$ and the matrix $S* = [S_{ij}]$. Since $S*$ must be positive definite by the logic of the utility maximization problem, the value of A-4 must be negative.

The message of this exercise is clear. The family earnings of those participating in a negative income tax experiment must decline. This suggests one reason why it is appropriate to concentrate empirical analysis on the effect of the experiment on family earnings. It is this quantity about which the classical theory is useful in making predictions.

A second reason for concentrating on the analysis of family earnings is that the change in family earnings induced by the program is proportional to the excess transfer cost of a negative income tax program over the cost calculated on the basis of preprogram incomes alone. Thus, if D^0 is the average subsidy calculated from A-1 on the basis of the preenrollment income of participants, $D^1 = -t[w_1 dh_1 + w_2 dh_2] + D^0$ is an approximation to the ultimate transfer cost. Although there is surely interest in the composition of the labor supply responses of family members to the negative income tax, the ultimate size of the total transfer cost of such a program will no doubt loom very large in any public discussions of the adoption of such programs.

14. Mark R. Killingsworth, "Must a Negative Income Tax Reduce Labor Supply? A Study of the Family's Allocation of Time," *Journal of Human Resources*, vol. 11 (Summer 1976), pp. 354–65.

Which Families Will Participate

Of course, the preceding analysis is incomplete until it is specified which families will be participants in the program. This problem has been discussed by Greenberg and Kosters[15] and the issue incorporated into their simulations of the cost of a negative income tax plan. Its importance has been emphasized more recently by Hall.[16] Of course, any family eligible for the plan will presumably opt into it if, at its preenrollment income level, it is entitled to a positive subsidy. After all, the family may then have more of consumption goods or leisure and therefore is unambiguously better off participating in the program. There will also be some families at preenrollment that are above the breakeven income level and that will opt to work less and thus become participants. The question naturally arises as to what determines which families make this choice.

To start with the simplest case, assume that only one family member works. Then if the family is in the program it needs unearned income of $E[(1-t)w_1, v]$ to reach the utility level v, while it needs unearned income of only $E(w_1, v)$ to reach the same utility level if it remains a nonparticipant. On the other hand, as a participant it has unearned income of $G + (1-t)Y$ dollars while as a nonparticipant it has Y dollars. Clearly, the family will choose to participate in the program if

(A-5) $$E[(1-t)w_1, v] - E(w_1, v) < G - tY,$$

that is, if the extra unearned income needed to compensate the family for the damaging effects of the tax rate is less than the extra unearned income actually transferred to the family as a result of the program. A natural procedure is to approximate the difference $E[(1-t)w_1, v] - E(w_1, v)$ by a second-order Taylor series around preenrollment equilibrium. In this case we have

(A-6) $$E[(1-t)w_1, v] - E(w_1, v) \simeq (\partial E/\partial w_1)dw_1$$
$$+ \frac{1}{2} (\partial^2 E/\partial w_1^2)(dw_1)^2$$
$$= -h_1 dw_1 - \frac{1}{2} S_{11}(dw_1)^2.$$

15. David H. Greenberg and Marvin Kosters, "Income Guarantees and the Working Poor: The Effect of Income-Maintenance Programs on the Hours of Work of Male Family Heads," in Cain and Watts, eds., *Income Maintenance and Labor Supply*, chap. 2.

16. Robert E. Hall, "Effects of the Experimental Negative Income Tax on Labor Supply," in Pechman and Timpane, eds., *Work Incentives and Income Guarantees*, pp. 115–56.

Putting $dw_1 = -tw_1$ into A-6 and the result into A-5 shows that a family will participate if

$$(A-7) \qquad\qquad D^0 + \frac{1}{2} S_{11}(tw_1)^2 > 0.$$

Since S_{11} is positive, it follows immediately that any family with a positive subsidy at preenrollment will participate, but also that some families above the breakeven will too. The preenrollment earned income level below which all families will participate may be called the opting-in income level and is simply

$$(A-8) \qquad\qquad w_1 h_1^0 = (G-tY)/t(1-0.5te),$$

where e is the compensated elasticity of labor supply. Since unearned income is very small for the negative income tax experimental group, the opting-in income for them is merely $(G/t)/(1-0.5te)$, so that the ratio of the opting-in income level to the breakeven income level is just $(1-0.5te)^{-1}$. As might be expected, the opting-in income level increases with the compensated labor supply elasticity and equals the breakeven income level when the compensated labor supply elasticity is zero. As an example, for a tax rate of 0.5 and $e = 0.1$, $(1-0.5te)^{-1} = 1.026$, so that participants will be those with preenrollment incomes no greater than 2.6 percent of the breakeven income level. Other calculations for this case are contained in table 1 of the text. By a similar argument it is straightforward to establish that the opting-in income level for a family with two workers is

$$(A-9) \qquad w_1 h_1^0 + w_2 h_2^0 = (G-tY)/t[1-0.5t(\theta_1 e_{11} + 2\theta_1 e_{12} + \theta_2 e_{22})],$$

where e_{ij} is the income-compensated elasticity of the ith family member's labor supply with respect to the jth family member's wage rate and $\theta_1 = w_1 h_1/(w_1 h_1 + w_2 h_2)$ and $\theta_2 = 1-\theta_1$ are the respective shares of each family member's earnings of total earnings at preenrollment. For the case where participants have negligible unearned income and the cross-substitution elasticity is negligible also, the ratio of the opting-in income level to the breakeven income level is merely $[1 - 0.5t(\theta_1 e_{11} + \theta_2 e_{22})]^{-1}$. As an example, with $\theta_1 = 0.8$, $e_{11} = 0.15$, $e_{22} = 0.6$ and a tax rate of 0.5, only families with incomes less than 6.4 percent above the breakeven level would participate.

Effects of Permanent and Temporary Programs on Labor Supply

One of the obvious difficulties in the application of the preceding analysis to the results of a negative income tax experiment is that it takes no account of the temporary nature of such experiments. In order to remedy this difficulty it is necessary to recognize that families must base their work decisions for the current period on both the wage rate and unearned income to be received in the current period and the wage rates and unearned income to be received in future periods. To take the simplest possible case, consider a family with only one worker and, since the expected relative wages in future periods will remain unchanged, represent future periods by a single composite measure of labor supply. More detail is contained in Metcalf's[17] discussion of this problem. Utility is now defined over lifetime consumption and, supposing that consumer-workers can borrow and lend freely at the interest rate r, their budget constraint requires that

$$(A\text{-}10) \quad p_1x_1 + (1+r)^{-1}p_2x_2 = w_1h_1 + (1+r)^{-1}w_2h_2 + Y_1 + (1+r)^{-1}Y_2;$$

the discounted present value of present and future consumption must equal the discounted present value of present and future income. In A-10 p and x are the price and quantity of consumption goods, while the subscripts on all variables denote the period of consumption or supply. Putting $(1 + r)^{-1}\hat{w}_2 = w_2, Y_1 + (1 + r)^{-1}Y_2 = \hat{Y}$ and ignoring the unchanging consumer prices, it should be obvious that the formal analysis of this problem is identical to the analysis of the two-worker family above and that $\hat{w}_2$ and $\hat{Y}$ play the roles that w_2 and Y played in the preceding case.

It is now a simple matter to distinguish between the effects of both permanent and temporary negative income tax programs on labor supplied in the current period for those who participate. In the permanent program all wage rates are changed from w_i to $(1-t)w_i$, while in the temporary program only the current wage rate is so changed. Likewise, in the permanent program the discounted present value of unearned income is increased by $G + (1+r)^{-1}G$, while in the temporary program this increase is only G. Referring to equation A-2 and recalling the new interpretation of each variable, it follows that a first-order approximation to the change in labor supply in the current period resulting from a permanent program is

$$(A\text{-}11) \qquad dh_1 = -t(s_{11}w_1 + s_{12}\hat{w}_2) + (\partial h_1/\partial \hat{Y})\hat{D},$$

where

$$\hat{D} = G - t(w_1h_1 + Y_1) + (1+r)^{-1}[G - t(w_2h_2 + Y_2)]$$

17. Charles E. Metcalf, "Making Inferences from Controlled Income Maintenance Experiments," *American Economic Review*, vol. 63 (June 1973), pp. 478–83.

is the discounted present value of the current and future subsidies evaluated in the absence of the program. Likewise, an approximation to the change in labor supply in the current period resulting from a temporary program is

$$(A-12) \qquad dh_1 = -t(s_{11}w_1) + (\partial h_1/\partial \hat{Y})D,$$

where D is the subsidy in the current period evaluated in the absence of the program. The decline in labor supply resulting from the income effect of the temporary program is only the proportion $D/\hat{D}$ of the decline resulting from a permanent program. Since $D < \hat{D}$, the income effect is smaller than the income effect of the permanent program by an amount that depends on the length of the worker's planning period and rate of interest. On the other hand, the decline in labor supply resulting from the substitution effect of the temporary program is in the ratio $s_{11}w_1/(s_{11}w_1 + s_{12}\hat{w}_2)$ to the change resulting from a permanent program. As we have seen from equation A-3, the current-period substitution effect of a permanent program on labor supply need not even be negative. In any case, if current and future leisure are substitutes so that $s_{12} < 0$, the substitution effect on current-period labor supply of a temporary program is smaller (in absolute value) than that of a permanent program.

Appendix B: A Simplified Analysis of Tax Evasion Possibilities in the Negative Income Tax Experiment

It is a straightforward matter to set out the implications of the possibility of tax evasion for the likely measured responses to the institution of a negative income tax experiment. Here I take up only the simplest possible case and concentrate on its implications for variations in reported income with variations in guarantee levels and tax rates.

For a more detailed analysis that concentrates on the implications of various attitudes toward risk, for example, see Allingham and Sandmo.[18]

To simplify matters it is convenient to take the case where labor supply is exogenous and the family has a true total income of N. If X is the income stated by the family and accepted as correct by the experimenters, $Z = N-X$ is the income on which tax is evaded. Presumably the probability of being caught evading, P, will depend positively on the amount of

18. Michael G. Allingham and Agnar Sandmo, "Income Tax Evasion: A Theoretical Analysis," *Journal of Public Economics,* vol. 1 (November 1972), pp. 323–38.

evasion, so that $P = P(Z)$ and $P' > 0$. It is unclear what penalties are assessed for those caught evading, but suppose that any pecuniary or non-pecuniary penalties are independent of the amount of evasion and may be represented as θ. Total income if the family is not caught evading is then $G - tX + N$, where G in the guaranteed income level and t is the tax, while it is $G - tN + N - \theta$ if caught. Expected income is merely

$$E = P(Z) [G - tN + N - \theta] + [1 - P(Z)][G - tX + N]$$

and will be maximized by choosing X so that

$$P' [\theta + t(Z)] = (1 - P)t$$

if the second-order condition is satisfied ($P'' > 0$ being sufficient, for example). This implies that at the optimum the amount of evasion is

(B-1) $$Z = (1 - P)/(P' - \theta/t).$$

There are three points worth drawing from this analysis. First, the optimum amount of evasion for a participating family *does not* depend on the guarantee level in the family's program. This result is generated by the simplistic assumptions of the model, but it no doubt contains a kernel of the truth even in more complex cases. Of course, for a family that is initially above the breakeven income level, the higher the guarantee and the lower the tax rate, the more likely it is that evasion will be profitable. Second, implicit differentiation of the equilibrium condition B-1 establishes that $dZ/d(\theta/t) = 1/(ZP'' + P' + P'') < 0$, so that increases in the penalty and decreases in the tax rate tend to decrease evasion. Finally, in this framework it is equally profitable to decrease the reporting of all income regardless of its source, so long as all income is taxed at the same rate and the probability of being caught does not depend on the source of reported income. Thus, tax evasion provides a rationale for expecting a decline in reported income not only from earnings but from other sources as well.

Comment by James J. Heckman

Orley Ashenfelter compares the labor supply results from the rural nonfarm negative income tax experiment with results from the urban experiment and with predictions based on estimates drawn from the literature on labor supply functions estimated from cross-section data. He performs the valuable service of reanalyzing the rural nonfarm data using econometric techniques that produce parameter estimates of labor supply functions, which can readily be interpreted within the framework of the classical theory of labor supply he exposits so well. His analysis, and that of the authors of the basic report, suggest that there was a work-reducing effect of the experiment. If those estimates can be used to measure the potential impact of a permanent negative income tax program, they imply that the loss in market output of such a program would not be negligible, and that program transfer costs could be quite high.

The basic question is whether or not these estimates can be used to make such an inference. In my view, the estimates presented at this conference are not reliable and contribute little to our understanding of the consequences of a permanent program. This is so for three reasons: (1) The findings reported here on the results from a limited duration experiment cannot be directly generalized to predict the consequences of a permanent program. (2) The models employed to analyze the data are inappropriate. (3) Limited sample size precludes precise determination of parameters.

In principle, the first two problems can be solved, even with the existing data. If more use of a priori theory is made, much more can be squeezed out of the data. This is demonstrated below. But there is a more basic issue. Many of the comments at the conference, and certain remarks in the Ashenfelter paper, suggest that social experiments provide a simple short-cut method for answering policy questions. No doubt this illusion provided the initial stimulus for collecting the experimental data. This view is misleading and has caused the full potential from the experimental method to remain unexploited. In the concluding section of this comment, some remarks on this topic are offered.

The Choice of an Appropriate Model

There are two issues here: one economic and the other statistical in nature. The analysts of the experiment implicitly utilize a one-period theoretical model of labor supply in formulating their expectations about experimental outcomes and in estimating program effects. A components of variance regression scheme is used to analyze the data. Although he qualifies some of his results in light of a conceptually more appropriate life cycle model, Ashenfelter has no quarrel with either the econometric or the economic specification, using a one-period model of labor supply throughout much of his analysis.

APPLYING A LIFE CYCLE THEORY FRAMEWORK. Life cycle theory provides a natural framework for analyzing an experiment that is, after all, a limited intervention into the life cycle of its participants. The life cycle framework can be used to (1) interpret received cross-section estimates and examine their relevance for predicting experimental effects, and (2) formulate an econometric model that exploits the dynamic nature of the experiment and permits use of limited duration experimental findings to estimate the consequences of a permanent program.[19]

In order to clarify what has been estimated, and contrast these estimates with what should have been estimated, it is useful to consider the following simple *dynamic* model of labor supply, which deliberately abstracts from many inessential aspects. Suppose that people live forever, face a constant real wage rate W at each age, a constant interest rate r, and possess a stock of wealth A_i coming into life cycle period i. For simplicity, assume a linear labor supply function so that labor supply in period i, L_i, is

$$(1) \qquad L_i = \alpha_0 + \alpha_1 W + \alpha_2 \frac{W}{r} + \alpha_3 A_i,$$

where α_1 is the effect of a current period wage change on current period labor supply, α_2 is the effect of a future (discounted) wage change on current labor supply, and α_3 is the effect of assets on current labor supply, traditionally assumed to be negative. Nothing restricts the sign of α_1 and α_2, although most analysts, including Metcalf[20] and Ashenfelter, follow the convention in life cycle theory that $\alpha_2 < 0$ (leisure in different time periods is a net substitute). Note that all future *discounted* wage changes of equal magnitude are assumed to have the same effect on current labor supply independent of their timing. Household aspects are ignored. The assumption of stationary wage rates may not be inappropriate for a poverty population.

19. Charles E. Metcalf has discussed the issue of the appropriate model for analyzing experimental data to estimate the effect of a permanent program from the limited data available. (See his "Making Inferences from Controlled Income Maintenance Experiments.") Unfortunately, his analysis seems to have had little impact on the methods used by the analysts of the experiment. In this section, I generalize his results, present some new ones of my own, and utilize a conceptually appropriate framework to analyze the results of the experiment.

20. Ibid.

Cross-section analysis of labor supply functions, obtained by regressing labor supply on wage rates and wealth, estimates the effect of wages on labor supply as

$$\left(\alpha_1 + \frac{\alpha_2}{r} \right)$$

and the effect of wealth on labor supply as α_3.[21]

Using this simple framework, consider the effect on active participants of a negative income tax experiment that lasts *two periods*.[22] Wage rates are reduced by tax rate t, and a guarantee level bonus of $\$B$ per period is received. The predicted change in labor supply in the initial period is

$$(2) \qquad \Delta L_i = - \left(\alpha_1 + \frac{\alpha_2}{1 + r} \right) tW + \alpha_3 B \left(1 + \frac{1}{1 + r} \right).$$

Cross-section coefficients would predict a change in labor supply given by

$$(3) \qquad \Delta L_i' = - \left(\alpha_1 + \frac{\alpha_2}{r} \right) tW + \alpha_3 B \left(1 + \frac{1}{1 + r} \right)$$

if the present value of the program benefit levels are used to measure the change in wealth. Following Ashenfelter's procedure, one might use only the current period transfer B to estimate

$$(4) \qquad \Delta L_i'' = - \left(\alpha_1 + \frac{\alpha_2}{r} \right) tW + \alpha_3 B.$$

Or, if wealth is annualized to yield a perpetuity flow equivalent, as is done in some cross-sectional studies, the predictions of the cross-section theory corresponding to 3 and 4 become

$$(3') \qquad \Delta L_i' = - \left(\alpha_1 + \frac{\alpha_2}{r} \right) tW + \frac{\alpha_3}{r} rB \left(1 + \frac{1}{1 + r} \right)$$

or

$$(4') \qquad \Delta L_i'' = - \left(\alpha_1 + \frac{\alpha_2}{r} \right) tW + \frac{\alpha_3}{r} rB.$$

A comparison of equations 2 and 4 suggests that the cross-section estimates provide a useful benchmark for predicting experimental results only

21. If unearned income is used as a regressor, instead of wealth, the estimated cross-section income coefficient is α_3/r. Given prior knowledge of r, one can move interchangeably between those two versions of the income parameters. In fact, most cross-section studies utilize a wealth variable.

22. I abstract from the program participation decision in this analysis, following the main theme of Ashenfelter's paper.

if the rate of discount (r) is large. Otherwise the cross-section estimates *understate* the true wealth effect but a comparison of wage effects is ambiguous. If the conventional assumptions of life cycle theory are maintained, $\alpha_2 < 0$ (leisure in different time periods is a net substitute) the response to the wage change would be more negative in the experiment than the response predicted from the cross-section estimates. Accordingly, predictions based on cross-section estimates understate the decline actually observed in the experiment. If comparisons based on 4' are made, the same conclusion holds.

The first point to note is that the appropriate econometric scheme to analyze the experimental effects involves a multiplicative *interaction* of the wage rate with the tax level and the *present value* of benefits, not just their current flow. The analysts of the experiment use variables t (the tax rate) and B (the breakeven level) as regressors. Ashenfelter notes that tW and not t is the appropriate variable but fails to note that the appropriate wealth measure is the present value of benefits.

The second point to note is that the cross-section estimates *do not* provide a proper benchmark with which the experimental results in equation 2 should be compared irrespective of whether equation 4 or 4' is used.

A third point to note is that even in a two-period experiment, it is possible to estimate the impact of a long-term program. To see this, assume that α_1 and α_2 are the same in each life cycle period. The effect of the experiment on the change in second period behavior (compared with what it would have been) is

$$(2') \qquad \Delta L_{i+1} = -\alpha_1 tW + \alpha_3 (A_{i+1} - A'_{i+1} + B),$$

where A'_{i+1} is the stock of net worth that the individual would have had at hand coming into period $i+1$ had he not participated in the program, a variable that could be estimated using data from the control group. Note that if $\alpha_2 < 0$ and fraction $\dfrac{1}{1+r}$ (or greater) of the first-period benefit is saved, the second-period labor supply declines more than the first-period labor supply, a phenomenon actually observed in the experiment.[23]

Regression estimates of equations 2 and 2' fitted on samples of experimentals *and* controls permit estimation of α_1, α_2, α_3, and r, and hence all of

---

23. Note that even if less than fraction $\dfrac{1}{1+r}$ of the initial period benefit, B, is saved, it is still possible to obtain this ordering result depending on the size and sign of α_2, r, and α_3. Note further that I assume $\alpha_1 > 0$.

the parameters required to estimate long-term effects.[24] Thus, if a simple dynamic theory is used, one can exploit the limited duration aspect of the negative income tax experiment to produce estimates of the parameters required to forecast the effects of a negative income tax program of any duration.

Of course, considerable caution would be required in using such estimates to predict the effect of a permanent program. The simple theory does not take account of the impact of widespread participation in the program, nor does it adequately account for personal investment decisions that would be made in a program with a long time-horizon.

OTHER CONSIDERATIONS ILLUMINATED BY THE FRAMEWORK. The framework developed above is a convenient one for making some other points. Ashenfelter makes the valuable point that one difference between the urban and rural experiments is that in the rural program benefit levels were set to ensure greater active participation. Hence there should have been greater reduction in labor supply in the rural experiment than in the urban experiment, not only because more people participated but also because the average rural plan is more generous. But this may not be the whole story. Even with the same mix of plans offered in both programs, if the cost of living is lower in rural areas than in urban areas, as seems likely, the real value of the income guarantee is greater in rural areas and hence the expected reduction in labor supply is greater.

This framework also helps to account for the observed ordering in labor supply response among the three demographic groups included in the experiment. Iowa whites are the most educated group while North Carolina whites are the least educated, and North Carolina blacks fell between the other groups. Since education raises the real wage, given an identical mix of tax-guarantee plans for all three groups, the participating Iowa whites experienced the greatest decline in real wages while North Carolina whites experienced the smallest decline as a result of participat-

---

24. The coefficient α_3 can be estimated from equation 2'. From equation 2, the coefficient on B is $\alpha_3 \left(\frac{2+r}{1+r} \right)$ so r is estimable. This method is *not* the same as that of Metcalf ("Making Inferences from Controlled Income Maintenance Experiments"). Note further that this scheme could be enriched by varying tax rates in different periods to identify parameters more precisely. Also, if wage rates differ in each period, greater precision would be possible for the estimates. For a discussion of some of these ideas and for estimates of a life cycle model see James J. Heckman, "Three Essays on the Supply of Labor and the Demand for Goods" (Ph.D. dissertation, Princeton University, 1971).

ing in the program. Accordingly, one would have anticipated that the
Iowa whites would have reduced their labor supply more.[25]

Statistical Issues

Consider the components of variance regression scheme employed
by the analysts. Despite its conceptual simplicity, as employed, it is not
without its problems. To examine these problems, consider a simplified
model based on this scheme. Let E_{io} and E_{it} be earnings for individual i
before the experiment and earnings in experimental period t, respectively.
The μ_{io} and μ_{it} are measurable factors determining earnings in periods 0
and t; ε_{io} is the error term in period 0 while ε_{it} is the error in period t. The
components of variance scheme assumes that

$$\varepsilon_{io} = U_i + V_{io}$$

$$\varepsilon_{it} = U_i + V_{it},$$

where $E(U_i) = 0, E(V_{io}) = E(V_{it}) = 0$, V_{it} is the transitory component
for individual i in period t, and U_i is the permanent component for period
i, and $E(U_i V_{io}) = 0$, $E(U_i V_{it}) = 0$, and $E(\varepsilon_{io}\varepsilon_{it}) = \sigma_U^2$. Random sampling is assumed.

Collecting these results, and letting T_i be a dummy variable indicating whether or not individual i receives treatment, we reach

$$E_{io} = \mu_{io} + \varepsilon_{io}$$

$$E_{it} = \phi T_i + \mu_{it} + \varepsilon_{it},$$

and

(5) $$E_{it} - E_{io} = \phi T_i + \mu_{it} - \mu_{io} + (V_{it} - V_{io}).$$

The analysts report regressions based on 5, sometimes with E_{io} taken over
to the right-hand side as a regressor.

Note that while the simple difference scheme of equation 5 eliminates
the permanent component in the error, it does not avoid the selection bias
that arises in assigning people to the program on the basis of preexperi-

---

25. In addition to this argument, note that both North Carolina blacks and Iowa
whites received a much larger fraction of their income from part-time farming than
did the North Carolina whites. If there is greater freedom to set self-employed hours
than to set market hours, or if Welch's investment in farming effect is at work (see
chapter 4), one would predict that North Carolina whites would be the least respon-
sive. Note that the argument in the text assumes that $\left(\alpha_1 + \dfrac{\alpha_2}{1+r} \right)$ is positive.

mental earnings except in the implausible circumstance that only permanent preexperimental earnings $(E_{io} - V_{io})$ are used to enroll people. Assuming that the poorest are the most likely to participate, the effect of such a selection procedure tends to give an upward bias to the measured effect of the program based on estimates of 5 (assuming $\varphi < 0$), that is, estimated effects of φ are too small in absolute value, so that the estimated decline in earnings understates the true decline.

To circumvent this bias, consider the following procedure.[26] Suppose that treatment T_i depends on prior earnings (E_{io}), and some bureaucratic assignment variables G_i, so that there is a participation equation for T_i:

$$T_i = \beta_0 + \beta_1 E_{io} + \beta_2 G_i + \eta_i$$

where $E(\eta_i) = 0$, and η_i is assumed to be uncorrelated with ε_{io} and ε_{it}.

If one inserts E_{io} and G_i as regressors in equation 5, in addition to those already present, one can consistently estimate the experimental effect φ since the value of T_i effectively being used in such a regression is that variable purged of its E_{io} and G_i (and μ_{it} and μ_{io}) components. This analysis suggests that the variables in μ_{it} and μ_{io} that are also in G_i play two roles: as direct determinants of earnings and as determinants of program participation. Accordingly, such control variables provide little information on the underlying earnings function and do not deserve the elaborate discussion accorded them in the original reports. Enrollment-determining variables that do not determine earnings properly belong in the modified equation 5. Note further that the regression coefficient for E_{io} is *not* predicted to have a value of one, contrary to assertions in the original report.

There is one further point. While the components of variance scheme is conceptually attractive, it is not necessarily empirically appropriate. In some of my own work on female labor supply, this scheme is rejected by the data in favor of a simple first-order Markov scheme.[27] If the true model for the errors is first-order Markov, but a components of variance scheme like equation 5 is used to estimate effects of a program, and if one abstracts from the correlation between T_i and the errors, it is easy to see

26. Similar procedures are discussed in G. Chamberlain, "An Instrumental Variable Interpretation of Identification in Variance-Components and MIMIC" (Cambridge, Mass.: Harvard University, 1976); and M. Keeley and others, "The Estimation of Labor Supply Models Using Experimental Data" (*Stanford Research Institute,* August 1976; processed).

27. Heckman, "Dynamic Models of Female Labor Supply" (University of Chicago, March 1977; processed).

that a regression of current earnings on the treatment variable, the treatment variable multiplied by duration in the program, and initial earnings, which is the model utilized by the analysts of the original experiment, leads to a negative measured effect of the duration interaction *solely* as a consequence of model misspecification. This explains the otherwise peculiar finding of a negative interaction effect reported by the analysts in the original report. Because of the crucial role played by the error structure in dictating the appropriate econometric model to be used in analyzing the results of the experiment it seems clear that more complete testing for the appropriate error structure is in order.

Uses of Social Experiments

At the conference and in the Ashenfelter paper, the belief is expressed that experiments provide a simple means of estimating the effects of social programs. This simplicity makes experimental evidence politically more valuable and intellectually less time-consuming than other evidence. Superficially, a "laboratory experiment" can be viewed as a short-cut that enables analysts to avoid articulating more precise models of labor supply.

If cost were no object, and if an experiment could be conducted that *exactly* resembles a proposed social program, this view would be correct. But these conditions are unlikely ever to be realized. For example, a negative income tax experiment of long duration might take a generation to conduct, surely too long a time for any politician to deem suitable to sponsor.

Under these circumstances, the notion that a meaningful experiment can be conducted without having a well-formulated model in hand is quite misleading. Precisely because an experiment will never, by itself, provide direct predictions of the impact of a program, it is important to realize that its goal should be to estimate economically meaningful parameters that can be used to make such predictions.

An experiment conducted under less than ideal conditions is likely to be most valuable when the key issues of model formulation have already been resolved and increased precision in estimates of a limited number of conceptually well-defined parameters is required. In view of the high cost of experimental observations, it is natural to ask that cheaper data sources be fully exploited before experimental observations are collected. Thus social experiments are likely to be most productive when they are viewed as a final step in model development and not as a "model free" alternative for estimating program impacts.

As it happened, the limited funds available for the rural experiment resulted in sample sizes too small to estimate any model with much precision. The limited amount of experimental data was utilized in an attempt both to explore alternative models and to estimate their parameters. Since so much was asked of so little data, and since so little use was made of prior information (both theoretical and empirical), it is not surprising that the results of the experiment presented at the conference shed so little light on the issue of the true impact of a permanent program.

Comment by Michael J. Boskin

I agree with James Heckman that although a considerable amount of simple labor supply theory went into the analysis and design of the negative income tax experiments, theory seems to have been abandoned in the analysis. The analysts did not try to estimate income and substitution effects. Essentially they looked at average differences in labor supplied by people in the control and experimental groups. I believe it is improper and misleading to limit attention to such a comparison.

Averages Can Be Misleading

There are several reasons why an average for all people in the experiment may be misleading. First, even if every individual in the sample had an identical labor supply curve, the average response could be a substantial misestimate of that of the population eligible for a general income maintenance program because of the aggregation bias.

Second, there will always be a large residual variation in any set of estimates. No matter how well any data set measures the right-hand variables—age, race, sex, education, wage rates, and so forth—many people with the same set of these variables will have different labor supply responses. Robert Hall and others have tried to deal with this problem, but a lot more work needs to be done to explain individual differences. It may be necessary to posit something about the distribution of responses—on the basis of tastes for leisure, and other variables—to arrive at more precise estimates.

Third, families with incomes above the breakeven points were included in the calculation of the averages. The effect of including people who did not have a change in their effective budget constraint is to underestimate the response.

Fourth, the implicit tax in the plan was not binding for all people. As Finis Welch pointed out, farmers are able to control the amount of income they report. When the basic data can be manipulated by the individual, the labor supply estimates must be suspect.

Fifth, there was a rather restrictive income cutoff determining eligibility for the negative income tax. The cutoff was market income, which excludes, for example, leisure and the imputed household income of wives.

Truncation of the Sample

So the sample was truncated on the basis of two left-hand variables that really should be studied carefully: earnings and income. This causes severe problems. If the true specification of a simple labor supply function were linear, the expected value of labor supply—given the wage, tax rates, income guarantee, and so forth—would be bx where x is the vector of the right-hand variables and b is the vector of coefficients to be estimated. That is the desired estimate for the general population, but the truncated sample introduces a bias.

The bias in the estimation of the conditional mean of labor supply is an increasing function of the standard error of the regression. This is important because the unexplained variance in every labor supply equation that has ever been estimated is large—typically 30, 40, or 50 percent. Therefore, the result will almost certainly seriously underestimate the expected value of labor supply, given the wage, tax rate, and guarantee. As a result, the estimated labor supply function will lie to the left of the true labor supply function.

There are methods available to adjust for this underestimation of the true elasticities. In subsequent analyses I would like to see a variety of these techniques—the techniques developed by other researchers dealing with life-cycle phenomena, unobserved wages, truncation of labor supply at zero, fixed costs, and moving in and out of the labor market—embedded into a fuller analysis of the data.

Let me conclude by saying that the report before us contains only the first wave of results. Given the pressure on the people who were doing the analysis, we should perhaps be more generous in interpreting what was done. Much more analysis can be expected both by those who prepared the report and by other analysts.

ROBERT T. MICHAEL

The Consumption Studies

The issues involved in the six consumption studies are fundamentally different from those in the labor supply analyses.[1] First, the estimated cost of an income maintenance program is directly affected by the labor supply response, but this is not the case, except by second-order or very long-run effects, when considering how families spend their income or how much they save. Second, the price incentives and choices are more complex with respect to consumption behavior. An income maintenance program alters the relative prices in the work-leisure choice in a well-defined direction, which reinforces the income effect and induces a shift in labor supply behavior. Thus the empirical question for labor supply is the magnitude of these two reinforcing effects. In the consumption studies, however, the program's effects on the relevant prices are not so clear a priori, and there are a multitude of consumption items among which families must choose. Third, there seems to be a generally held normative judgment about the socially desirable labor supply response: it is less costly for the program and preferred if families do not substitute leisure for work to any great extent. There is not any comparable normative judgment about the consumption response.

Thus the researchers conducting the consumption studies are not armed

The author wishes to thank Robinson G. Hollister, Edward P. Lazear, Stanley H. Masters, and John H. Pencavel for comments on an early version of this report.

1. The six papers, in D. Lee Bawden and William S. Harrar, eds., *Rural Income Maintenance Experiment: Final Report* (University of Wisconsin–Madison, Institute for Research on Poverty, 1976), vol. 5, are: "Housing Consumption," by Aaron C. Johnson, Jr.; "Consumer Durables, Cars, Liquid Assets, and Debts of Wage-Working Families," by W. Keith Bryant and Christine J. Hager; "Consumer Durables, Cars, Liquid Assets, Short-Term Farm Capital, and Nonreal Estate Debts of Farm Families," by W. Keith Bryant; "Clothing Expenditures," by Christine J. Hager and W. Keith Bryant; "State of Health and the Utilization of Medical Care," by Stuart H. Kerachsky; and "Nutrition," by J. Frank O'Connor, J. Patrick Madden, and Allen M. Prindle.

with a clear-cut social issue (a socially preferred response) or an urgent programmatic issue (an implication for the cost of an income maintenance program) on which to focus their efforts. We might expect this lack of focus to result in a relatively diffuse set of consumption papers. Indeed, the six papers reviewed here are not integrated with one another in focus, theoretical structure, or empirical technique. Before discussing the papers themselves, however, it is appropriate to ask what one might wish to learn from consumption studies based on data from relatively poor rural families.

What Might Be Learned?

Taking the rural income maintenance experiment sample and survey instruments as given, the studies overlook two of the most important issues on which these data might have shed light. First, there is the issue of simply describing the ownership of durables, the level of purchases of items, and the debt-liquidity position of participating families and comparing these purchases and holdings with those of other rural families, other poor families, and median-income families. Relatively little is known about the economic circumstances of the rural poor and the rural experiment data provide an opportunity to learn something about the pathology of poverty for this segment of society.

Unfortunately, that opportunity is still unrealized—none of the six papers makes any effort to compare the circumstances of those in the sample with other families;[2] one of the papers does not even indicate the mean value or the within-sample variance of the variable studied. In general, the papers focused almost exclusively on partial regression coefficients of "treatment" (whether or not a family was receiving an experimental payment) or experimental "payment" (the amount of the payment) variables.

2. There is the question of feasibility in the suggestion of intersample comparisons. The New Jersey experiment contained some appropriate information for a rural-urban comparison as does the U.S. Department of Agriculture's 1973 Farm Family Living Expenditures Survey of 2,500 families, and the U.S. Bureau of Labor Statistics' Survey of Consumer Expenditures, which contain detailed information on several thousand rural households by income level. An April 1976 report by the U.S. Department of Health, Education, and Welfare provides much information for such a comparison. See HEW, *The Measure of Poverty*, A Report to Congress as Mandated by the Education Amendments of 1974 (HEW, 1976), and especially the supplemental Technical Paper XVIII (HEW, 1976).

Learning More about Poverty

There are at least two questions that might have been addressed by a descriptive analysis. First, the official definition of poverty is based on far from omnipotent judgments that a particular level of money income is needed in today's world for the maintenance of a socially adequate life style. What does that definition yield in terms of real standards of living for families designated as "in poverty"? Conversely, if the poverty standards had been set in terms of real consumption inflow instead of money inflow, how would the number and composition of those designated as in poverty be altered?

Second, the delineation of those in poverty on the grounds of any one-year income figure is, of course, bound to encompass a disproportionate number of families who happen to have temporarily low income but who are not in poverty in a longer run sense. The question of movement into and out of poverty has received considerable attention in recent years, and by one recent estimate for the late 1960s and early 1970s, the probability of whites in poverty one year remaining so for another year was only about 50 percent.[3] The information on ownership of durables and cars, housing tenure and consumption, health levels, nutritional intake, and the like could provide a valuable additional dimension to the research on poverty mobility since transitory fluctuations in the use of consumer goods are generally smaller than year-to-year fluctuations in money income.

I do not suggest using durable stocks or actual nutritional intake adequacy as some new way of defining poverty. That would not be a practical or analytically tractable alternative. But some consideration of the *real* analogue to the monetary definition of poverty could provide insight about

3. That is, if one were "in poverty" in one year, the probability of being in poverty the next year was roughly 0.5 for whites and 0.7 for blacks; the probability of being in poverty five years hence was about 0.3 for whites and 0.4 for blacks. These estimates are made by Lillard and Willis using an error components model applied to seven-year panel data for some 1,100 men 18–57 years of age from the University of Michigan Panel of Income Dynamics. Lee A. Lillard and Robert J. Willis, "Dynamic Aspects of Earning Mobility" (National Bureau of Economic Research, April 1977 [revised]; processed); forthcoming in *Econometrica,* tables 4 and 5. Other studies of poverty-mobility include John J. McCall, *Income Mobility, Racial Discrimination, and Economic Growth* (Heath, 1973); Frank Levy, "How Big is the American Underclass?" (University of California, Berkeley, Graduate School of Public Policy, June 1976; processed); Bradley R. Schiller, "Inequality, Income, and Opportunity: II," *Public Interest,* no. 43 (Spring 1976), pp. 111–20.

the average level and dispersion of well-being among those in poverty at a particular time, and about the variability of well-being over time. The absence of any attention to these issues is a major disappointment.

Learning More about Consumption Responses to Different Sources of Income

The second issue on which the rural experimental data might provide insight, and on which several of the studies partially focused, is the difference in consumption responses to various kinds of income. The permanent and transitory income distinction was pursued in varying degrees in the papers under discussion.[4] The papers on durables, debts, and assets made a substantial and generally successful effort to measure separately the permanent and temporary components of income (by source). The housing and health studies mentioned the issue but despite using the same income variable (preexperiment, 1969 family income), one described this variable as a "proxy" for permanent income while the other characterized its use as reflecting a decision to "abandon the permanent income concept."

Another important income distinction, emphasized in the clothing and durables studies, is the source of the income. The analytical justification for this distinction is that the availability or costs of other resources differ by income sources.[5] Hence income received from one source does not reflect the same impact on the family's total resource constraint as the same income from some other source. For example, additional income might result from an increase in one or another family member's wage rate (which implies a change in his or her time value), or from an increase in hours of work (which implies a reduction in the available nonmarket

4. See Friedman's pathbreaking analysis of permanent income and its relation to durable expenditures and the outstanding empirical study of family budget data in Prais and Houthakker. Milton Friedman, *A Theory of the Consumption Function* (Princeton University Press for the National Bureau of Economic Research, 1957); S. J. Prais and H. S. Houthakker, *The Analysis of Family Budgets* (Cambridge University Press, 1955; abridged and updated, 1971).

5. An additional $1,000 of, say, permanent family income in the form of husband's earnings, is obtained through an exchange of the husband's time for money or a difference in the value of his time. If instead the $1,000 is received in the form of nonwage (capital) income, it is obtained through an exchange of prior-year consumption or a difference in investment proficiency or the risk or liquidity of investments. If received in the form of public transfer income, it may be obtained without affecting other resources but possibly at some psychic cost or some extraneous conditions imposed as prerequisites for eligibility.

time), or from a shift in the family's asset holdings (which may imply a change in their liquidity or risk-bearing position); the behavioral response to the additional income may be quite different in these cases.[6]

The third issue about which we might expect to learn from the rural income maintenance studies is the one on which these six papers primarily focused—how the income maintenance provisions themselves affect consumption. This issue involves estimation of the impact of income by type and also the impact of the program per se.

Channels through Which Income Maintenance Might Affect Consumer Behavior

An income maintenance program might be expected to affect consumption patterns through at least three channels—raising income, altering the relative prices of goods and services, and providing a minimum income guarantee that reduces year-to-year income variations. According to one study of consumption patterns by income levels, the increased income would imply increases in expenditures on all categories of goods with proportionately small increases in groceries, tobacco, utilities, household supplies and appliances, children's clothing, medical insurance, and personal care items, and proportionately large increases in restaurant expenditures, alcohol, lodging out of town, household services, men's and women's clothing, automobiles, dental services, sports and recreation equipment and fees, education (tuition), and special lessons.[7] The precise nature of such shifts, however, will depend partly on the extent to which the increase in income is transitory or permanent.

6. More fundamentally, as most income is affected by the characteristics and behavior of family members, it can be thought of as a proxy for those characteristics—their health, schooling, age, motivation, and so forth. Public transfer income, which is not generated in the same manner, is not so obviously a proxy for these characteristics. Hence, in a regression of consumption on income, one source of income may be reflecting the effects of individual characteristics while the other income does not. So a basic identification issue is involved in the interpretation of effects of income by source.

7. This particular list is based on nationwide and income-wide consumption patterns in 1960 (Robert T. Michael, *The Effect of Education on Efficiency in Consumption* [Columbia University Press for the National Bureau of Economic Research, 1972], p. 62) and may not be applicable at very low-income levels. But that, presumably, is a question one might resolve with the low-income budget data. These general income effects also abstract from the different effects of various types of income.

Raising Family Income

Suppose a family has a given permanent income apart from any income maintenance program. If the introduction of the program resulted in no behavioral response affecting income, the family's permanent income would rise by the amount of its average income maintenance payment. However, if the family responds to the program by substituting nonmarket time for wage income, the increment in permanent income attributable to the program is less than otherwise even though the average transfer payment is higher. The average payment would no longer be a measure of the increment in permanent income; the payment would reflect a partial substitution of one source of income for another. Furthermore, beyond any permanent income that an income maintenance program provides, monthly payments also partially offset transitory fluctuations in other income. The payments are in part insurance against the guaranteed income.

Clearly, the relationship between the income maintenance payments and the permanent income component of an income maintenance program is a complicated one. In an income maintenance *experiment* (as opposed to an established program) the payment is only a temporary source of income even if family income remains at low levels.[8] Thus, in the experiment itself, the payments partly represent transitory income, partly offset transitory income fluctuations in other income sources, and partly reflect a substitution of payment income and nonworking time for labor income.

Altering the Relative Prices of Goods and Services

The second channel through which an income maintenance program might affect consumer behavior is through changes in the relative prices of consumer goods and services. The reduction in after-tax wage rates reflects a reduction in the price of time compared to the price of market goods and services; families facing the marginal tax rate of an income maintenance program are thus induced to substitute some of their nonmarket time for market goods in obtaining the final goods they consume. Thus they presumably buy fewer convenience (preprepared) foods, perform more household and auto repairs themselves, frequent medical and other professional services that are available with longer waiting lines but

8. Of course, high enough discount rates would imply a sufficient discount on income received several years later and would nearly offset the fact that the experiment lasted only three years. For example, at discount rates above 19 percent, income earned four years hence is discounted by more than 50 percent.

lower dollar costs, and so forth. This is not to say they consume less of the final good—nutrition, service flow from durables or health, for example—just that they have greater incentive to produce these things in a somewhat more time-intensive way. Compared to families that don't face the higher tax rate, their time is cheaper relative to market goods. To take the point a step further, the consumption of some goods and services requires relatively more time per dollar of expenditure, and families will be induced by the lower market time value to substitute among commodities toward these.[9]

So, the experimental payments shift the relative prices of the items families consume. These price shifts would be expected to influence spending patterns quite aside from the pure income effects of income maintenance payments. It would be convenient, therefore, if price and income effects were captured separately in a regression model by a "treatment" variable and a "payment" variable, but that is not the case in the rural income maintenance analyses. These price effects are combined with the income effects in the estimated coefficients. Without information on the relative time intensities, production coefficients, or price elasticities of various market goods and services, one cannot predict the impact of income maintenance payments on consumption patterns resulting from these price shifts.

Reducing Income Variance

The third channel through which the income maintenance program may affect spending patterns is by reducing the variance in income for low-income families. It is surprising how neglected this aspect has been as one of the unique features of the program is the provision of a guaranteed income floor.

Income, in general, is not highly predictable in any year. Unexpectedly low incomes, especially at levels near the poverty line, are presumably a determining factor in decisions about such things as housing, durables, liquidity, and long-term obligations. A family's inclination to hold reserve money balances, insurance, and certain long-term contracts is influenced by income uncertainty. Reductions in the variance of income at low-income levels may be expected to influence expenditure and savings behavior of families. Moreover, a guaranteed income floor may be expected to affect the availability of credit to low-income families.

9. Qualifications on this scenerio abound but for the point that is to be made, I will not discuss intrafamily substitution, corner solutions, or the like.

The Influence of the Limited Duration of the Experiment

Of these three channels of influence in the experiment—income effects, price effects, and reduced income instability—none seems comparable to the change that would prevail in a long-term income maintenance program of similar structure. Regarding price effects, long-run elasticities exceed short-run elasticities, so the behavioral responses are presumably muted by the short-run nature of the experiment.[10] In terms of the income effects, while the payments represent more than 20 percent of average family income, they partly reflect a substitution of this kind of income for wages and other income transfers. So the increase in money income may also reflect an increase in the nonmarket time of some family members. Moreover, since the payments are known to last only three years, they represent only about half as large a percentage (about 10 percent) of the present value of the family's income stream.[11] The impact of the experiment on the reduction in the variance of income is also considerably less than that of a long-term program. Thus, the observed consumption effects are primarily a reflection of short-run responses of the family to the transitory experimental payments. These also incorporate a short-run response to the price changes caused by the reduction in the market value of time.

Findings from the Studies

The following brief discussion indicates the nature of some of the more important findings in the consumption papers. Obviously, a few pages

10. Metcalf has pointed out, however, that compared to a permanent reduction in a wage rate, a temporary reduction in the after-tax wage rate embodies a positive income component (the present value of the wage increment when it subsequently returns to its initial level) that further reduces labor supply. Thus the measured short-run "current income-compensated" labor supply elasticity may be *larger* than the elasticity resulting from a permanent reduction in the wage rate. Furthermore, as the price changes are known to be temporary, an effort to build inventories of temporarily cheaper commodities might be expected. Charles E. Metcalf, "Making Inferences from Controlled Income Maintenance Experiments," *American Economic Review*, vol. 63 (June 1973), pp. 478–83.

11. Assuming payment income of $375 per quarter and other income of $1,400 per quarter, the former is 21 percent of total income received in three years. However, the present value of the payment income over three years is only 9.8 percent of the present value of total income received in a ten-year period (at $r = 0.1$; or 11.9 percent if $r = 0.2$) and 7.3 percent of the income received in a twenty-year period (at $r = 0.1$; or 10.4 percent if $r = 0.2$).

cannot adequately summarize the findings of some four hundred manuscript pages of the rural income maintenance report, and this discussion
should not be viewed as a comprehensive summary. Additional details
about the studies, their methodologies, and limitations are indicated in
the appendix to this paper.

Nutrition

The study of the nutritional adequacy of a one-day diet indicates that
Iowa families have substantially more adequate diets than North Carolina
families (89 versus 79 on a nutritional scale in which 100 is ideal and below 67 nutritionally inadequate or dangerous to health). Inadequate intake of calcium, iron, and vitamin A was most severe, with at least one-
fifth of Iowans and over 60 percent of North Carolinians receiving less
than 67 percent of the recommended amount of calcium. The most important demographic characteristic related to suboptimal diets has to do with
age: families in which the head was over sixty-five years of age had substantially poorer diets—about 10 percentage points lower—than families
in which the head was under thirty-one years of age. Income does not appear to be a determining factor in the within-sample regression analysis
although a variable defined as the family's "net equity" does show a very
slight but significantly positive effect (about 1 or 2 percentage points per
$10,000 increase in equity) on nutritional adequacy.

There was no ascertainable effect of experimental payments on nutrition in Iowa but a persistent, small (3 percentage point) positive effect in
North Carolina (that is, higher levels for those on the experiment),[12]
which is positive for nine out of ten separate nutrients as well as average
nutritional intake. The authors emphasize that the effects appear somewhat stronger over a longer time interval (for example, stronger effects
by the eleventh quarter than in the third quarter of the experiment).

I do not know how a 79 or 89 on the nutritional scale for these poor
rural families compares with the averages of median-income or urban
families, nor how substantial that 10-point difference between the states
might be in terms of health. The small or nonexistent effect of income on

12. The description of the variables in the ordinary least squares regressions is
not complete in the paper but there appears to be a redundancy in the four experimental control variables, estimable by suppression of the intercept. It appears more
information would have been obtained by replacing the "NC-Iowa experimental"
variable by a dummy defined as one for Iowans (control and experimental) and
zero for North Carolinians, which would have yielded levels as well as differentials.

measured nutritional intake in the sample is not surprising.[13] But it would *not* be appropriate to conclude that differences in income among these relatively poor families do not affect the nutritional adequacy of their diets: the ordinal scale used in this study implies that an increase from 85 to 95 has the same nutritional weight as an increase from say 60 to 70, while the authors imply that there is in fact a critical threshold somewhere around 67. Additional study with a nonlinear loss function might reveal a substantially different picture.[14]

Clothing

The most interesting findings relating to clothing purchases involved the differences in marginal propensities to spend by source of income. Table 1 reflects the implied expenditure from an additional $500 of income from each of three sources. For wage earners, the marginal propensity to consume out of the wife's income and experimental payments is substantially higher than the marginal propensity to consume out of the primary source of income (that is, the household head's earnings and transfer payments, which account for about 75 percent of the wage earner's quarterly family income and as much as 89 percent of the non-wage earner's).[15] For nonwage earners experimental payments have a much smaller implied effect. While they appear to be spent on both sexes' clothing, the spouse's income is spent predominantly on her own clothing (or perhaps, but less likely, her daughter's). Much of this difference is

13. In an unpublished study some years ago, I did a somewhat comparable analysis converting sixty-five foods into their nine nutritional contributions, deflated each by the daily adult nutritional requirement, weighted each equally, and deflated the average by the price paid for each food, in order to get a nutrients-per-dollar measure. I found for a sample of several thousand households from the U.S. Department of Agriculture's 1955 Household Food Consumption Survey that household income was strongly and negatively related to the nutrients-per-dollar index, but that both rural and farm households had relatively higher indices. The negative relationship with income reflected, I think, the greater variety of foods and less use of cost-efficient nutritional items such as beans and rice. So as incomes rise, nutrients-per-dollar may fall as total dollars spent on food rise. If the proportionate changes in opposite directions are about equal, the observed correlation between income and nutrient intake may be near zero.

14. An illustration of the bluntness of the measurement instrument is seen in the comparison of Iowa, quarter three, control and treatment groups. The average nutrition index, MAR, was 89.2 and 87.6 for the two groups—very little difference. But the percent of families with MAR below the 67.0 threshold differed by 80 percent (from 7.0 percent of the control group to 12.8 percent of the experimental groups).

15. Hager and Bryant, "Clothing Expenditures," table 2, p. 34.

Table 1. Additional Clothing Expenditures from a $500 Increase in Each of Three Sources of Income, by Wage and Nonwage Earners
Dollars

Source of income	Total[a] clothing	Men's and boys' clothing	Women's and girls' clothing
	Wage earners[b]		
Head's earnings and transfer payments	3.50	2.00	1.00
Spouse's earnings	25.00	3.00	20.00
Experimental payments[c]	31.05	14.18	9.86
	Nonwage earners[d]		
Head's earnings and transfer payments	2.00	0.50	1.00
Spouse's earnings	20.00	4.00	15.00
Experimental payments[c]	6.29	2.14	4.72

Source: Derived from data in Christine J. Hager and W. Keith Bryant, "Clothing Expenditures," in D. Lee Bawden and William S. Harrar, eds., *Rural Income Maintenance Experiment: Final Report* (University of Wisconsin–Madison, Institute for Research on Poverty, 1976), vol. 5, chap. 4, tables 4 to 9, and text, pp. 10–23.
   a. Total includes infants' clothing and miscellaneous items as well as the two categories listed.
   b. 795 observations for 265 wage-working family units.
   c. Experimental effects are estimated with a fixed component (a treatment effect per se) and a variable marginal propensity to consume (MPC) component. The estimated MPC is negative in all those nonwage earners regressions and is statistically significant in *none* of these six regressions.
   d. 678 observations for 226 families whose head did not work.

probably attributable to employment-related clothing needs of working spouses.

It is unfortunate that the major income source was not more finely delineated than husband's and transfer income. Nevertheless there is evidence here that with respect to clothing expenditures, families treat experimental payments differently from the bulk of their other income.

Durables, Assets, and Debts

The two chapters dealing with the durables, assets, and debts of households reveal much about the households in the experiment. Table 2 shows the means and standard deviations (in parentheses) of holdings. Although there is substantial net financial indebtedness, these households possess significant quantities of durable goods, cars, and especially farm capital. Of course, these averages mask the impoverished circumstances of the poorer families in the study, as evidenced by the sizable standard deviations, especially for loan indebtedness. A similar table by household characteristics would be far more revealing, but even this much general information about the sample was unusual in the six consumption papers.

Table 3 summarizes the estimated long-run effects of a $1.00 increase in household income (by source of income) on the holding of stocks of

Table 2. Mean Values of Selected Durables, Debts, and Assets Held by Households in the Rural Income Maintenance Experiment, 1970–72[a]
Dollars

Item	Wage-working households[b]		Farm households[c]
	White	Black	
Stock of durables	1,572	1,126	1,781
	(806)	(600)	(1,022)
Appliances	615	439	...
	(324)	(276)	
Entertainment durables	471	309	...
	(390)	(237)	
Furniture	481	376	...
	(347)	(343)	
Stock of cars	976	761	813
	(1,069)	(1,095)	(1,120)
Store debt	280	199	753
	(545)	(299)	(1,721)
Loan debt	1,112	823	1,891
	(7,558)	(7,929)	(4,662)
Liquid assets	823	63	1,354
	(2,639)	(191)	(3,646)
Farm capital (short term)[d]	...	...	13,524
			(16,957)

Sources: Wage-working families, W. Keith Bryant and Christine J. Hager, "Consumer Durables, Cars, Liquid Assets, and Debts of Wage-Working Families," in Bawden and Harrar, eds., *Rural Income Maintenance Experiment*, tables 4 II.1–4 II.8; farm families, W. Keith Bryant, "Consumer Durables, Cars, Liquid Assets, Short-term Farm Capital and Nonreal Estate Debts of Farm Families," in ibid., tables A5.1–A5.6.
a. The numbers in parentheses are standard deviations.
b. The number of households in the sample is 124 white and 95 black.
c. The number of observations in the sample is 918.
d. Consists of farm machinery, livestock, and grain inventories.

durable goods, cars, store and loan debts, and liquid assets. The table pertains to nonfarm, wage earner households. For whites, an additional dollar in experimental payments appears to raise the value of holdings of durables and cars by less than 10 cents; by contrast, 25 cents is spent on these items out of the family head's income and even more from the wife's income. For blacks, the experimental payments effect is considerably higher; the authors argue that this is partly because blacks had much lower stocks of these items at the outset.[16] I think some of the explanation is also found in the way in which the marginal propensities to consume

16. That explanation raises the question why the MPCs for durables from the head of family's income and wife's income are not also much higher.

Table 3. Long-run Effects of $1.00 of Additional Income on Holdings of Durables, Assets, and Debts of Wage-working Households, by Source of Income

Source of income	Stock of durables	Stock of cars	Store debt	Loan debt	Liquid assets
	Marginal propensity to consume				
	Whites				
Household head's earnings	0.12	0.13*	0.03	0.44	0.30
Spouse's earnings	0.20	0.22*	−0.06	0.66	0.04
Experimental payments	0.05	0.03	0.07	0.23	0.29*
	Blacks				
Household head's earnings	0.16	0.43	0.00	1.71	0.00*
Spouse's earnings	0.19*	0.21	0.11	−0.17	−0.01
Experimental payments	0.27*	0.44	0.01	3.51	−0.02

Source: Bryant and Hager, "Consumer Durables, Cars, Liquid Assets, and Debts of Wage-Working Families," table 4.3.
*Based on regression coefficients that are statistically significant at the 5 percent level.

(MPCs) were calculated.[17] The experimental payments' effect on financial debts and assets for whites is similar to that for the income of household head, but I find these results strange—apparently a $1.00 increase in normal income induces whites to borrow about 50 cents and to hold about 30 cents of it as increased liquid assets. The results for blacks are even less believable. Of course, the pattern of MPCs in table 3 does not warrant extensive scrutiny given the generally insignificant coefficients on which they are based.

The positive effect on loan debt of experimental payments is explained by the following. Bryant and Hager estimate the long-run effects of a permanent income maintenance payment. They contend the average size of that payment to whites in the experiment is $626 per year, and they estimate its effect to be an increase in the stock of durables ($170), cars ($130), and liquid assets ($187), an increase in store debt ($57), and a *reduction* in loan debt (−$1,245). This estimated reduction in loan debt

17. Where income variables were included nonlinearly, MPCs were computed at the mean income of *whites;* thus the blacks' MPCs pertain to levels of income above the average income of blacks for head-of-family's income and below the average income of blacks for maintenance income. For example, for blacks the functional form of the maintenance income, Y_m, effect on durables, cars, and loan debt was $(b_1 Y_m - b_2 Y_m^2)$ so the MPC evaluated at the whites' mean Y_m yields an MPC that is higher than would be estimated using the blacks' mean Y_m. Furthermore, the functional form of Y_m for blacks for store debt was linear and for liquid assets was $(-b_1 Y_m + b_2 Y_m^2)$, which explains why these two MPCs for blacks in table 3 are not exceptionally high. The very large MPC from head's income for loan debt for blacks, 1.71, is also explainable along comparable lines.

results from a large negative "treatment effect" (a fixed component) and a positive "payment effect" (a variable component). The MPC in table 3 simply reflects that positive variable component.[18]

A similar analysis of durable stocks, cars, store and loan debts, liquid assets and, additionally, short-term farm capital was conducted for farm households. Here income was not decomposed into permanent and transitory components. The resulting estimates of long-term marginal propensities to consume out of experimental payments were statistically insignificant except for an MPC of 0.08 for durable goods. Generally, these MPCs were small and positive for durables and cars, larger and positive for loans but small and negative for liquid assets. In this sample as with white wage earners, the MPC for cars was substantially higher when derived from the spouse's income rather than from "primary income" sources; income from most secondary sources was used to lower debt. The long-run combined treatment and payments' effect of the average experimental payment of $1,276 annually was estimated to be an increase in durables ($122) and liquid assets ($19), and a reduction in car stocks ($-\$87$), in store debt ($-\$60$), in loan debt ($-\$268$), and a very questionable reduction in short-term farm capital ($-\$2,120$).[19]

An Assessment

All of the papers on consumption behavior focused nearly exclusively on the demand response to the income maintenance treatment and payment variables. In my judgment that focus was unfortunate. Much might have been learned about the real (as opposed to monetary) circumstances of the rural poor in particular, and about poverty in general, by a detailed study of the inventories, expenditures, and outcomes of consumption processes among these families. The levels and variations in consumption behavior within this sample, and a comparison of this group with other rural groups, other poor, and nonpoor, would have been illuminating. To have bypassed this descriptive analysis seems to suggest that this informa-

18. Derived from Bryant and Hager, "Consumer Durables, Cars, Liquid Assets, and Debts of Wage-Working Families," tables 4 II.1–4 II.8. The comparable estimates of long-run effects of the average income maintenance payment of $1,064 to blacks are an increase in the stocks of durables ($173), cars ($166), and assets ($42), and a reduction in store debt ($-\$12$), but an increase in loan debt ($654).

19. Bryant, "Consumer Durables, Cars, Liquid Assets, Short-Term Farm Capital and Nonreal Estate Debts of Farm Families," table 5.5.

tion is already known, but that is not the case so far as I am aware and the authors of these papers give no reason to think otherwise.

There was surprisingly little coordination of research effort among the authors of the consumption studies. One of the most basic properties of a system of demand equations is the "adding-up" property. Despite the focus in some of these papers on marginal propensities to consume certain market goods, no effort was made in the surveys or in the analysis to apportion the increase in income among an exhaustive and mutually exclusive set of consumption and savings components. The papers do not use a consistent concept or measure of income, do not use similar functional relationships to describe demand curves, and either do not attempt themselves, or make it possible for others, to bring their estimates together using the insights derived from the study of systems of demand equations. Consequently, the set of consumption papers does not yield any results beyond the separate findings of the individual papers. The whole is no bigger than the sum of the parts although that need not be the case.

All of the studies exclude from analysis families that were not in the experiment for the entire three-year period as well as those that were not maritally stable throughout the three years. According to the Middleton-Haas study of marital dissolution using these data, slightly more than 5 percent of the initially intact families dissolved during the three years, and differential rates of dissolution were not small—for example, 4.8 percent of the control group and 5.7 percent of the experimental families broke up, and, more substantially, 1.7 percent of the families of Iowa whites, 2.8 percent of those of North Carolina whites, and 11.1 percent of the North Carolina black families had their marriages dissolved.[20] The dissolution rates also vary with socioeconomic characteristics. Thus the sample attrition due to marital instability is correlated with some of the independent variables, and more importantly, with some of the dependent variables. Marital dissolution will surely affect housing and durables consumption, although it may have a less important impact on such consumption components as nutrition. This selective attrition will introduce bias into the estimation of the regression coefficients. The use of only maritally stable families thus renders the analyses conditional to an extent not sufficiently emphasized in the papers.

Despite the criticism, numerous interesting effects are reported in the

20. See Russell Middleton and Linda Haas, "Marital Dissolution and Family Interaction," in Bawden and Harrar, eds., *Rural Income Maintenance Experiment*, vol. 6, pt. 1, chap. 8.

lengthy papers. The broad sweep of the findings suggests that the additional income and the income guarantee provided by the experiment improved average nutritional intake in the North Carolina sample (but not in Iowa where the levels were initially more nearly adequate), increased consumption of clothing (somewhat less for male than for female clothing), slightly increased household inventories of durable goods and cars (except for cars in farm households), reduced short-term farm debt, and increased farm liquid assets somewhat.

One remaining question should be addressed. Why are we interested in how the income maintenance payments are used? Sheer intellectual curiosity does not appear to be the answer. Apparently, the satisfaction derived by taxpayers at least partly depends on how the transfer income is used, perhaps because taxpayers or policymakers believe they can judge the relative merits of various expenditures. Evidence of such social concern is found in the preference for transfers in-kind (via food stamps, medical services, housing subsidies, et cetera) rather than in-dollars. Scientific analysis permits one to evaluate the net present value of various investment alternatives and rank them; to compare two production processes for a given output and rank them; and to determine that some level of intake of, say, a nutrient such as riboflavin is necessary to sustain good health. But I know of no scientific insight by which one can judge the merits of an expenditure for one consumer good compared to another.

It is one matter to make a collective determination that the consumption of some items should be encouraged by subsidy (for example, higher education, religion, or rural mail delivery) while for various reasons consumption of other items should be discouraged by tax (for example, cigarettes, alcohol, or gasoline); it is quite another matter to determine the optimal bundle of consumption for anybody but oneself. I suggest that there should be no policy implications drawn from these consumption studies for no set of findings of experimental effects could demonstrate the wisdom or meritoriousness with which the income transfers were spent.

Had these studies discovered some particularly large use of the transfer income, it might be appropriate to infer that the rural poor act as if that item is of special need; we might then ask if it could be provided more generally or more cheaply. That strategy would permit the poor to reveal what they find most lacking. But the consumption studies in the rural income maintenance report did not pursue that tack. Nor, as I have indicated, is that the focus I would have preferred to see these studies take.

Appendix A: Description and Discussion of the Research Papers on Consumption Behavior

This appendix provides a brief description and discussion of the six research papers on consumption behavior in volume 5 of the rural income maintenance experiment, all of which are cited in text note 1.

"Nutrition," by O'Connor, Madden, and Prindle

In this study of the effects of the experiment on nutrition, the authors use a twenty-four-hour recall diary of food consumed in the third and eleventh quarters of the experiment for over seven hundred families. Information about food quantities consumed (net of waste and leftovers and adjusted for method of food preparation, vitamin supplements, and food eaten away from home) is converted into the percentages of the recommended daily allowances of ten nutrients, for families of given size, age, and sex composition. These percentages or nutrient adequacy ratios (NARs) for the ten nutrients separately, and an unweighted average of the ten (the mean adequacy ratio [MAR]), are used as dependent variables in ordinary least squares regressions. The ratio is bounded at 100 percent of the recommended allowance; thus excess intake of one nutrient does not offset deficiencies in another. The mean value of MAR in the Iowa sample is about 89 (percent) while in North Carolina the mean is around 79. According to the authors, diets supplying less than 67 percent of the recommended intakes are considered nutritionally inadequate.

A few quibbles with this paper: (1) Although one of the summary reports on the rural experiment implies that food stamps were available to at least some of the families in the experimental and control groups,[21] no discussion of the food stamps appears in this paper on nutrition. Even if experimental effects are the only concern, some effort to determine how the availability of food stamps interacts with these experimental effects would seem appropriate. (2) The paper attempts to estimate the cost efficiency of the program in terms of nutritional improvement (the percentage change in MAR) per dollar of maintenance income—a cost of about $1.50 per unit of MAR in North Carolina and an unmeasured cost

21. U.S. Department of Health, Education, and Welfare, "The Rural Income Maintenance Experiment: Summary Report" (HEW, November 1976; processed), p. 58.

in Iowa where the effect is negative. (This figure is compared in the paper to a cost-effectiveness of $0.11 to $1.04 estimated for food stamps from other data, and a cost of "mere pennies" for direct food [such as milk] supplements.) The calculation is misleading. Were cost defined per dollar *spent* by the family on food it would suffer only from the arbitrariness of the scale and from the disregard for the evidence on groups for which there was no positive effect. But the present calculation also ignores non-payment programmatic costs and the diffused usage of the payment income. (3) Noting that treatment improvements in the MAR in North Carolina resulted from increases in the intake of six deficient nutrients, the authors state that the result is "quite important, because it shows that families used the additional resources . . . to acquire foods which improved their intake" of deficient nutrients (p. 65). The implication of purposiveness here is not well-founded. A general random increase in the variety and quantity of foods will decrease these deficiencies absolutely.

"State of Health and the Utilization of Medical Care," by Kerachsky

One of the few dimensions of life quality about which there is practically no dispute is health status. The rural income maintenance experiment data include a considerable amount of information on the number of visits for, and expenditures on, medical care, and on several measures of health status. Kerachsky's paper focuses exclusively on estimating the effects of the experimental variables on health and medical care and, in brief, finds essentially no effects. The focus is unfortunate as more information about levels and within-sample variations in health levels, mortality and morbidity rates, and medical care could have been instructive.

The analysis is carefully constructed to standardize each dimension of medical care usage during the experiment by the individual's own pre-experimental usage (in the year prior to the start of the experiment). So persistent (several-year) individual variations in health and medical care usage are adequately controlled in the sample of 554 families analyzed separately as 472 adult men, 541 adult women, and 441 families with children under sixteen years of age.

Of those sets of health-related variables, the author judges the medical care usage information as "the most reliable." The expenditure data exclude medical insurance and cannot be apportioned to individual family members; the health-status information does not provide "viable measures of the state of health," partly because "poor health is a convenient excuse to work less" and because the maintenance program "allows them to recognize and treat real conditions that they had ignored prior to benefiting from the program" (pp. 6–7). So the analysis centers on the impact of the experiment on the number of visits to physicians, clinics, hospitals, specialists, and dentists. The results are interpreted by the author as implying that "it cannot be concluded . . . that a negative income tax has any effect on the utilization of medical care by adult males" (p. 23), or for adult females (p. 24), and generally so for children as well (p. 24).

Likewise, on the medical care expenditures, data which the author distrusted but analyzed, "no significant or strong patterns of experimental results were found" (p. 38). Similarly on self-assessed health status of men, the author concludes that "almost all indications of significance disappear by the end of the experiment, but so does any pattern of experimental effects, even when significance is ignored" (p. 39). For women there appears to be a slight deterioration in health among those in the experiment and no effects on children (p. 44). All of which leads the author to conclude candidly "the expectations of experimental effects on medical care utilization and on the state of health have not been borne out" (p. 44).

How is this finding to be understood?

The author's explanations are: (1) that the incomes are "so low that, after fulfilling more basic needs such as food, clothing, and shelter, the families have little income left to spend on medical care"; (2) that the effects on the price of medical care were "misunderstood by the participating families" (the expenditures on medical care were subsidized directly by the experiment as an income deduction for expenditures in excess of $30 per family); or (3) "the level of payments or the length of the experiment was insufficient to alter medical care utilization or health" (p. 47). I find none of these explanations satisfying—health is not such a luxury; poor families are not necessarily stupid; the experimental income and guarantee were not so slight.

I am not as convinced that I know the correct explanation as I am that it would be incorrect to conclude on the basis of this study that income transfers to poor families do not improve health levels. I do have two explanations to suggest. As the experiment tends to lower the value of time for many families and subsidizes dollar outlays on medical care, there is surely a reduction in the relative price of medical care compared to other nonmarket commodities like shelter. However, a recent detailed study of the price-responsiveness of demand for one kind of health care, pediatrics, found a significant price effect for quality of medical care but an insignificant price effect for visits.[22] In that study people appear to adjust the quality of care (defined in terms of characteristics of the physician such as whether Board-certified or whether a specialist) but not the number of visits. If the findings on pediatrics apply to medical care of adults in rural areas, then it is not surprising that no significant effect is observed in the rural experiment's data on visits. As Kerachsky stresses, the expenditure data are flawed and so not to be given much weight; on health levels the study did find some positive effect by the mid-period of the experiment although none remained by the last year of the experiment.

More important, I think a part of the explanation for the findings on health rests with the study's definition of income. According to the HEW summary report of the experiment, income (excluding maintenance income) was somewhat higher for families in the control than experimental groups ($1,484 compared to $1,350 a quarter, a difference of $536 a year); the discrepancy apparently grew somewhat larger as time passed, so by the third year the control familes had an average of over $600 more annual income (excluding experiment payments) than the experiment families. The health study used preexperiment 1969 income as the only income measure, and according to the summary report, in *that* year the experimental families averaged about $100 more per year than the control families ($1,206 compared to $1,180 per quarter, according to summary report's table 16).[23] Therefore the treatment dummy variable in the regressions in this study reflects (1) participation in the experiment, (2) the maintenance income payments, and (3) on average, about $700 less in family income (excluding experimental payments). My inference is based on information from the sample as a whole, but could easily be checked by the authors for their 554 observations. If the point is correct, it is little wonder that no substantial income effect is observed.

"Housing Consumption," by Johnson

While the "guiding question" of the housing chapter may have been to determine "whether or not a guaranteed annual income program might result in an improvement in the quality of housing for low-income families residing in rural areas" (p. 44), no useful answer is provided here. The author acknowledges that with regard to the housing data the experiment

22. Fred Goldman and Michael Grossman, "The Demand for Pediatric Care: An Hedonic Approach," *Journal of Political Economy,* forthcoming.
23. HEW, "The Rural Income Maintenance Experiment: Summary Report," table 16.

"was beset with problems" (p. 46), and that regarding several dimensions of the housing data studied, "at best the results should be viewed as merely suggestive" (p. 39). The principal finding of interest is that holding constant a set of socioeconomic characteristics, the families in the experiment had somewhat higher (5 to 7 percentage points higher) probabilities of purchasing a first home within the three-year duration of the experiment; the effect was stronger at younger ages and perverse (that is, lower) for Iowa nonfarmers.

While measuring the quality of housing is not an easy matter, I think the methodology used in this study suffered primarily from the severe sample censoring imposed on the data. Home ownership and housing quality are especially sensitive to the life cycle and the age composition of families. So to select for study those households that had not yet purchased a home at the beginning of the experiment (instead of at some particular age) yields a sample with considerable heterogeneity in terms of propensity to purchase, which in turn can yield biased estimates of the impact of both background and experimental variables on the likelihood of purchase. By further restricting the study to families that did not undergo any change in structure during the three-year period, additional censoring is imposed. The resulting samples of 321 families (out of 729) for the analysis of home purchase, 55 families for the analyses of age at purchase and value of purchased home, and 41 families for the analysis of improvements in rental dwellings, could explain many of the anomalies in this study. Moreover, the description of the study suggests so much pretesting of variables and functional forms that the tests of statistical significance that are reported are not of much relevance.

This study would have benefited from a detailed description of the housing conditions in which these poor rural families lived, and from some simpler efforts to ascertain if improvements were discernible over the three-year period. The study does not indicate, for example, except by inferences from sample sizes, how many of these families owned their homes (it would be useful to have such information by age of head of household or income level), what the characteristics of their housing were, how mobile these families were with respect to housing, et cetera). No means or distributions of even the dependent variables are given.

"Clothing Expenditures," by Hager and Bryant

Expenditures on total clothing, men's and boys' clothing, women's and girls' clothing, infants' clothing, and miscellaneous items and sewing materials, are studied for wage-earning families and nonwage-earning families separately. Information was analyzed for the first, fifth, and ninth quarters (December, January, February of three consecutive years), pooling the data using quarter-specific dummies to standardize for inflation and other date- and duration-specific factors.

"Consumer Durables, Cars, Liquid Assets, and Debts of
Wage-Working Families," by Bryant and Hager

This paper is the most substantive of the six consumption papers. Using a portfolio analysis approach, short-run and long-run adjustments in consumer durable goods, cars, liquid assets, and some aspects of financial indebtedness are estimated. The effects of several sources of income are distinguished, as are permanent and transitory components of each source in a framework that also takes account of state, race, age, year, education, family size, and several asset and occupation differences. The data demands in this project were large, but unlike many of the other papers that mentioned data limitations, this research effort included estimation of the value of durables and autos for four years (1970–73), as well as loan and store debts and financial assets for 219 households. Perseverance in research (apparently there was information on such diverse durables as waffle irons, snowmobiles, and encyclopedias) was matched by ingenuity (where no purchase prices of owned items were listed, the items "were assigned prices from Sears catalogs published in the year of purchase" [p. 50]); such details as a three-month gap in information about the purchase and sale of cars were somehow overcome and "algorithms were devised" (p. 48). For all the creating-something-out-of-something-less, this study seems quite useful in indicating the financial and durable goods holdings among rural households in the lower tail of the income distribution, and some indication of the adjustment in these holdings to income changes of various kinds.

One might question the underlying behavioral assumptions of the simultaneous estimation of the permanent income of the family head, spouse, and dependents, including the assumption that the entire four-year-average error is a household-specific, persistent component of the error. Furthermore, the distinction between a permanent maintenance income payment (measured as the guarantee minus the product of the negative income tax rate and the estimated permanent household income) and a transitory maintenance income payment seems to me to stretch credibility

for a program advertised to run only three years. But the authors emphasize deficiencies in their estimates themselves, and their results, on balance, offer a useful indication of how these relatively poor rural households utilized a portion of their additional money income.

"Consumer Durables, Cars, Liquid Assets, Short-Term Farm Capital and Nonreal Estate Debts of Farm Families," by Bryant

This study is similar to the companion study for wage-earning families
except that no decomposition of income into permanent and transitory
components was made, the analysis was not performed for whites and
blacks separately, and short-term farm capital was included in the household's "portfolio." The paper states that 918 observations were used, but
does not indicate how many separate households these yearly (1970–72)
observations cover. (Oddly, in the other durable goods study the authors
indicate how many households were included in the analysis [219], but
not how many observation points were used.)

Comment by Stanley H. Masters

Robert Michael is critical of the expenditure papers
from the rural experiment on the ground that they focus too heavily on
experimental-control differentials. I share this criticism, at least in the
sense that the papers I have seen generally include little motivation for
the analysis.

Michael's primary suggestion is that more attention should have been
given to a descriptive analysis comparing the expenditures of the poor
rural families in the sample to corresponding expenditures of average
families, average rural families, and poor urban families. The goal of such
an analysis would be to determine how badly off the rural poor really are.
I believe this suggestion is one useful purpose to which the expenditure
data could be put.

There are also other important uses for expenditure data from this and
other income maintenance experiments. As Metcalf has emphasized,[24]
for example, expenditures on durable goods represent a form of saving
and thus can be used to gain some insight into time preference regarding

24. For example, see Charles E. Metcalf, "Predicting the Effects of Permanent
Programs from a Limited Duration Experiment," *Journal of Human Resources*,
vol. 9 (Fall 1974), pp. 530–55.

consumption of the experimental families, an important issue in evaluating the labor supply results from short-term income maintenance experiments.

My primary disagreement with Michael concerns his view that, because of effects on program costs, there are normative issues with regard to the labor supply effects of an income maintenance experiment but no such issues with regard to consumption effects. Although I share Michael's view (and that of most economists) that we should not make value judgments about how people spend their money, it is my view that the general voting public has a different opinion. Thus the primary concern with labor supply effects is one stemming from the work ethic in our society and not just a concern with program costs. Similarly, most people are not indifferent to whether the poor spend income from government income maintenance programs on milk or scotch (for example, witness the recent growth of the food stamp program and the failure of Congress to enact the family assistance plan). If I am correct in this assessment, an analysis of experimental effects on expenditures may have a direct bearing on the likelihood of Congress passing new cash assistance programs, especially for people who are prime-aged, employed, and healthy but who still earn little income.

Starting from this perspective, the main question to be addressed with the expenditure data is, "Do the recipients of the negative income tax payments spend their new income on goods and services that are pleasing to the rest of the country?" In this way, results that may be relevant for the political debate can be obtained and some of the stereotypes about the poor can also be addressed. The labor supply analysis is relevant for the stereotype of the poor as lazy bums. The expenditure analysis could be relevant for the stereotype of the poor as profligate boozers.

To do such an analysis, the researchers need to ask questions such as how much is spent on alcoholic beverages, fancy clothes, and flashy automobiles. Such expenditures should also be contrasted with those for items highly valued by society, such as food and clothing for children.

In my view, the normal categories of expenditures are not good enough for such an analysis. For example, expenditures on clothing can (and have been) disaggregated by whether the clothing is for children or adults. If it is possible, it would also be useful to break down the adult items into fancy apparel versus utilitarian items. Expenditures on alcoholic beverages should certainly be looked at separately from other expenditures on food and beverages. And the interesting results for debt found in the rural experiment should be examined to determine what was purchased with the debt.

In many cases, the data I have in mind may not have been collected; in some cases, it may not have been possible to make my suggestions operational. My guess is, however, that the main reason this approach has not been emphasized in any of the income maintenance experiments is because it is based so obviously on value judgments. Economists do not like such value judgments. In fact, they generally make the value judgment that such value judgments are bad. Perhaps they are bad, in which case doing the analysis I have suggested would have the unfortunate consequence of increasing their frequency. On the other hand, I believe that such an analysis might be valuable in reducing stereotypes about the poor and might increase the chances that a more generous income maintenance system could be achieved with fewer horizontal inequities. In my view, the gamble is worth taking.

Comment by Robinson G. Hollister

At the outset, I think we owe apologies and condolences to the authors of the studies under review. Having been in a similar position—as an author of a study in the New Jersey negative income tax experiment reviewed at a previous Brookings conference—I understand the frustration and irritation authors can feel in this situation. Often commentators berate the authors for not carrying out some obvious piece of analysis that the authors *have* carried out but did not report because of space limitations. In addition, since there are so many pages for any reviewer to read, it is inevitable that they will not get through all the studies with equal care. Thus authors often feel, sometimes with a great deal of justification, that their work has not even been read.

I will begin by commenting on several of the general observations and methodological points that Robert Michael makes in his paper. Then I will discuss some of the substance of the original papers and comment on Michael's observations about them.

General Observations and Methodological Points

Professor Michael sets the policy framework for his review by stating: "the researchers conducting the consumption studies are not armed with a clear-cut social issue (a socially preferred response) or an urgent programmatic issue . . . on which to focus their efforts." Toward the close of the paper he notes that society seems to care how transferred income to the poor is used: "Evidence of such social concern is found in the preference for transfers in-kind (via food stamps, medical services, housing subsidies, et cetera) rather than in-dollars." Yet he goes on to urge us to ignore these concerns: "I suggest that there should be no policy implications drawn from these consumption studies, for no set of findings of experimental effects could demonstrate the wisdom or meritoriousness with which the income transfers were spent."

A curious aspect of this downgrading of the policy import of the consumption studies is that just prior to introducing it Michael notes "there seems to be a generally held normative judgment about the socially desirable labor supply response: it is less costly for the program and preferred if families do not substitute leisure for work to any great extent." And Michael seems to accept this norm as a relevant policy guide. This strikes me as inconsistent. I can't see why the normative judgment about labor supply (or consumption of leisure) should have any more standing (wisdom or meritoriousness) than the admittedly ambiguous norms about consumption of goods purchased from transfer payments.

THE POLICY RELEVANCE OF THE FINDINGS. Consistency aside, it is clear that some findings regarding consumption out of transfer income could have a major impact in the policy arena. If the data could support the contention that raising nutritional levels through cash transfers is equally effective as through food stamps, this could influence policy on the desirability of "cashing out" food stamps. If housing consumption is as effectively upgraded through cash transfers as through housing allowances, the policy on special in-kind housing programs might be affected. Findings regarding utilization of health services could yield useful insights about the integration of income maintenance programs and a national health insurance program.

Thus, while most of us would accept the view that the labor supply response is of first-order policy interest, there are plenty of "urgent programmatic issues" to focus the analytical efforts on the consumption side. This is not to say that the consumption data in the rural experiment will yield definitive findings impinging on these issues, but at least the potential should be recognized and the studies should not be downgraded a priori.

INSUFFICIENT ANALYSIS OF ASSET-DEBT PATTERNS. Perhaps because of his willingness to downgrade the experimental findings regarding effects on consumption, Professor Michael laments that the rural data were not utilized sufficiently to describe the asset-debt patterns of the rural poor. This is a laudable suggestion but two points should be made about it. First of all, authors themselves were not asked to provide such descriptive studies, and I understand in some cases they were explicitly directed not to do so. As an author of this type of paper, I know how it feels when one could write ten papers on the subject and has to decide which of them to write for which type of audience. For better or worse, one cannot follow the grammar school imperative to "show all your work" in the Final Report on such projects. The second point is that there are some pitfalls in trying to use the data to describe conditions and behavior of low-income families. The major problem is that the eligibility criteria for the experiments often introduce serious truncation biases. This requires that analysis be carried out using the recently developed sophisticated techniques for dealing with truncation bias as described and utilized by Amemiya, Bryant and Hager, and Hausman and Wise.[25] For example, in a follow-up study on the New Jersey negative income tax, Hausman and Wise show that if you estimate the rate of return on education by ordinary least-squares in the experimental sample, you get a figure of 0.8 percent and no statistical significance. But if you use the appropriate maximum likelihood estimate taking into account truncation bias, you get a statistically significant rate of return estimate of 1.6 percent. Other coefficients in the earnings function were two to three times larger in the maximum likelihood estimate compared to ordinary least squares estimates.

SAMPLE CENSORING. A general methodological point should be made regarding sample censoring. At several points, Professor Michael complains about elimination of observations from samples used for analysis. In particular, he dislikes the convention broadly adopted in the rural (and in the New Jersey) experiment of limiting the analytical sample to families that remained intact throughout the experiment. The problem is that he fails to propose any alternatives to this mode of analysis. How one creates comparability in units when going from intact to nonintact families is not clear. One solution, which has been resorted to in some of the

25. See Takeshi Amemiya, "Regression Analysis When the Dependent Variable is Truncated Normal," *Econometrica,* vol. 41 (November 1973), pp. 997–1016; W. Keith Bryant and Christine J. Hager, "Consumer Durables, Cars, Liquid Assets, and Debts of Wage-Working Families," in Bawden and Harrar, eds., *Rural Income Maintenance Experiment;* and Jerry A. Hausman and David A. Wise, *Social Experimentation, Truncated Distributions, and Efficient Estimation,* Technical Analysis Series 4 (Mathematica Policy Research, n.d.).

studies in the experiments, is simply to run single cross-sections for each quarterly time period, including all family units as they are at that period. The problem with this is that it loses certain advantages of time-series data, and differences from quarter to quarter show variations that confound changes in unit structure with changes in within-unit behavior. This problem certainly deserves more attention but the present results should not be discarded because they have not solved the problem.

Michael also complains about sample censoring in the housing studies. In the case of the limitations on renters that chop the sample to forty or fifty families, the complaint is surely justified; one could draw no conclusions on such a limited sample. However, when dealing with the limitation of a sample to those not owning a home prior to the experiment, which was done to estimate the probability of home purchase, he seems unreasonably severe, particularly given the availability of the control group and the regression control variables for age, and so forth.

CHANNELS THROUGH WHICH CONSUMPTION IS AFFECTED. A final methodological point concerns Professor Michael's review of the channels through which income maintenance might affect consumption. There are a couple of comments to be made about this review. First, with regard to his third channel, the reduction in variance in income due to the guaranteed income floor, some work on the effects of variance (or reduced risk) was done in the labor supply studies of the New Jersey experiment and is being done for the Seattle-Denver experiment as well. On the basis of that work, I would guess that the rural experiment sample is too small, and the consumption data too weak, to hope to detect any risk-reduction effects in this area. Second, Michael's discussion—and the original author's papers—ignore the work by Charles Metcalf, which explicitly analyzes the effect of a limited duration experiment on estimates of income and substitution effects. Metcalf shows that in the simplest case, the limited duration of the experiment leads to data that *underestimate* the long-run income effects and *overestimate* the long-run price effects.[26] In more com-

---

26. The underestimate of the long-term income effect occurs because, as Michael recognizes, the present discounted value of the maintenance payments for a short-duration experiment will in general be less than those for a permanent national program. However, the price effects may be overestimated (not underestimated as Michael suggests) because there is a short-term "sale of leisure" due to the reduction in the price of leisure caused by the marginal tax rate on wage increments. See Charles Metcalf, "Predicting the Effects of Permanent Programs from a Limited Duration Experiment," in Harold W. Watts and Albert Rees, eds., *Final Report of the New Jersey Graduated Work Incentive Experiment* (University of Wisconsin–Madison, Institute for Research on Poverty, and Mathematica, 1974), vol. 2, pt. c, chap. 3, pp. 6–14.

plicated cases, the income effect may be overestimated or underestimated.[27] He then develops a strategy for using the variability in expenditures on leisure and goods *within* the experimental period in order to
estimate the magnitude of the biases due to duration. While the data in
the rural (and New Jersey) experiments are not wholly adequate for the
implementation of the model Metcalf works out, he was able to obtain
for New Jersey at least a rough estimate of the order of magnitude of the
biases due to the limited duration of the experiment. Metcalf's work indicates the potential for using the experimental data on consumption to
estimate long-term income and price effects. To that extent, it seems to
me, Michael's assessment of the usefulness of the experimental consumption data in inferring permanent income maintenance program effects is
overly pessimistic.

Having suggested that the potential for useful insights from the experimental consumption data is perhaps gerater than Professor Michael's
review suggests, I want immediately to reemphasize some practical reasons why that potential is not likely to be fully realized. To carry out
consumption studies appropriately, one should have data that covers the
utilization of income exhaustively and systematically, that is, estimates
over a given period for all expenditures and savings. This would allow
estimation of complete demand systems in which all cross-effects—including those between work-leisure time and goods or savings—are taken
into account. However, in order to get such data it would probably be
necessary to use diary techniques and in experiments such as these, investigators are concerned (probably correctly) that attempts to use diaries
in such exhaustive detail might cause serious fatigue on the part of subjects, irritation with the study, and higher rates of attrition. As a result,
given only a secondary interest in consumption, decisions were made
quite early in the experiment to compromise and to use less adequate measurement techniques.

In the case of the rural experiment, when the problem of incomplete
and weak consumption data is combined with small sample size—particularly when divided between two sociocultural extremes in Iowa and
North Carolina—one should expect few significant results, and should
trust only those results that prove to be robust under alternative formula-
tions and that can be shown to be generally consistent with the findings
in other experiments.

27. Ibid., p. 17.

Substance of Papers

With these general methodological points as background, I will now turn to some discussion of the substance of particular papers.

NUTRITION. I found the paper on nutrition interesting and I would guess it might have considerable impact in policy debates. If findings on improved nutrition, combined with those on improved school performance, were replicated for the other income maintenance experiments, they might do more to increase the likelihood of a broadened national cash transfer program than all the findings on labor supply responses. Michael's suggestion that we look more directly at effects in the lower tails of the nutrient adequacy ratios is an excellent one and it should be followed up. However, I think both Professor Michael and the authors of the nutrition paper miss a central aspect of the cost-effectiveness calculations. The authors calculate estimates of cost per day to raise the mean nutrient adequacy by one point using the income maintenance payments, food stamps, or a direct dietary supplement. The authors emphasize that the diet supplements are much more cost-effective and Michael complains, correctly, that this comparison is unfair because it fails to take into account that income maintenance payments are spent on other things besides food. The important point is that the authors find the cost-effectiveness of the income maintenance payments to be within the general range of the cost-effectiveness of food stamps. This clearly is of relevance to debate about integration of food stamps with cash transfers.

For the other studies upon which I intend to comment, I would like to stress comparisons with similar findings from the New Jersey experiment data.

HOUSING. First, with regard to the housing study, analysts in the New Jersey experiment[28] also studied the probability of home purchase among families that did not own a home prior to the experiment. They found a statistically significant response to the experimental treatment yield, about a 5 percent increase in the probability of home ownership. I believe this comparability across experiments should lead us to take the rural experiment results of a 5 to 7 percent increased probability of home ownership

28. See Judith Wooldridge, "Housing Consumption in the New Jersey-Pennsylvania Experiment," in Watts and Rees, eds., *Final Report of the New Jersey Graduated Work Incentive Experiment,* vol. 3, pt. D, chap. 3(a), and Walter Nicholson, "Expenditure Patterns in the Graduated Work Incentive Experiment: A Descriptive Survey," in ibid., chap. 3(b).

more seriously than Professor Michael seems to be inclined to do. The New Jersey study also found significant effects in the rent category but as already indicated, the rural sample of renters was too truncated to be of much use. Comparisons between these results and the forthcoming housing allowance experiments should be of considerable interest.

HEALTH. Professor Michael comes down hard on the study of health and medical care utilization. This appears to be primarily—and quite naturally—because he finds the results implausible. Michael attacks the analytical framework and the definition of income that was used. The author of the health and medical care study, Stuart Kerachsky, after he had completed the work on the rural experiment, applied essentially the same framework[29] to a follow-up study of the New Jersey experiment.[30] There he found significant effects of the experimental payments on the pattern of utilization of health services. In this light, I think Michael's complaints about the framework are misguided. His complaints about the definition of income used are also off the mark, I believe. Since the level of income is endogenously determined, partly in response to the experimental treatments, some proxy for normal income should be used and preexperimental income is a reasonable choice. All this is not to say that Michael should not be skeptical about the lack of experimental effects on patterns of utilization but I think the problem is not with the analytical methods.[31] The lack of effects on health status is not at all surprising since the ability to measure health status is limited and the inability to find programmatic effects on health status, particularly in small samples, is well known.

CONSUMER DURABLES, ASSETS, AND DEBTS. I must agree with Professor Michael's assessment that the study on consumer durables, assets, and debts is the most substantive—and ambitious—of the consumption studies. However, in this case I'm afraid that ambition may have carried the authors a bit too far and created some of the anomalies pointed out by Professor Michael. I think this can be seen most clearly by comparing the rural results with the New Jersey experiment's analysis of durables,

29. The framework, contrary to Michael's characterization, does allow for quality of care differences in response as it measures shifts away from clinics and hospitals toward specialists.

30. The publication reporting the follow-up study is forthcoming. Results are discussed in Stuart H. Kerachsky, "Health and Medical Care Utilization," MPR working paper B-5 (Mathematica Policy Research, 1976), pp. 10–11.

31. In fact, for the New Jersey experiment Kerachsky's analysis picked up experimental effects on health utilization that had been missed in previous analyses.

assets, and debts. This comparison proves extremely difficult to carry out. The problem is that the models adopted for analysis differ sharply. For the New Jersey study there are three different sets of analysis by Metcalf and Nicholson.[32] Unfortunately, the rural study develops still another model that does not match well with any of the New Jersey models. However, the match that comes closest yields the results shown in table 4.

Disregarding the low level of statistical significance[33] of any of these estimates, it is clear that there is virtually no comparability between the estimates in the two studies.

In trying to determine the reason for the noncomparability, it became apparent to me that a major part of the problem arose from the fact that the rural study entered the normal income and payments functions in a highly nonlinear fashion. This strikes me as a particularly questionable procedure where the underlying data are shaky *and* the standard deviations of the variables are so large (as is shown in Professor Michael's table 2). When evaluated at a particular point—as is necessary to calculate a marginal propensity to consume—these nonlinear functions can be taking rather sharp twists in order to allow the function to reach points at either extreme. This is the reason for the apparent conflict for loan debt (which Professor Michael points out in his discussion of table 3) between the marginal propensity to consume results, which are sharply different for whites and blacks, and the average effects results (which he gives in his informal table), which are more nearly the same for whites and blacks.[34]

This is just one illustration of the lamentable fact that within the New Jersey and rural experiments, and more clearly across the two experi-

32. See Charles E. Metcalf, "Consumption Behavior under a Permanent Negative Income Tax: Preliminary Evidence," in Watts and Rees, eds., *Final Report of the New Jersey Graduated Work Incentive Experiment,* vol. 3, pt. D, chap. 3(c); Charles E. Metcalf and Walter E. Nicholson, "Low-Income Households and the Permanent Income Hypothesis: Implications of the Urban Experiment" (paper prepared for delivery at the 1973 annual meeting of the American Economic Association; processed); and Walter Nicholson, "Expenditure Patterns in the Graduated Work Incentive Experiment: A Descriptive Survey."

33. One can only guess at significance of the rural estimates since the estimates of marginal propensity to consume are a weighted sum of regression coefficients and the authors do not calculate the standard error of the sums.

34. Unfortunately, for loan debt even the average effect is probably not a good indicator of the experimental impact since the distribution of loan debt is highly skewed, as indicated by a mean of $823 and a standard deviation of $7,929. The results suggest, as the authors themselves note, that probably there is a specification error in the model, which, if rectified, would change the results substantially.

Table 4. Estimates of Marginal Propensities to Consume, Families in the New Jersey and Rural Experiments, by Race, Selected Consumption Items

| Item and race | New Jersey | | | Rural | |
	Family normal income	Normal negative income tax payment	Transfer income[a]	Family heads' normal wage	Normal negative income tax payment
Durable stocks					
Whites	0.0090	0.0159	−0.0286	0.1228	0.0535
Blacks	0.0165	0.0420	−0.0079	0.1564	0.2672
Loan debt					
Whites	0.0147	0.0142	0.0294	0.4402	0.2337
Blacks	0.0208	−0.0192	0.0644	1.7145	3.5124
Liquid assets					
Whites	−0.0128	−0.0041	0.2149	0.3026	0.2889
Blacks	0.0008	0.0338	−0.0627	−0.0016	−0.0166

Sources: For the New Jersey experiment: Charles E. Metcalf and Walter E. Nicholson, "Low-Income Households and the Permanent Income Hypothesis: Implications of the Urban Experiment (paper prepared for delivery at the 1973 annual meeting of the American Economic Association; processed), tables 6, 7; for the rural experiment: W. Keith Bryant and Christine J. Hager, "Consumer Durables, Cars, Liquid Assets, and Debts of Wage-Working Families," in Bawden and Harrar, eds., *Rural Income Maintenance Experiment*, table 4.3.

a. Transitory income including negative income tax payments offset.

ments, authors have used sharply different models to analyze the same phenomena—and this holds for the labor supply studies as well. In many cases, one simply cannot tell whether differences are due to differences in behavior or simply to differences in models.

The marginal propensities to consume for the rural experiment, reported in the table above, are the long-run marginal propensities. The authors also estimate short-run marginal propensities using stock adjustment models. Unfortunately, the short-run estimates are even less useful than the long-run estimates. This is because the desired stock level, which is estimated as a first step toward the short-run adjustment estimates, causes the desired stock to shift from year to year by as little as 10 percent for some items to as much as 300 percent for others.

The durables, debts, and assets studies in the two experiments are filled with interesting ideas that deserve further study. The problem is that each author pursued a different idea and we are at a loss when we try to draw any clear conclusion. All the studies recognize that the experiments offer an unusual opportunity to estimate marginal propensities to consume out of different sources of income. Metcalf uses the time patterns of consumption during the experiment to draw inferences about the effects of the short-term duration on behavior. Bryant and Hager use the time patterns in order to estimate stock adjustment. If the consumption data in the Seattle-Denver experiment are in reasonably good shape, they should offer a unique opportunity to pin down all three of these areas of inquiry since the variations in duration of payments within the experiment would allow both estimates of stock adjustment and duration effects as well as rates of consumption out of different income sources. But before we get to that, let us hope that someone will do us the service of at least estimating relatively simple, comparable models for the New Jersey, rural, Gary, and Seattle-Denver experiments.

MICHAEL T. HANNAN

Noneconomic Outcomes

Analysis of noneconomic[1] outcomes is given consider-
able attention in the final report of the rural experiment. A multidiscipli-
nary team has prepared chapter-length reports treating impacts on marital
dissolution and marital interaction, migration, nutrition, school performance, educational and occupational aspirations, delinquency, political
participation, and psychological well-being. I find these analyses on the
whole thoughtful, detailed, and comprehensive. In a sense they are too
detailed and comprehensive. At times the analysts seem to be over-
whelmed by the mass of results and this often leads them to overlook interesting experimental effects. I will therefore concentrate on comparing
broad patterns of findings across diverse chapters.

The outline of the paper is as follows. First, to put the issues in scientific and policy perspective, I intend to review the rationales for investigating noneconomic outcomes of income maintenance programs. Then I
will summarize the findings concerning the main outcome measures for
each chapter. This is followed by a more detailed consideration of the
procedures and findings in each chapter. The final section contains a
methodological critique of the set of reports.

Rationale for Studying Noneconomic Outcomes

Labor supply impacts have direct consequences for program costs. This
is clearly true for only one of the noneconomic outcomes, impacts on

1. The term *noneconomic* outcome is a somewhat misleading label for the outcomes considered. It connotes a secondary importance to these issues that I do not
think is accurate; and it seems to indicate that the issues are not subject to economic
analysis, which is decidedly not true (just as the so-called economic outcomes can be
studied within an anthropological context). However, the term was proposed to me
in the original outline of this conference and I have been unable to come up with a
better brief title for the bewildering variety of outcomes covered here.

rates of change of marital status,[2] and possibly true for migration.[3] The rest of the outcomes considered here do not affect program costs directly. Arguments have been made, however, that impacts on nutrition, school performance, and so forth, have possible indirect effects on program costs by influencing the cycle of poverty. The view is widespread that poverty persists in the United States, at least in part because it is a self-perpetuating system with deprivation passed on from generation to generation. The best argument for such a cycle can be made with respect to nutrition. Inadequate prenatal and early childhood nutrition has been shown to diminish intellectual functioning and physical health. Individuals who experience such nutritional deprivation will have shorter and less productive lives than those exposed to more adequate diets. To the extent that their lowered productivity produces further prenatal and childhood malnutrition, the cycle will persist.[4]

Similar, if less persuasive, arguments are made with respect to each of the other noneconomic outcomes by authors of the final report. I do not wish to dispute the point that an individual's occupational and marital career will be affected by school performance, delinquency, political participation, and psychological functioning since the nonexperimental literature suggests that some such effects do exist. But there is some doubt that these effects are strong enough to account for the persistence of poverty. However, if the persistence of poverty is due in large measure to characteristics of the poor rather than to structural features of the economy and society, impacts on individual psychology and careers will influence long-run program costs.

2. If income maintenance programs alter the rates at which men and women enter and leave marriages, they will tend to change the composition of the population below the breakeven point of the program. For example, if a certain program raises the rate of marital dissolution and does not affect the remarriage rate, it will increase the number of families headed by females in the population. Since such families are more likely than families with two parents to fall below breakeven points, the total payments under such a program will be higher than one would calculate from modeling the labor supply effects alone. (Of course labor supply and marital status change are likely to affect each other.) It is easy to show that relatively small effects on rates of marital dissolution may have very large effects on eventual program costs.

3. If some unemployment is frictional and localized to specific areas, increased fluidity of movement might result in small decreases in unemployment and thereby lower the sum of transfer payments.

4. For an examination of the nutritional effects of the income maintenance program see J. Frank O'Connor, J. Patrick Madden, and Allen M. Prindle, "Nutrition," in D. Lee Bawden and William S. Harrar, eds., *Rural Income Maintenance Experiment: Final Report* (University of Wisconsin–Madison, Institute for Research on Poverty, 1976), vol. 5, chap. 6. (Hereafter, *Rural Income Maintenance Experiment.*)

Microexperiments, such as that under discussion here, cannot address an issue of this sort. All they can tell us is whether salient features of individual psychology and individual careers are affected by an income maintenance program. But this sort of information is crucial for evaluating the social science theory that serves as the foundation for most work on poverty cycles: the theory of the culture of poverty. This theory is explicated by Lewis, and popularized by Moynihan, Banfield,[5] and many others, makes a very strong hypothesis about poverty. The argument is that individuals do not respond to material deprivation singly. Rather, as is always the case with our species, people adapt collectively. An important part of collective adaptation is the development of a culture that sustains and constrains individuals in the face of high levels of uncertainty and threat. Poverty culture is a generic response to material deprivation that improves individual existence for those exposed to the deprivation. It does so by valuing the possible and minimizing concern with the future, which is both uncertain and dangerous. Lewis lists some seventy specific characteristics of the culture of poverty. Each of them is to be understood as a specific feature of this adaptive system. However, collective adaptation by means of a highly specialized cultural system is a double-edged sword. The culture has real adaptive value in environments to which it is specialized. But it also takes on a life of its own—as is so often the case with cultural systems—so that it persists after the environment has shifted away from one of extreme deprivation. At that point the culture is maladaptive.

Whether or not the culture of poverty is an important causal factor in the persistence of poverty depends on whether or not individuals are able to shift living styles once the culture becomes maladaptive. Lewis adds a specific social-psychological theory to the poverty culture theory, arguing that individuals are trapped for life in such cultures:

The culture of poverty, however, is not only an adaptation to a set of objective conditions of the larger society. Once it comes into existence, it tends to perpetuate itself from generation to generation because of its effect on the children. By the time slum children are age six or seven, they have usually absorbed the basic values and attitudes of their subculture and are not psychologically

5. Oscar Lewis, "The Culture of Poverty," in Daniel P. Moynihan, ed., *On Understanding Poverty: Perspectives from the Social Sciences* (Basic Books, 1969), pp. 187–200; Daniel P. Moynihan, "Employment, Income, and the Ordeal of the Negro Family," *Daedalus*, vol. 94 (Fall 1965), pp. 745–70; Edward C. Banfield, *The Unheavenly City: The Nature and Future of Our Urban Crisis* (Little, Brown, 1970).

geared to take full advantage of the changing conditions or increased opportunities that may occur in their lifetime.[6]

One can accept the cultural theory without accepting the social psychological theory, which amounts to a theory of imprinting. But it is the latter that has captivated so many social scientists and policy analysts.[7] And it is this theory that has direct relevance to the present study. If adults are indeed trapped by their origins, they cannot respond to environmental changes such as that afforded by income maintenance programs.

Virtually all previous work that bears on these issues considers socioeconomic status and does not separate effects of culture and class from those of current variations in employment or income. As the authors of the relevant chapters in the final report of the experiment point out, we know a good deal about the relationship of socioeconomic status to each outcome, but very little about the effects of income variations. The work that does separate the effects of origins from those of the current socioeconomic situation does not support the extreme hypothesis advanced by Lewis (see, for example, Duncan).[8] However, a great deal of additional research is needed. The income maintenance experiments offer a unique opportunity to clarify the issues since income environments are manipulated in a way that provides a very clear separation of the effects of origins from those of the current situation.

Having stated the opportunity provided by this experiment, I must add a major caveat. The duration of the experiment was only three years. We know almost nothing about the dynamics of response of, say school performance, to changes in economic environments. We must recognize that three years may not be a sufficiently long period to observe a full response. Thus the absence of a response neither proves nor disproves the social origins perspective.

Experimental Impacts: An Overview

The analyses of noneconomic outcomes present enormous detail. Each outcome is measured in many ways and usually at several different times, typically during the second and eighth quarters of the experiment. More-

6. Lewis, "The Culture of Poverty," p. 188.
7. See, for example, Charles A. Valentine, *Culture and Poverty: Critique and Counter-proposals* (University of Chicago Press, 1968).
8. Otis Dudley Duncan, "Inheritance of Poverty or Inheritance of Race?" in Moynihan, ed., *On Understanding Poverty*, pp. 85–110.

over, most chapters present three (sometimes four) parameterizations of the experiment. The various possible permutations yield an enormous number of experimental analyses. In some of these chapters, virtually all of the details are reported. This leads to the presentation and discussion of thousands of experimental effect measures; in the chapters on marriage and psychological well-being alone, just under 1,600 experimental effect measures are presented.

The reader cannot see the forest for the trees. At times, neither can the analysts. We see this clearly in Russell Middleton's summary of the entire set of papers:[9] "As this and subsequent chapters indicate, the improvement of levels of consumption [in the experiment] tended to have little impact either positively or negatively on behavior or attitudes in noneconomic areas."[10]

This opening statement, and my own reservations about the possibility of finding subtle effects in a short duration experiment on a small sample, did not quite prepare me for what I found. Each chapter has one or a few main outcome measures. In this overview I consider only the main outcomes. At the risk of advancing too optimistic a view, I offer the following summary of the main findings.

Marital Dissolution

The overall experimental effect is a rate of marital dissolution of experimental families one-third higher than that for control families. The effect, however, is not significant at even the 0.10 level. This may reflect both estimation problems (with the linear probability model treatment of rare events) and the size of the sample. There is a nonmonotonic pattern of treatment effects (as in the New Jersey and Seattle-Denver results), with the low support treatments tending to increase the rate of dissolution and the high support treatments lowering the rate.

Nutrition

The financial treatment has positive and significant impact on mean nutritional adequacy of diets for the North Carolina sample but not for

9. Middleton, a sociologist, as sole author of one paper and senior author of three others, apparently exercised a major leadership role in the analysis of noneconomic outcomes.

10. Russell Middleton, "Psychological Well-Being," in *Rural Income Maintenance Experiment,* vol. 6, pt. 1, chap. 7, p. 69.

the Iowa sample. The analysts attribute this to the fact that the North
Carolina sample started at a lower level of nutritional adequacy and that
response depends on starting point.

Geographic Mobility

There are positive experimental impacts in the sense that those on the
experiment are more likely to move. The effect is significant at the 0.05
level for all families and at the 0.09 level for those families with a wage
earner.

School Performance

The treatment produces decreases in absenteeism and increases in comportment scores, in grade point average, and standardized achievement
test scores for the North Carolina sample; these effects are significant for
primary grade students. The impact is negative but insignificant in the
Iowa sample.

Delinquency

There appears to be a nonmonotonic pattern of effects in the sense that
delinquency rates for most experimental plans are higher than that for the
controls, while the rate for those on the most generous plan is below the
control rate. Moreover, there is a significant negative effect of guarantee
level on overall rates of self-reported delinquency.

Political Participation

There are positive experimental inpacts on voting and more comprehensive measures of political participation for married men, married
women, and female heads of families for both the 1970 and 1972 elections. The effects are significant only for married women.

Psychological Well-being

There is a strong nonmonotonic pattern of effects on overall psychological well-being for heads of families, with those on the least generous plan
always below the control families and two of the three most generous

plans significantly higher than the control families. There is a significant positive guarantee effect on overall well-being. For teenagers only the most generous treatment (50/100) group has significantly higher well-being scores than the control group. However, the guarantee effect is positive and significant.

Aspiration-Expectation Gap

Income maintenance lowers the gap between the occupational aspirations of teenagers and their realistic expectations. The effect is significant overall with only one of two occupational metrics. The most generous treatment group has significantly smaller gaps by both measures.

Experimental Impacts: A Closer Look

A more accurate assessment of the findings requires considerably more detail. Therefore let us turn to consideration of the theoretical arguments, methodology, and findings of each new chapter.

Marital Dissolution and Marital Interaction

The literature on the sociology and economics of marriage indicates that the probability of marital dissolution declines, apparently monotonically, with improved socioeconomic status of the family. But as Middleton and Linda Haas point out, the impact of income maintenance is likely to be complex.[11] One possible effect is a pure income effect that will raise levels of satisfaction with living standards, reduce marital strain, and lower rates of marital dissolution. The second effect, sometimes called an independence effect, lessens the financial dependence of partners on the marriage and thereby lessens constraints on marital dissolution. So the total experimental effect can be positive or negative depending on which of these effects dominates. Since these effects need not be linear, it is possible for one effect to dominate in some programs and the opposite to dominate in others. If this occurs, the experimental response will be non-monotonic in support levels (or tax rates or both).

11. Russell Middleton and Linda Haas, "Marital Dissolution and Family Interaction," in *Rural Income Maintenance Experiment*, vol. 6, pt. 1, chap. 8.

The adjusted annual dissolution rate per thousand marriages for each of the experimental treatments are presented in table 1.[12] We see that the impact is indeed nonmonotonic. At the lowest levels of guarantee-tax rate, the dissolution rate is much higher for the experimental group than that for the control group. But as the programs become more generous, the rate of dissolution drops so that for the most generous program the dissolution rate is actually below that for the control group (though this difference is not significant). Other analyses show that the guarantee has a negative effect on the dissolution rate that is statistically significant.

Since the sample is small, the number of events analyzed is very small. I would not make much of this pattern of effects were it not for the fact that two other income maintenance experiments have reported very similar results.[13] In the light of these other findings, those of the rural experiment take on a heightened importance.

12. These rates are adjusted (in a linear regression) to be the rates for those at the mean of race, state, education, length of most recent job, 1969 family income, family size, welfare status at beginning of experiment, farm occupation, age, nights in hospital, disability, net equity, preexperimental labor supply, and a social desirability bias measure.

13. Analysis of the New Jersey data shows that there is a positive impact for the least generous plans that declines in such a way that the most generous plans have dissolution probabilities that are below those of the control group (Jon Helge Knudsen, Robert A. Scott, and Arnold R. Shore, "Changes in Household Composition," in Harold W. Watts and Albert Rees, eds., *Final Report of the New Jersey Graduated Work Incentive Experiment* [University of Wisconsin–Madison, Institute for Research on Poverty, and Mathematica, 1974], vol. 3, pt. D, chap. 8). Since neither standard errors nor significance tests are reported, we cannot tell whether these effect measures are dependable; they are large relative to the effects of background variables such as age and education. Analysis of impacts on dissolution rates in the Seattle-Denver experiment finds much the same pattern. Nancy B. Tuma, Lyle P. Groeneveld, and Michael T. Hannan, "First Dissolutions and Marriages: Impacts in 24 Months of the Seattle and Denver Income Maintenance Experiments," research memorandum 35 (Stanford Research Institute, Center for the Study of Welfare Policy, August 1976; processed), and Michael Hannan, Nancy Tuma, and Lyle P. Groeneveld, "The Impact of Income Maintenance on the Making and Breaking of Marital Unions: Interim Report," research memorandum 28 (Stanford Research Institute, Center for the Study of Welfare Policy, June 1976; processed). The impact of the low support treatment for marriages formed before enrollment in the experiment (only slightly more generous than the combination of aid to families with dependent children and food stamps) is to increase significantly the rate of dissolution for the black and white samples. The medium level of support has a somewhat weaker, but still significant, effect for whites, but a stronger effect for blacks. The highest level of support does not differ significantly from the control situation in terms of dissolution rates. For chicanos, none of the support levels are significant. This pattern holds when the data are analyzed by a linear probability model such as

Table 1. Impact of the Rural Income Maintenance Experiment on Marital Dissolution, by Tax and Guarantee Levels[a]

Adjusted annual dissolution probability

Description	Control group	Experimental group (percent guarantee and tax rate)				
		50/50	70/75	50/75	30/75	50/100
Adjusted mean	0.04	0.08	0.19[b]	0.05	0.04	0.03

Source: Russell Middleton and Linda Haas, "Marital Dissolution and Family Interaction," in D. Lee Bawden and William S. Harrar, eds., *Rural Income Maintenance Experiment: Final Report* (University of Wisconsin–Madison, Institute for Research on Poverty, 1976), vol. 6, pt. 1, chap. 8, tables 1 and 2.

a. The control group consisted of 336 families at the beginning of the experiment, the experimental groups of 280 families, for a total of 616 families.

b. Rho < 0.05.

An explanation for this pattern of effects is presented elsewhere.[14] Hannan and associates suggest that income maintenance has a nonpecuniary independence effect in that it provides a nonstigmatizing alternative to the conventional welfare system. This change is a substantial one (even at the same levels of support) for those women who have remained in marriages because they were either unaware of their welfare rights or had a moral aversion to adopting the role of the disreputable poor. In addition, the way in which the income maintenance subsidy was suddenly made available may have upset existing equilibria (a set of accommodations and compromises), affecting what Becker calls the gain from marriage.[15] Both types of effects operate at each level of support and tax. Thus there is a component of the independence effect that does not depend on the parameters of the experiment and that tends to increase the rate of dissolution.

Suppose there is also an income effect as described above. The income effect is almost certainly a function of guarantee and tax rates. Its strength will increase with the generosity of the program and more and more offset the constant independence effect. On the least generous programs, the weak income effect does little to offset the program effect; but on a more

that used by Middleton and Haas and by a log-linear model of the instantaneous rate of leaving a marriage.

14. Hannan, Tuma, and Groeneveld, "Impact of Income Maintenance," pp. 118–19, and by the same authors, "Income and Marital Events: Evidence from an Income-Maintenance Experiment," *American Journal of Sociology,* vol. 82 (May 1977), pp. 1186–1211.

15. Gary S. Becker, "A Theory of Marriage: Part I," *Journal of Political Economy,* vol. 81 (July/August 1973), pp. 813–46, and Becker, "A Theory of Marriage: Part II," ibid., vol. 82 (March/April 1974, pt. 2), pp. S11–S26.

generous program, the two opposing forces appear to cancel each other.[16] Testing these hypotheses demands a different sort of analysis from that presented in the report in question. However, there appears to be a genuine need for such additional analysis.

Besides analyzing impacts on marital dissolution, Middleton and L. Haas also explored experimental effects on husband-wife interaction, particularly with respect to division of labor and power, and marital happiness and conflict. In none of these areas are there any meaningful patterns of effects. It is possible that the absence of effects is due partly to the fact that the analysis was restricted to couples that stayed married. Possible experimental effects on other aspects of marriage may be confounded with effects on dissolution.

An equally extensive analysis of parent-child interaction patterns also fails to reveal any systematic experimental response. This is true both of responses by mothers and of the children themselves.

Nutrition

Analyses of nutritional effects are especially interesting and important. As I noted earlier, the causal link between nutritional deficiency and persistence in poverty is much better documented than the other causal effects I will discuss. Poverty programs have historically concerned themselves with nutrition and this continues to be the case today with the food stamp and commodity distribution programs. Typically, food transfer programs, like other in-kind benefit programs, have been justified on the grounds that the poor will not consume in a manner that meets individual and collective needs if they are given free choice. Surely the many features of Lewis' account of the culture of poverty—personality disorganization, short time-horizons, and so forth—lead to such a conclusion. In light of the continuing debate over the relative advantages of income programs and in-kind benefit programs, it is important to investigate whether income programs have negative consequences for the nutritional status of families.

The methodology employed by O'Connor, Madden, and Pringle is as follows. In the third and eleventh quarters, reports were obtained from individuals responsible for preparing meals in each household on food consumption for the previous 24 hours. The report included quantities

16. Middleton and Linda Haas view the absence of a high guarantee effect as conclusive evidence that "the Income Maintenance Experiment had (any) real effect —positive or negative." "Marital Dissolution," p. 29.

and weights of food consumed as well as reports of meals consumed outside the household. The choice of a 24-hour recall method involves a trade-off of typicality with accuracy. Apparently previous research in this area has indicated that total intakes for groups are measured more reliably with the 24-hour recall as opposed to recall over longer periods.

These basic data are converted into measures of intakes of ten nutrients: energy, protein, vitamin A, calcium, iron, phosphorus, niacin, riboflavin, thiamin, and ascorbic acid. Consumption of each nutrient is then expressed as a percentage of the "recommended daily allowance" proposed by the Food and Nutrition Board of the National Research Council. Analyses concern consumption of each nutrient and the mean adequacy of the ten.

Analysis of the control groups indicates generally low levels of nutritional adequacy. About 20 percent of the control families in Iowa and North Carolina had diets that were deficient in consumption of calcium, iron, and vitamin A. The problem is much more intense in North Carolina, where 60 percent of the sample had inadequate calcium intake, 50 percent had inadequate iron intake, and more than a third had inadequate vitamin C intake.

As mentioned in the overview, the experiment had a significant positive impact on mean nutritional adequacy of the North Carolina but not the Iowa sample. Looking at the ten individual nutrients, we find that in the eleventh quarter, ten of the ten impacts are positive for the North Carolina sample. Of these, impacts are significant (at the 0.05 level) for energy, calcium, phosphorus, iron, riboflavin, and vitamin C. Note that there is substantial and statistically significant improvement in intake of the three nutrients for which the North Carolina control sample was particularly deficient. In the Iowa sample, seven impacts are positive. Only one impact (on total energy) is significant (at the 0.10 level); and that effect is negative.

The same sort of findings hold when the experiment is parameterized in terms of transfer payments. Unfortunately no analysis of effects of variations in tax rates and guarantees was reported.

O'Connor and associates suggest that the reason why no experimental impact was observed in Iowa is that there was little room for improvement. The implicit model made response conditional on preexperimental status. Since no nutritional data were available for experimental families prior to the experiment, one cannot model this sort of response directly. Still I suggest that models be estimated in which the response is conditional on background variables that are associated with nutritional adequacy. It would also be worth exploring the change between the third and eleventh quarters in the framework of a dynamic model. Nonetheless, the analysis is convincing as it stands. The results stand in sharp disagreement with poverty culture theory and with the arguments in favor of in-kind benefit programs.

Geographic Mobility

The chapter by Aaron Johnson on geographic mobility makes almost no effort to tie the voluminous literature on migration to the experimental problem.[17] Instead, Johnson offers three hypotheses: (1) income maintenance may increase rates of movement by defraying costs of moving; (2) income maintenance may decrease rates of movement by smoothing out income fluctuations during periods of unemployment; and (3) income maintenance may have no effect on geographical movement either because family income is not an important determinant or because the full effect cannot be observed in a three-year experiment.

Analysis is restricted to heads of household who did not change marital status and did not drop from the sample for the entire experimental period. There seems no justification for the first exclusion. It is certainly possible to study the migration of those who leave marriages; and marital dissolution seems associated with geographical movement.

I can find no description of the dependent variable other than that it indicates a "move." What is not clear is whether this refers to all changes of residence or to moves out of a town, or what. Some subsidiary analysis is referred to in which the categories are moves more than 25 miles and more than 50 miles. It is obviously critical to know whether or not the moves occurred within a labor market or not. If they did, they are relevant to questions about impact on housing consumption but not to more general questions about migration.

At any rate, very little analysis is reported. As I mentioned in the overview, there is a positive experimental impact on "propensity to move." This is significant at the 0.05 level for all families, and at 0.09 for those families with wage earners, and is stronger in North Carolina than Iowa. This suggests that more careful and deeper analysis of these data ought to be carried out.

17. Aaron C. Johnson, Jr., "Geographic Mobility," in *Rural Income Maintenance Experiment,* vol. 6, pt. 1, chap. 9.

School Performance

Maynard and Crawford analyze impacts on four aspects of school performance: absenteeism, comportment, academic grade point average, and achievement on standardized tests.[18] Unlike the other analyses, this offers a series of well-reasoned hypotheses concerning overall experimental impacts, effects of expected gain from the experiment, the dynamics of the experimental response, differential response among subpopulations, and differential response by outcome. Moreover, the analysis in this chapter is both more subtle and more statistically sophisticated than that of the other chapters.

Analysis is conducted separately for the North Carolina and Iowa samples for two reasons. The data are more complete in North Carolina, and the educational environment is very different in the two states; for example, the mean percentile ranking on nationally standardized tests was the 25th percentile for North Carolina and the 52nd percentile for the Iowa sample. Because these researchers hypothesized that younger children would respond more to income maintenance plans, they also analyzed second through eighth graders and ninth through twelfth graders separately.

Maynard and Crawford hypothesized that the experimental impact would be greatest on absenteeism—days of school missed in a year for any reason[19]—since this outcome is dependent directly on economic factors and subject to short-term variations. They expected the response to be next greatest for comportment scores, that is, average scores on a wide variety of school behavior and such characteristics as cooperation, courtesy, initiative, and self-control, since these seem subject at least to some short-term variations. Scores on academic grade point average, the average grade on all academic subjects weighted by credit hours, and nationally standardized achievement tests should be more dependent on past learning and relatively insensitive to recent environmental change.

Within the North Carolina sample this pattern is borne out, particularly for second through eighth graders. For this group the adjusted mean on absenteeism is significantly lower (at the 0.05 level) than that of the control group. Comportment scores, academic grade point average, and standardized achievement test scores are all significantly higher for ex-

18. Rebecca Maynard and David L. Crawford, "School Performance," in *Rural Income Maintenance Experiment,* vol. 6, pt. 2, chap. 12.
19. The North Carolina analysis includes measures of the reasons for absences.

perimental children. For those in this category in Iowa, the experimental impact is negative though never significant. As expected, the effects are smaller (and not significant) for high school students.

Considerable analysis of the response in subpopulations and the dynamic of the response is provided. Here the results are more variable than those concerning the main experimental effects. This analysis is hampered particularly by the fact that the response was so different in the two sites. Since space limitations prevent full consideration of the more detailed analysis, it seems preferable to focus on the site difference.

Maynard and Crawford offer several explanations for the difference in response between North Carolina and Iowa. First of all, there were substantial differences between the two samples in demographic and other characteristics: heads of families in North Carolina had on the average three years less schooling than those in Iowa, approximately 30 percent of the North Carolina sample were farmers compared with almost 50 percent in Iowa, and 67.9 percent of the North Carolina sample was black, while the Iowa sample was all white.[20]

Second, the North Carolina sample was relatively poorer than the Iowa sample; 62.1 percent of the North Carolina sample was below the poverty line at the beginning of the experiment compared with 36.8 percent in Iowa. Therefore, a given level of support had a higher relative importance in North Carolina than in Iowa.

Third, in Iowa there was a low correlation between predicted and actual payments. This indicates considerable income fluctuations in the Iowa sample. Maynard and Crawford advance the view that a much greater portion of the Iowa population was only temporarily poor.

Finally, the Iowa sample children were performing at about the national norm on standardized tests while those in the North Carolina sample performed at a much lower level, that is, the samples do not include the same type of students.

Finally, as noted earlier, there were differences in the data bases available in the two sites. When the North Carolina analysis was redone using only school data similar to that used for variables measured in Iowa, the experimental response diminished. Therefore, at least some of the difference between sites depends on the structure of the data.

The first three explanations can be summarized in the statement that the Iowa sample had substantially higher socioeconomic status than the North Carolina sample. If the culture of poverty thesis is correct, the Iowa

20. Maynard and Crawford, "School Performance," table 1.

sample should be more able to take advantage of the opportunities afforded by income maintenance. Instead, we find just the opposite.

Delinquency of Teenagers

Middleton and Ain Haas are somewhat skeptical that income maintenance programs affect rates of delinquency.[21] It is their view that the literature offers only equivocal support for the hypothesis that socioeconomic status affects delinquency rates and that delinquency may be an element of a larger life-style organization that is resistant to situational changes (that is, it may be part of a poverty culture). Moreover, they argue that delinquency has been extremely resistant to policy measures.

Three theories of delinquency are relevant to this study. The first is a version of poverty culture theory—"gang culture" theory. According to this perspective, youths are socialized into a gang culture that emphasizes such qualities as toughness and excitement. This may be intensified by more general features of a poverty culture such as short time-horizons that may induce criminal behavior. The second theory, termed "control theory," rejects the view that there are significant subcultural variations in morality and life styles. Instead it attributes the high rates of delinquency in the lower classes to inadequate ties to agents of social control—parents, teachers, the school. Consequently, rewards for conformity with the moral order are relatively slight and punishments for transgressions are weak. The third perspective, called "strain theory," attributes delinquency and other deviant behavior to the strains generated by the discrepancy between high achievement goals (generated by the system) and low achievement expectations (generated by the structural barriers to mobility). One way to resolve the conflict is to reject the dominant goals and seek success in the more achievable ones, for example, status in a delinquent subsociety.

From the poverty culture perspective, delinquent behavior is not subject to modification by environmental change. However, both control and strain theory suggest that improvements in economic circumstances may have an effect on such behavior. Control theory suggests that income maintenance does so by reducing strains in relations between teenagers and their families, schools, and community organizations. Strain theory suggests that if income maintenance reduces some barriers to achievement

21. Russell Middleton and Ain Haas, "Delinquency of Teen-Age Youth," in *Rural Income Maintenance Experiment*, vol. 6, pt. 2, chap. 11.

(for example, barriers to educational attainment), it will have a beneficial effect on rates of delinquency by lowering the gap between aspirations and reasonable expectations. This gap is the subject of an impact study that will be discussed below.

The data on delinquency in the experiment consists of self-reports of youths aged fourteen through eighteen years of age who had not graduated from high school or started college. These data were collected by questionnaires (to maximize privacy and ensure accurate responses) in the twelfth experimental quarter. The most important measure is the self-reported delinquency scale.[22] The respondents were asked how many times in the previous two years they had engaged in each of a series of offenses: theft at three levels of seriousness, receiving stolen property, vandalism, trespassing in a house or building, assault, extortion, and using marijuana, narcotics, and other illegal drugs. One scale is simply the sum of frequencies of all delinquent acts for the two-year period divided by the number of items.

A more complex scale was constructed to take seriousness of the offense into account. Since there were no published seriousness weights appropriate for this analysis, Middleton and Ain Haas conducted a survey of a random sample of juvenile court judges to obtain such ratings. Mean seriousness indexes obtained from the 202 judges were employed as weights in constructing a self-reported delinquency scale.

The weighted and unweighted scales are very highly correlated, 0.997, suggesting that those with the highest delinquency rates were also the ones with the most serious offenses. Consequently, results using the two scales are almost identical.

Analysis of the adjusted means of each scale indicates a nonmonotonic pattern of effects. The adjusted means for most experimental plans are higher than those for the control groups. Only one of these is significant. However, the mean for those on the highest level of support is substantially lower than that for the control group. We see this guarantee effect more clearly in results from a model that contains guarantee levels, tax rates, and a dummy variable that distinguishes experimental from control families. In this formulation, the simple experimental effect is positive

---

22. Self-reports yield more comprehensive measurement of delinquent acts than other methods. Yet it is those acts that are detected and recorded by the police and courts that affect life changes, for example, mobility opportunities. Therefore, it would be preferable to use both self-reports and official records.

and the guarantee effect is negative (both significant at the 0.05 level). Middleton and Ain Haas remark:

The opposite signs for the guarantee and the experimental vs. control dummy seem incongruous when one considers that the latter incorporates the element of having some guarantee (vs. no guarantee). Because of the counterbalancing, the net effect of the experimental variables was negligible for all of the dependent variables.[23]

I have difficulty with this interpretation. If one is unwilling to interpret effects of individual program parameters, there is no point in estimating them. If, on the other hand, the model is meaningful, then one should conclude that there is a genuine effect of the guarantee. As was the case for the analysis of marital dissolution, the problem lies in the nonmonotonic pattern of effects. Yet the estimates of the model indicate that further increases in the guarantee would in fact produce a systematic decrease in the frequency and seriousness of delinquent acts.

A great number of interactions of experimental variables with various background variables were estimated. We are told that only 9 out of 150 were significant at the 0.05 level so that it is likely there was no substantial nonadditivity in the delinquency response. One of the interactions that is reported as significant but difficult to interpret is that teenagers in families with both parents present were more likely to respond favorably to the experimental treatment than those in families with female heads. I find this intriguing since it suggests that there is some interdependence of effects on marital dissolution and delinquency. Recall that the pattern of impacts on each variable is similar. Therefore, those plans that increased the rate of marital dissolution were also those that tended to raise the delinquency rate and vice versa. This suggests that the effect on delinquency is indirect and depends on an effect on marital relationships. Reanalysis of these data could easily test speculation about the interrelationship of the two. In the meanwhile, I do not think it accurate to conclude that income maintenance had no impact on delinquency-related measures.

Political Behavior

The very large literature on participation in electoral politics reveals a strong positive association with socioeconomic status. But there is only scanty evidence concerning the effects of income variations per se. How-

23. "Delinquency of Teen-Age Youth," p. 22.

ever, Heffernan points out two well-developed lines of argument in political science and political sociology on how income redistribution affects
the functioning of democratic political institutions.[24] As is so often the
case in political science, the two arguments correspond to the classical
left-right polarization. One holds that some minimal level of income
equality is a prerequisite for the survival and functioning of democratic
politics. The second view is that if the more numerous low-income citi-
zens are permitted to vote themselves a larger and larger share of the
system's wealth, they will bankrupt the society. Clearly a microexperi-
ment cannot answer these questions. However, the centrality of these
issues highlights the value of analyzing the effects of an income maintenance program on political behavior.

Although Heffernan does not mention it, the income maintenance experiments should create a new and potentially strong link between the
individual and the state. Just as participation in school and other organizations linked to the state can lead to increased political activity, so too
should participation in government programs. This should be particularly
true for participants in policy experiments for in a real sense, the state is
enlisting their aid in designing welfare policy. It is not difficult to imagine
that participation in this manner might induce increased participation in
other forms, such as voting.

Data were obtained on involvement in the 1970 statewide elections and
the 1972 presidential election. Participation was measured in two ways.
The first measure was simply whether or not an individual voted. The
second was a scale of various forms of participation, for example, talking
about the election, recalling candidates' names, displaying bumper stick-
ers, wearing campaign buttons, and so forth.

Analysis was conducted separately for husbands and wives in two-
parent families, and for female heads of families. For reasons that are not
explained, individuals who changed marital status were not included in
the analysis.

For each of the three groups, the two measures of participation were
investigated by multiple regression for each of two elections. The experimental impact in all twelve of these cases is positive but it was significant
in only two, both for wives. This group had voting probabilities that exceeded the comparable control group by 0.098 and 0.061 in 1970 and
1972, respectively. The impact is larger in the election with lower over-

24. Joseph Heffernan, "Political Behavior," in *Rural Income Maintenance Experiment,* vol. 6, pt. 2, chap. 13.

all participation levels; in the 1970 election, 37 percent of the experimental wives voted, compared with 26 percent of those in the control group; the comparable figures for 1972 were 43 percent and 37 percent.

Heffernan remarks that these impacts are either large or small, depending on one's perspective. Although I am not well versed in the study of electoral politics, I would imagine that increases of 5–10 percent in voting percentages that are localized in the population—for example, in the lower class—are enough to alter a good many election outcomes.

Psychological Well-being

The study of the social psychological impact of the experiment considers measures of life satisfaction, self-esteem, sense of anomie, sense of powerlessness, psychosomatic and nervous symptoms, worry, and assorted other characteristics. The selection of items was presumably intended to be broad enough to include virtually every dimension of possible impact on individual psychology. Middleton points out that to the extent that low levels of psychological well-being are associated with financial problems, income maintenance will have a positive impact. But also important, he argues, is the search for possible negative effects, "unintended dysfunctional consequences."[25] Nonetheless, Middleton's and Allen's earlier research on these questions in the New Jersey experiment revealed little or no experimental impact.[26]

Various scales of well-being and other more specific dimensions were constructed from responses of both male and female heads of families and teenage children at the second and tenth experimental quarters. The scales for the most part have been used in published research. Nonetheless, Middleton conducted careful analysis of the dimensionality and reliability of each scale. The major aims of the chapter are summarized in a single scale of overall psychological well-being that adds the scores of all the positive indicators (for example, self-esteem) and subtracts all the negative indicators (for example, self-deprecation).

Looking first at the summary measure for adults, we find a nonmonotonic pattern of effects. As mentioned in the overview, those on the least generous treatments have lower overall well-being scores than the control

25. "Psychological Well-Being," p. 2.
26. Russell Middleton and Vernon L. Allen, "Social Psychological Consequences of the Graduated Work Incentive Experiment," in Watts and Rees, eds., *Final Report of the New Jersey Graduated Work Incentive Experiment*, vol. 3, pt. D, chap. 5.

group. Two of the three more generous plans are significantly higher than the control group. There is a positive guarantee effect that is statistically significant.

There are so many items and subscales that it is difficult to find a further pattern of effects. However, one other measure seems particularly relevant both to the culture of poverty thesis and to policy choices. That is the measure of psychosomatic and nervous symptoms. This scale uses items from psychiatric epidemiology studies that validated items against clinical judgments of psychiatric impairment. Thus this scale should be an approximation to a clinical judgment of psychiatric (particularly neurotic) symptomology. There is no obvious pattern in the adjusted means, except that one of the least generous treatments (70T/75G) is significantly above the control group in both the second and tenth quarters and the most generous plan is below the control group in each quarter. However, when the effects are analyzed in a model containing the tax and guarantee variables, we find a significant negative effect of the guarantee in each of the two quarters and positive tax effects that are significant in the tenth quarter.

It would be particularly valuable to see if these effects remain while controlling for significant life changes during the experiment, such as marital status change, change in employment, and so forth. This is another area in which a joint impact study appears needed.

The results for teenagers, although somewhat weaker, are not very different. Those on the most generous support plans are significantly higher on the summary index of well-being. The guarantee effect is positive and statistically significant. Here, too, the experimental impact on psychiatric symptoms appears negative, though none of the effects are statistically significant.

Middleton concludes that there is no evidence of negative effects on psychological well-being. The summary scale gives a much more optimistic view: it appears that the experiment had a mild positive effect.

Aspirations, School Attitudes, and School Behavior of Teenage Youth

This chapter focuses on the subjective side of school experience and with the possible role of aspirations and expectations in the achievement process. The orientation follows the recent sociological preoccupation with the role of social psychological factors in what has come to be called the status attainment process, the process of obtaining occupational status. The view is that both aspirations and expectations are important determinants of the effort expended in educational and occupational attainment. Moreover, as Middleton and Ain Haas argued in their chapter on delinquency, the discrepancy between the two has distinctive effects.[27] Middleton, Haas, and Haas hypothesize that income maintenance is more likely to affect expectations than aspirations.[28] It may eliminate barriers to achievement, thereby raising expectations.

Other more or less loosely related issues are also addressed. They include perceptions of discrimination, subjective importance of money, self-ratings of school performance, subjective importance of grades, parents' interest in grades, attachment to school and teachers, rebellious behavior in school, participation in extracurricular activities, number of friends, dating frequency, religious behavior, and leisure expenditures.

All of these measures are collected at the end of the experiment from teenagers who had not graduated from high school or started college. The procedures are largely the same as those used in other chapters that analyze subjective data.

Those on the least generous program have significantly lower educational aspirations and expectations than the control group. Other than this, there is no apparent experimental effect. And, while there is no effect on occupational aspirations and expectations, there is some evidence of an impact on the discrepancy between the two. The overall experimental effect is to lower this discrepancy, but the effect is significant for only one of the two occupational measures. For each measure there is an indication of a nonmonotonic effect, with those on the least and most generous plans having smaller differences than the control group but those on some middle plans significantly higher than the control group. No explanation is offered for this result.

Conclusion

As indicated earlier, I was quite surprised that so many of these noneconomic outcomes were affected by the income maintenance program. Given the small size of the sample and the short duration of the experiment, it appeared likely that few subtle effects would be detected. But this

27. "Delinquency of Teen-Age Youth."
28. Russell Middleton, Linda Haas, and Ain Haas, "Aspirations, School Attitudes, and School Behavior of Teen-Age Youth," in *Rural Income Maintenance Experiment,* vol. 6, pt. 2, chap. 10.

does not appear to have been the case. Certainly the results do not square with the view that many low-income individuals are trapped in a poverty culture that prevents them from adapting to changes in the environment. The environmental changes produced in this income maintenance experiment were relatively slight. Nonetheless, we observed social, psychological, and political effects.

At least one of these effects, that on marital dissolution, has immediate policy relevance. Unfortunately, the design did not permit an equally precise analysis of impacts on the rate of remarriage; no analysis of the remarriage of single heads is reported. It is not enough simply to know the impacts on dissolution.

Several other impacts have quite immediate relevance to policy choices. I am particularly impressed with the findings concerning nutrition and school performance. Not only do improvements in these two areas bear on long-run financial costs of income maintenance programs, they are also important elements in any evaluation of the social cost of the program. Most important, the fact that nutritional adequacy of diets and school performance of children apparently improve with the program should help assuage doubts about the side effects of cash transfer programs. There is no evidence of negative side effects and at least some convincing evidence of positive consequences.

I have several comments about the analysis of noneconomic outcomes. On the whole, the analysis is careful and well done. The attention paid to measurement precision and to alternative hypotheses—particularly in those chapters authored by Middleton—is impressive and rare in research of this sort. Most chapters contain extensive reviews of relevant literature and deal with their implications for the experimental analysis. The fact that the social science literature so rarely gives clear guidelines cannot be blamed on the analysts.

These virtues are at least partially offset by some less desirable features of the analysis. I have concentrated on revising what I consider an overly negative and pessimistic tone concerning findings. Possibly I have overstated the case in the opposite direction in an effort to make plain the value of certain findings. But as the final report stands, it does not do justice to all the findings and should be revised accordingly.

The negative tone of the conclusions presented by Middleton is due partly to a reluctance to raise false hopes concerning income maintenance programs. In his summary of the results on psychological well-being, he writes: "In terms of policy, the findings reported in this chapter imply that a modest income maintenance program is not likely to be a panacea for all the social and personal ills of the poor in rural America."[29] Probably his pessimistic tone reflects an awareness that policy research in general has produced many false positive findings. The caution that typifies ordinary scientific activity tends to be heightened when we believe our findings may influence policy.

As one in the same position, I have sympathy with both views. We will do considerable damage to the prospects for the reform of the welfare system by raising hopes that cannot possibly be met by feasible programs. And false positive findings have similar consequences. But I am also concerned with false negatives.

An added reason for the negative tone of the final report may be the shotgun strategy employed in certain chapters. As already indicated, so many results are reported that one cannot see the larger structure of the findings. Not all the results are equally important to either policy or social science theory and they should not all be given the same weight in drawing conclusions. A second relevant factor is that too much attention is paid to statistical significance (a criterion I have followed because that is the approach of the analysts) and too little to patterns of effects over the main outcomes (as opposed to the many items that are summarized in scales).

Several features of the analysis also trouble me. First, although attrition from the experiment is frequently mentioned as a confounding factor, no analysis of the sensitivity of findings to attrition is reported. This is true in the analysis of marital dissolution, which ignores possible changes in marital status in the attrition group when intuition suggests that such change is a likely cause of attrition. This does not seem reasonable. Instead, it would have been more informative to have tested different hypotheses about the rates of marital dissolution among those leaving the experiment. It may be that the rates are the same as for those remaining in the experiment. But what would happen if they were higher, say double that of the treatment group? Such a sensitivity analysis would indicate how likely it is that the findings (or nonfindings, depending on how one looks at it) depend on nonrandom attrition.

Second, in a number of chapters the statistical analysis depends on a model with less than optimal properties. Although the analysts continually refer to the difficulties with the linear probability model for rare events (for example, marital dissolution, moves, voting), more suitable

29. "Psychological Well-Being," p. 68.

models are not sought. Some alternatives are widely available and should be tried on these data.

Third, the models of experimental response rely very heavily on classical experimental design considerations that do not always appear appropriate. In several chapters the analysts suggest that the response differs depending on the initial position on the outcome variable. But the response models (except in the chapter on school performance) do not incorporate such heterogeneity. In a few places, blackground variables that might be associated with heterogeneity are interacted with treatments. But even this crude procedure is not pursued systematically. In other places in the report, we are told that the response is dynamic and that it varies in intensity with the duration of the experiment. This is true for nutrition and school performance; for some other outcomes we do not know whether or not it is so. However, only in the report on school performance are the response models dynamic.

Each of these issues has at least some well-known solutions. The last issue I wish to raise does not, as far as I know. At several points in this discussion, I have suggested that impacts on one outcome appear to interact with other outcomes. Some examples are change in marital status and in labor supply, marital dissolution and behavior of children, nutrition and school performance. If we are to understand such complex results, we cannot continue to analyze impacts outcome by outcome. Instead we must design models that permit the analysis of joint impacts. What is tricky about this is that some relevant outcomes are discontinuous variables, such as marital dissolution, that can be located in time while others are continuous variables that may change slowly over a period—for example, labor supply, nutrition, school performance. Our usual ways of thinking about simultaneous causal systems (for example, the well-developed econometric theory for estimating systems of simultaneous linear equations) must be modified to deal with such questions. I suggest that research along these lines and the design of models appropriate to such analyses, should be given a high priority in policy studies of this kind.

Comment by Robert J. Lampman

This paper and some of the others in this volume distinguish the economic from the noneconomic concerns of the experiment, which can be a somewhat troublesome distinction. It might be better to distinguish between work responses and other—or nonwork—responses.

The experiment's principal aim was to estimate the cost of a nationwide negative income tax. Part of that cost has to do with changes in work effort that may be caused by the introduction of a negative income tax, and from variations in the guarantee and the tax rate. But there are other ways to change work effort, and hence the cost of the negative income tax. Among those are variations in other parts of the negative income tax formula aside from the guarantee and tax rate; for example, a change in the income definition, a change in the income period, or a change in the family filing unit. Those were not varied in the rural experiment, although a new income definition was introduced for self-employed farmers.

I think it is useful to separate work concerns from other concerns. But some of what are grouped together here as separate research topics are in fact closely related to the work concern. The separate investigations of migration, job search, and occupational shift are clearly tied in with the process by which people change their work and their incomes from work.

The other responses are hard to interpret for policy purposes or for their implications for further research. These include the various types of consumption behavior discussed in the Michael paper, and some responses that have to do with behavior other than consumption.

Edward Schuh grouped several of these under the heading of the accumulation of conventional capital and human capital that goes on in the household and on the farm. He is focusing on the question of whether the negative income tax influences the accumulation of capital.

Then he suggests that attention be directed at psychological well-being and political behavior. Most people would agree that it is good for families to save, to invest, and to improve their health and their education. But what about marital stability? If it turns out that a negative income tax does induce a higher rate of family separation, is that good or bad? It is possible that a major result of a negative income tax is to remove some of the financial obstacles to separation and divorce. With the increased economic independence of the wife, the divorce and separation rates of poor people may increase. So it appears that one of the desired outcomes from the point of view of poverty families may be a change in marital dissolution rates. I suppose there is a similar kind of question regarding teenage delinquency.

I agree with Hannan that there ought to be more analysis of the links between these several outcomes and process changes. For example, more effort should be devoted to studying the relationship between nutrition and health care, the relationship between family stability and school performance, and the relationship between teenage behavior and some of the other measures.

Hannan suggests that some of these outcomes may be so critical that an experiment should be designed especially to get at them. The elements in the negative income tax formula and in the selection of the sample of the rural experiment were clearly designed to get a better understanding of work responses. Suppose the objective was to know about family stability responses. What would have been done differently? I suppose the sample would have been drawn in a different fashion in order to identify family status as well as poverty status at the outset. Similarly, the sample might have been standardized with reference to children or political behavior if these were of primary concern. In addition, the elements in the negative income tax formula would have been altered. For example, instead of varying tax rates, variations might have been introduced in the treatment of the incomes of wives, child-care expense, and the guarantees for families of different size.

Comment by Aaġe B. Sørensen

The so-called noneconomic outcomes of the rural experiment are hard to find. Most of the chapters reviewed by Michael Hannan present a large number of insignificant and apparently unsystematic experimental effects. The lack of statistical significance is obviously partly a function of the small sample, the liberal use of control variables in the regression equations employed in the various analyses, and the low reliability of many outcome measures. However, in most instances the experimental effects not only fail to reach statistical significance, they also apparently fail to form a coherent and interpretable pattern. Hannan argues that the overwhelming number of results of this nature has led the investigators to overlook some interesting and important patterns of effects of the experiment. Most convincingly, Hannan argues the experiment had such an effect in the case of marital dissolution. He also points to the possible existence of meaningful effects in some other instances (psychological well-being, occupational aspirations and expectations of teenagers, juvenile delinquency), where the chapters leave an impression of no interpretable impact.

Hannan's reevaluation is plausible. It is difficult, however, to fault the analysts of individual chapters for the nature of the conclusions they draw, given the way the research was organized and the experiment designed. There are some lessons to be drawn from the differences in opinions concerning the existence of interpretable findings. One obvious lesson is the need for larger sample sizes, particularly when dealing with outcomes that have rather low reliability measures, as is the case with many of the noneconomic outcomes. Equally important is the need for a better integration of analysis across different outcomes. I strongly endorse Hannan's plea for an analysis of the interdependency of outcomes. Very little of this type of analysis was done as different dependent variables were assigned to different investigators. More meaningful patterns could have emerged as a result of a better coordinated effort. Admittedly, however, the methodology for such analysis is still in its infancy.

It should be noted that Hannan's reevaluation of the experiment's effect on marital dissolution is evidently inspired by his own research on the Seattle-Denver experiment. In that experiment, the effects are stronger and more unambiguous. As Hannan notes, the pattern is complicated, because it can reflect two opposing tendencies: on one hand, an independence effect, due to reduced financial dependency, and on the other hand, an easing of marital strains with receipt of a guaranteed income. Without the results from the Seattle-Denver experiment, it is difficult to find the pattern in the rural experiment. The example suggests that a reevaluation of findings (or lack of findings) from the completed experiments will be useful as new results become available. These large-scale experiments clearly represent a unique opportunity for replication and cumulative research.

Perhaps because of the many negative results, one finds nowhere in the analysis of the rural experiment any systematic analysis of possible Hawthorne effects of the experiments. Hannan's paper does not raise the issue either. However, I feel it is a crucial one that ought to have received more attention. The frequent contact between the participants and the staff in the experiment could conceivably make a difference in the lives of the participants not caused by the experimental parameters as such. The contact should have established a link between the participants and the larger society, particularly for the more isolated North Carolina sample. This linkage could have transmitted behavioral expectations that led to some of the experimental effects established. In particular, the results on nutrition, on school performance, and on political participation could be the result of the increasing interaction between these poverty groups and society as a whole. With respect to nutrition and school performances, the largest gains were observed for North Carolina families, and the effect on political participation was largest for wives—all results consistent with the hypothesis advocated here. Against this explanation, it might be argued that the control groups were also in frequent contact with the staff of the experiment. But since the contact was less intense and the staff controlled nothing of interest for the control group, it would presumably have had less influence on this group.

The possibility of the existence of such an effect suggests that Hannan's conclusion that the findings are at odds with the culture of poverty thesis should be qualified. If the experimental staff served to link these poverty groups with the larger society, the results are not inconsistent with the culture of poverty thesis, since this culture could be influenced by increasing interaction with nonmembers of the culture.

Let me finally draw the attention to a set of results—those dealing with job mobility and job search—that are not discussed by Hannan or in other presentations at this conference though mentioned in the overview papers. These results are nevertheless important. They seem to imply that a permanent negative income tax will lead to a reduced supply of labor for the most unsatisfying jobs in society. This in turn might lead to a reduction in the number of such jobs offered by employers. Since the major alternative to a negative income tax seems to be a job subsidy or public employment program, the possible labor market effects of a negative income tax in terms of the number and distribution of jobs of varying quality would seem to be a very significant issue.

G. EDWARD SCHUH

Policy and Research Implications

The urban and rural experiments have generated a massive amount of research results. To seek the policy implications in the mass of detail is not a simple task and I have not been able to do it entirely to my satisfaction. What follows is an attempt to focus on some of the key issues raised by the experiment. I have purposely cut through some of the detail in order to provide a somewhat more orderly set of comments.

My paper is divided into three main parts. In the first section is a brief discussion of the causes of poverty in agriculture. This provides a background for the policy analysis that follows as well as a framework for the evaluation of the experimental results. The second part is devoted to the main policy issues arising from the imposition of a comprehensive income maintenance program in rural areas; here I attempt to draw some of the policy implications of the results. In the third part are some suggestions for additional research.

Causes of Poverty in Agriculture

Some perspective on the causes and nature of poverty in agriculture is necessary if we are to understand the experimental results and to draw policy implications from them. Rural America continues to have more than its proportional share of the nation's poor. In 1969 the rural population represented 26.5 percent of the total U.S. population, but represented 35.5 percent of the poor people, as poverty is officially defined.

The concentration of the poor in the rural sector is a consequence of the

Helpful comments on an earlier draft of this paper were received from Theodore W. Schultz, Robert D. Emerson, and Richard L. Kohls.

nature of economic development in a market economy and of past deficiencies in policy. At least three dimensions to the problem are important.[1] In the first place, due to the conditions of demand and supply in
agriculture, some labor almost inevitably has to leave the sector.[2] Agricultural products have a low income elasticity of demand and, except when
export potential is great, a low price elasticity of demand as well. But
technical change tends to shift the supply curve of agricultural products
to the right at a fairly rapid rate, and to the extent that the new technology
is embedded in capital goods, it raises the productivity of these inputs.
Moreover, capital goods tend to be substituted for labor as real wages
rise.

Because of the limited opportunities for nonagricultural use of land,
farm labor has to bear the burden of the adjustment of resources. When
the adjustment is sluggish, labor tends to be dammed up in agriculture, and
its income declines relative to that of labor in the nonfarm sector, even
though it may rise in absolute terms as a result of the migration from
agriculture that does take place.

U.S. policymakers failed to give serious attention to this human resource problem until about ten years ago. The farm income problem was
dealt with by policies that focused on the product market, and very little
attention was given to facilitating the appropriate resource adjustment.
To take one example: the disparity in formal schooling between the rural
and urban sectors has traditionally been large, and training and vocational
programs in nonagricultural fields have not been readily available to rural
populations. Moreover, until fairly recently farm people were generally
excluded from such programs as unemployment insurance and social security, while at the same time many of the poor were being victimized by
commercial farm policy.

The third dimension to the poverty problem in agriculture is its uneven
regional development. For reasons that are beyond our present interests,
poverty within the agricultural sector has tended to be concentrated in the
Southeast. Even in the other regions, however, there have been local

1. For more detail, see G. Edward Schuh, "Neoclassical Economic Theory,
Poverty, and Income Distribution," in Robert O. Coppedge and Carlton G. Davis,
eds., *Rural Poverty and the Policy Crisis* (Iowa State University Press, 1977), pp.
87–110.
2. Johnston describes this as a universal aspect of the transformation of agriculture. See Bruce F. Johnston, "Agriculture and Structural Transformation in De-
veloping Countries: A Survey of Research," *Journal of Economic Literature*, vol. 8
(June 1970), pp. 369–404.

pockets of poverty associated with the uneven geographic dispersion of urban-industrial development.

The Policy Issues

In this section I have selected eight issues for discussion. Where possible I have attempted to draw out the unique features in the experimental results as well as their policy implications.

Disincentives to Work

The rural negative income tax experiment included a number of groups not covered by the urban experiment.[3] In what follows, attention is focused only on the results for the self-employed and for households headed by male wage earners. The self-employed are of interest since their labor response is expected to be different from that of wage earners. Since rural labor markets are sufficiently different from urban labor markets, the response even of the male wage earner was expected to be different. An important policy question is whether there are different behavioral responses between the rural and urban populations that would affect the policy parameters.

Broadly speaking, the results for the rural wage earners and their families were quite similar to those obtained for urban wage earners. The percent of experimental husbands employed in any quarter was virtually the same as for control husbands for all three subpopulations. And there was a statistically significant experimental/control difference in hours worked per quarter by husbands for only one of the three subpopulations. Hence, there was little tendency for the able-bodied male heads of household to abandon work and live on welfare. There *was* a tendency for them to work fewer hours but the difference, similar to that in the urban experiment, was quite small. From a policy standpoint, these results suggest there would be little need for a work requirement to keep husbands working, nor for different policies for the rural and urban populations.

The results for the wives were also similar to those in the urban experi-

3. The experiments are discussed in D. Lee Bawden and William S. Harrar, eds., *Rural Income Maintenance Experiment: Final Report,* vols. 1–6 (University of Wisconsin–Madison, Institute for Research on Poverty, 1976) (hereafter *Rural Income Maintenance Experiment*), and Joseph A. Pechman and P. Michael Timpane, eds., *Work Incentives and Income Guarantees: The New Jersey Negative Income Tax Experiment* (Brookings Institution, 1975).

ment. There was a negative and significant experimental response on the part of all three subpopulations in terms of the participation rates for wives, and this difference in participation rates accounted for most of the decline in hours worked by wives. The labor force participation rates of wives in the rural experiment were higher than those in the urban experiment. Hence, the aggregate supply effect could be expected to be larger for the former group.

Among dependents, there appeared to be a negative experimental response in wage income and hours worked for all three subpopulations, but the response was statistically significant only for Iowa dependents. In comparing the results from the rural and urban experiments, it should be noted that rural youth usually have greater access to employment opportunities because work laws are less effectively enforced in these areas.

Finally, contrary to the urban experiment, the results for blacks were not anomalous. Despite some individual cases of disparity, their responses were not substantially different from those of the whites.

In interpreting the labor supply response of self-employed farm families, the importance of multiple job-holding, especially for the farm poor, should be kept in mind. Of the experimental sample, 58 percent of the farm operators in North Carolina and 33 percent of the farm operators in Iowa worked for wage work. If the labor market activities of husbands *and* wives are considered jointly, 78 percent of the North Carolina families and 50 percent of the Iowa families had one or more members who worked for wages. These participation rates are consistent with other data indicating that more than 50 percent of the income of poor farm families comes from off-farm sources.

Contrary to expectations, hours of farm work by the operators increased both in North Carolina and in Iowa.[4] The response of wives was similar. The policy implications of these unexpected results depend on our understanding of how they came about. Unfortunately, no satisfactory explanation is given in the reports, although a number of plausible hypotheses are offered. First, other farm inputs may have increased as a

4. In North Carolina the increase was statistically significant at the 90 percent level. In Iowa it was less. Caution should be used in interpreting these results, however, since the samples were small. Moreover, it may be somewhat easier for the self-employed to overreport their hours worked than for wage earners because verification may be more difficult. Wendell Primus in a personal communication has indicated that he distrusts the positive response, and believes it arose as a Hawthorne effect due to the greater contact with this group. Despite these caveats, I accept the results at face value for present purposes.

result of the program, thereby increasing the productivity of farm work and in turn the implicit wage. Second, farm people may have a preference for farm work, and the higher incomes may have enabled them to honor these tastes, or to put it another way—to purchase conditions of employment. Third, the program may have provided more security against risks, thereby permitting farm activities to be undertaken that required more labor input. And finally, the results may be due to the short time horizon for the program. What might have been happening was that the families were undertaking investment activities on their farms that would give them a larger resource base for the future. However, there seems to be no evidence of this kind of investment.

If the increase in hours worked in agriculture were to continue under a permanent negative income tax program, this would be an important policy consideration. As noted earlier, agriculture has been chronically characterized by an excess supply of labor. Employment in the sector peaked around 1916, and from that date until the end of the 1960s there was an almost uninterrupted outflow and an overall decline in the rural population.

Since about 1969–70, however, employment in agriculture has remained relatively stable. Moreover, in two years, 1973 and 1974, per capita incomes of farm people in the aggregate were actually larger than those of people in the nonfarm sector. In addition, since the early 1970s there has been a reversal of the rural-urban shift, with a tendency for the population to move back to the rural areas.

Despite this apparent approach to equilibrium, the need to transfer labor out of agriculture is likely to persist, especially in regions such as the Southeast. A major increase in farm labor input by the rural poor could exacerbate the adjustment problem for agriculture as a whole since the number of such poor families is relatively large. The resulting increase in output would lower farm prices somewhat, other things being equal, and push a larger number of farm families below the poverty line.

It should be noted, however, that the increase in farm work is at the expense of wage work, and an important source of wage work for farm people is on other farms. This is especially the case in the Southeast. The labor adjustments in this sense could be offsetting, although whether they would be so or not requires more analysis of both the sample and aggregate data.[5]

5. Important shifts in product mix could be induced if this wage work is on larger farms producing labor-intensive crops, such as tobacco.

Hours of wage work declined for both the farm operators and their wives. The largest adjustments were for the wives—a result consistent with the urban experiment and the wage-earning rural families. In Iowa, the overall labor force participation rates actually increased for both husbands and wives. Hence, there was a considerable amount of partial withdrawal from the labor force.

Despite the rather sizable shifts in where farm operators worked, there was no evidence of a decline in total work effort. To the contrary, there was virtually no change in total hours of work for North Carolina farm operators, while in Iowa these operators actually worked more hours. Thus any concern about the fostering of idleness among farm operators seems to be misplaced.

When considering the drop in the participation rate of wives in North Carolina, however, the result is a sharp reduction in the work activity of the farm family as a whole—some 16 percent. This is due to the relative importance of wage work in that location, with both husbands and wives reducing both their participation rates and their hours worked in such activities. This is a very sizable reduction in labor suppy. However, it is due to a reduction in work activities on the part of the wives. Although the short-run labor market implications may be severe, the long-run (possibly positive) effects may be offsetting. I have more to say on that issue below.

There were also sizable regional differences in the labor response of farm families. These differences were probably due to the basic differences in labor market conditions between the two regions, and to the differences in poverty levels per se. The North Carolina sample was drawn from a poorer population group, and from a region of more generalized poverty compared to the Iowa sample. The combination of these factors suggests that there could be rather sizable interregional transfers of income as a result of a universal income maintenance program.

The final issue on work disincentives has to do with the labor supply response to different levels of marginal tax rates. The overall results were rather inconclusive just as they were with the urban experiment, although there is somewhat more evidence among some population groups that a stronger disincentive effect is associated with a higher tax rate.

The Mahoney-Mahoney paper on the urban experiment flushed out most of the issues on the tax rate issue,[6] and there is little that I might add.

6. Bette S. Mahoney and W. Michael Mahoney, "Policy Implications: A Skeptical View," in Pechman and Timpane, eds., *Work Incentives and Income Guarantees*, pp. 183–97.

However, on the question they raised about vertical equity, there is little one can say as an analyst or social scientist. In the first place, there is a trade-off between the effect the program has on income distribution and the efficiency with which that distribution is altered. Although we can say something about the nature and dimensions of the trade-off, only policy-makers or society at large can make the choice.

Second, the experiment has told us little about alternative *systems* that differ in the amount of income differentials they preserve at both the upper and lower ends of the income distribution. It could be that both savings rates and work effort will be different depending on the tax rate imposed. Should tax policymakers opt for a posttax income distribution that narrows rather than eliminates income differentials on the upper end of the income distribution, symmetry—for whatever it is worth—would require the same thing on the lower end.

Other Labor Market Issues

The experiment provides information about several other important and interrelated aspects of the labor market, all concerned in one way or other with mobility. These are intersectoral adjustments of labor, mobility between geographic regions, and occupational mobility and job search behavior. In general, from a micro standpoint, a program that facilitated labor mobility should enable individuals and the family to earn larger incomes, thus enhancing human capital. From an aggregate or macro standpoint, any improvement in mobility should aid in the adjustment of the economy to changing conditions of supply and demand, and, in turn, affect the total output of goods and services produced by the economy.

INTERSECTORAL LABOR ADJUSTMENTS. Until recently, the labor markets in the farm and nonfarm sectors have been in almost continuous disequilibrium. The conditions of economic development required a transfer of human resources out of agriculture but because the intersectoral labor market was imperfect, incomes of farm people chronically lagged behind those in the nonfarm sector. Because of the low earnings that have prevailed through most of the postwar period, and the seasonality of farm work, members of the rural labor force have often held more than one job—in both the farm and nonfarm sectors.

Theoretically, a program such as the negative income tax should provide more income security, thereby enabling the rural worker to shift from wage work to self-employed activities. This would reflect a better capability to control conditions of employment and would provide an increase in welfare in the form of nonpecuniary income. In addition, if the shift were toward more labor-intensive activities, there could be a long-term increase in family income since the expected future income of the more risky venture might be larger than the realized income from the more secure activity chosen in the absence of a program.

The results from the rural experiment proved consistent with this theory. Multiple job-holding declined and there was a general tendency to reduce nonfarm wage work in favor of farm activities. There are a number of implications to be found in these trends. First, farm families are likely to become less dependent on nonfarm income than they would be in the absence of a negative income tax program. In principle, an important source of income stability for farm families would be lost although presumably this would be compensated for by the negative income tax program.

To the extent that a program results in a shift of labor from nonfarm activities to farm activities, short-term output would be affected as well as the short-term equilibrium in the intersectoral labor market. Should there be additional capital accumulation in agriculture as a result of the program, both tendencies would be even larger.

A withdrawal of farm labor from nonfarm activities would have important implications for the nonfarm labor market in rural areas. Wage rates would tend to rise in these markets, other things being equal. Since an important share of the employment previously held by these groups would tend to be unskilled, there might be a tendency to attract unskilled labor from the urban centers back to rural areas. This would further the recent shift of population to the countryside, while partly alleviating the congestion and unemployment in urban centers.

The intersectoral labor market now appears to be much closer to equilibrium than in the past, but there are still rather obvious farm income problems in the Northeast and Southeast. At the same time, there could be further shifts back to agriculture in other regions if present trends continue. Moreover, if the United States should lose its trade advantage in agricultural products because of developments here and abroad, there could be a renewed need to transfer additional resources from the agricultural sector.

GEOGRAPHIC MOBILITY. Aaron Johnson's analysis of the effect of the experiment on geographic mobility indicates that experimental families had a significantly higher incidence of mobility than control families when controlling for other family characteristics.[7] For all experimental families, the response rate was 5 percent higher than that for control families. If this is applied to a 30 percent mobility rate, the relative increase in mobility is 17 percent. When the self-employed were removed from the sample and wage earners alone were considered, the response was even larger —9 percent, or an increase in mobility of 30 percent.

Overall, the results suggest that the experiment did enhance the propensity of a family to move. There was a difference in response by race and region, however, with both black and white families residing in the South exhibiting positive and significant experimental responses, while there was no apparent experimental effect in Iowa. Hence, to the extent that increased mobility was toward higher income opportunities, the program helped families improve their long-run income-earning capability. At the same time, it increased resource mobility, thereby leading to a more efficient allocation.

OCCUPATIONAL MOBILITY AND JOB SEARCH BEHAVIOR.[8] Theoretically, an income maintenance program should increase the control that individuals have over the timing of their work activity. The extent to which this potential flexibility is exercised, the purposes to which it is applied, and the job search methods used, are all key issues in the evaluation of an income maintenance program. Consideration should also be given to the disincentive effects of a program, which might lead to higher rates of job departures, longer periods of unemployment, and some indifference to the earnings characteristics of the job selected. However, support payments may enable individuals to make strategic job changes or to engage in longer and more rewarding job searches. Another possible outcome is that income transfers may be viewed as earning subsidies, increasing the job stability of some workers or supplementing income from jobs with good earnings prospects but low initial wages.

The experiment provides a good deal of useful information about the labor market in the rural study areas and how members of the labor force went about their job search. On the first point, the two study areas severely lacked permanent employment opportunities, as evidenced by the number of respondents reporting they were out of a job, who were laid off or released from temporary or seasonal jobs, and who reported no jobs avail-

7. Aaron C. Johnson, Jr., "Geographic Mobility," in *Rural Income Maintenance Experiment*, vol. 6, chap. 9.
8. Luther G. Tweeten, "Job Search Behavior and Its Impact on Earnings," and Richard E. Miller, "Job Change Behavior," both in ibid., vol. 3, chaps. 7 and 8, respectively.

able as the reason for not taking a job.[9] From a policy standpoint, this suggests that an alternative to the negative income tax is a program to provide more jobs. Whether that is a more desirable solution than an income transfer program, however, is an issue that requires considerably more analysis.

On the second point, the individual interviews suggest that comparatively little use was made of the public employment service in seeking jobs. The rural respondents relied heavily on direct contact with private employers to find work. This may suggest the need for educational and informational programs to make rural wage earners more aware of the public employment service and the wider access to information it might provide. Alternatively, the results may reflect a lack of effectiveness of the employment service in rural areas. If this is the case, then policy should be directed to improving this service.

Overall, the program appears to have had desirable effects on occupational mobility and job satisfaction. For example, individuals in the experimental groups who initially had desirable positions were less likely to leave their employers than were individuals in the control group, while those with less desirable positions were more likely to change employers. This suggests that workers with relatively good jobs viewed the support payments as a wage subsidy, increasing their satisfaction with their present jobs. Individuals with low-paying and lower status jobs, on the other hand, would have had more to gain from a job shift, and the support payments should have enabled them to schedule their work activity accordingly.

Similarly, individuals in the experimental group who could expect to increase their total income the most with reemployment tended to be unemployed the least, while those who could anticipate less net gain in income were unemployed more weeks. In effect, the workers who were most disadvantaged in the labor market—the older and less educated—tended to substitute leisure for work activity when the support level was sufficient. Hence, there appeared to be a natural selection process, with those least able to compete in the labor market being more dependent on the income transfers, and those more able to compete doing so. Most observers would probably agree that this is a desirable outcome of a transfer program.

The analyses of the effects of tax rates and guarantee levels on search activities indicate they had more distinctive effects than were apparent in the direct analysis of supply behavior. For example, in a special analysis of unemployment-prone wage earners, the employment disincentives

9. Tweeten, "Job Search Behavior."

associated with high tax rates and high guarantee levels more than offset the potential gain from effective job search, causing net wage losses from search. But the reverse was true with low tax rates and low guarantees; these more than offset disincentives for employment, causing net wage gains. For the standard plan (guarantee at 75 percent of the poverty level, 50 percent marginal tax rate), the effect of more search effort dominated slightly, causing net wage gains from job hunting and unemployment associated with it of 3.6 percent per search.

In general, disincentives to employment seemed to dominate the data for high tax and guarantee levels, but were overshadowed by other factors at low tax and guarantee levels when unemployment frequency was reduced. These results suggest that within the range of parameters considered, lower tax rates and guarantee levels facilitate the search process, enabling individuals to improve their own lot and at the same time making for a more efficient allocation of resources.

The Accumulation of Conventional Capital

The expenditure data from the participants in the program can be interpreted in a number of different ways. In one sense, they have policy implications in terms of where effective consumer demand can be expected to grow as a result of transfer payments. When combined with expenditure data from those paying the positive income taxes to support the transfer program, the data could be used to determine the kind of problems that might arise with the implementation of a universal cash transfer program.

I prefer to emphasize a different aspect of the data, however. In a longer-run context, a key question is whether participants in the program use the cash transfer to enhance their material well-being, or whether they use it to substitute for alternative means of support. An important question is whether they use the income to make investments in assets that increase their earning ability in the future, or whether they use it in direct consumption. The accumulation of assets, either in the form of human capital or conventional capital, is an important means of building income-producing capability.

There are at least two dimensions to the accumulation of conventional capital. For the self-employed farm operator, for example, the accumulation of machinery and equipment, buildings, and other physical improvements on the farm can be an important source of income streams in the future. But the accumulation of capital assets in the household, both of the wage earner and the self-employed, is also important. Consumer durables such as dishwashers, washing machines, and other substitutes for household labor represent an improvement in household technology. Such improvements can release time of the housewife either for work in market activities or for more intensive activities with her children and husband. In the long run, such developments increase the lifetime earning potential of the family.

There is some evidence that the program does lead to such developments both for household and farm activities.[10] Summary measures of the effects of the program indicate an increase in nonreal estate net worth of both black and white rural wage-working families, and a decrease in the net worth of farm families. The increase in net worth for black families is less than for white families, a result of large marginal propensities for loan debts. The decline for farm families resulted from the large effect of the program on farm production capital.

On the surface, the large debt incurred by the black rural wage-working families might suggest the need for educational and training programs that provide instruction on how better to handle their financial affairs. However, if this debt is used to build up stocks of durable goods under the protection of the income maintenance program, the implication might be very different. And there is evidence that at least part of the debt was used for this purpose.

Certainly this appears to be the case for the farm families who increased their farm production capital. In fact, their accumulation of capital appeared to have been sufficiently large to lower the technical efficiency of farm production in the short run, inasmuch as output did not immediately expand as much as total input. If the short-run nature of the experiment caused the families to use most of the income transfer for durable goods, the longer-run effect on technical efficiency might be different. But here we come up against the problems associated with the short-run nature of the experiment. The savings-investment behavior of the families might be quite different if the program were permanent, so conclusions from these experimental results should be drawn with caution.

10. W. Keith Bryant and Christine J. Hager, "Consumer Durables, Cars, Liquid Assets and Debts of Wage-Working Families," and Bryant, "Consumer Durables, Cars, Liquid Assets, Short-term Farm Capital and Nonreal Estate Debts of Farm Families," both in *Rural Income Maintenance Experiment,* vol. 5, chaps. 2 and 3, respectively.

The results from the analysis of housing consumption[11] seem consistent with the above findings, although the results are mixed and limit the robustness with which conclusions can be formed. However, among those who did not own their housing at the beginning of the experiment, the rate of home purchases was higher for experimental families than for control families. In addition, there was a tendency for home purchases to be made at a younger age. These results are consistent with those that showed families building their stock of conventional capital with income transfers.

The Accumulation of Human Captial

The accumulation of human capital may have more important effects on the long-run income-producing capability of the families than the accumulation of conventional capital. Although the results are again quite mixed, a rather consistent picture emerges that suggests increased accumulation of human capital as a result of the program. The story has to be told by piecing together bits and pieces from various studies.

One significant aspect of the picture is the rather large proportional withdrawal of wives from the labor force. Unfortunately, no time accounting within the household was undertaken so we do not know whether the wives devoted more of their increased household time to care of their children. Moreover, at least one indirect test of such a hypothesis was negative. For the rural wage earners, the experimental/control differentials were larger for wives with school-age children than for wives with preschool children.[12] Had this result been the opposite, we could have surmised that time withdrawn from the market economy was at least influenced by the need to take care of children. But in any case, the shift from market activities to household activities at least makes it possible for wives to give more time to household production, and to the rearing of their children.

There was a similar tendency for dependents in the experimental group to work and earn less than dependents in the control group. Moreover, for all three subpopulations of wage earners, the experimental response was largest for dependents eighteen to twenty years of age. One possible explanation for this differential response is that more dependents in experi-

11. Aaron C. Johnson, Jr., "Housing Consumption," in ibid., chap. 1.
12. See U.S. Department of Health, Education, and Welfare, "The Rural Income Maintenance Experiment: Summary Report" (HEW, November 1976; processed), pp. 27–31.

mental families entered post-secondary educational institutions.[13] Again, answers to this question require further analysis of the data. All we can conclude is that the observed withdrawal from market activities would have permitted dependents to give more time to education and training. The presumption that this would occur is strong because of the short time horizon of the experiment and the fact that future income would not be taxed at the relatively high program tax rates. With a permanent program, this form of evasion would probably be less, leading to rather different results from those of a temporary experiment.

Another aspect of human capital formation is improved nutrition. Here also there were some rather encouraging and positive results suggesting that some of the disadvantaged did use their increased income to improve their diets.[14] It should be noted that the extent of dietary deficiencies was more widespread in North Carolina than in Iowa, a reflection in part of the lower per capita income in that region in the absence of the program. Fully 60 percent of the families in the North Carolina sample had inadequate calcium intake, with the figure for iron almost 50 percent. About a third of the sample families in North Carolina had inadequate vitamin C intake.

The tax had little, if any, influence on the quality of diets of the Iowa families. However, there is strong evidence that it had a beneficial effect on the overall quality of diets of the North Carolina families. Furthermore, there is considerable evidence that the families used the additional resources at their disposal to acquire foods that improved their intake of nutrients in which their diets were particularly deficient.

In their chapter, O'Connor, Madden, and Prindle point out that the cost-effectiveness of the negative income tax as a means of improving diets was low compared to other means of accomplishing this goal.[15] However, the comparisons are not quite valid, since there is no reason for the full costs of the program to be charged against nutrition per se. The significant point is that the program did lead to improved nutrition for low-income groups with dietary deficiencies, and that this enhances human capital formation within the household.

The results for health care, another aspect of human capital formation,

13. Ibid., pp. 31–34.
14. J. Frank O'Connor, J. Patrick Madden, and Allen M. Prindle, "Nutrition," in ibid., chap. 6.
15. Ibid., pp. 68–73.

were more mixed.[16] Perhaps the most significant finding was that children appear to have had an improved health status as a consequence of the experiment. Although the relationships were not statistically significant, a relatively large estimated experimental effect was observed for each of three indicators: the number of days in bed, the incidence of chronic conditions, and the incidence of chronic conditions that limit school attendance—all of which declined in association with the experimental effect.

For the adults, on the other hand, the expectations that a negative income tax program would increase the use of medical care and improve health status received little support from the empirical analyses. There was never a coherent overall pattern, and many apparent effects contradicted the theory. It should be noted with respect to health status, however, that the data were largely from self-evaluation. As Kerachsky notes, reporting chronic conditions may be an ex post rationalization when there is an experimentally induced disincentive to work. This phenomenon is less likely with young people, and it is here that the positive response was found. So we can conclude that the program probably does improve the health status of the population.

The results for school performance of children also provide evidence of a positive effect on human capital formation.[17] Improvement in school performance in Iowa was negligible, as it was in the sample of older children from North Carolina families. But the sample of second-through-eighth-grade students from North Carolina families exhibited statistically significant responses for four measures of school performance. Here there was a 30 percent reduction in absenteeism, a 6.7 percent increase in comportment grade point average, a 6.2 percent increase in academic grade point average, and an 18.9 percent improvement in the deviation between achievement test scores and expected grade equivalent.

The sample is representative of an intellectually impoverished group in both states. Although the results were not uniformly supportive, the results from North Carolina for the elementary school students do suggest that a universal income maintenance program may lead to overall improvements in school performance and increased educational attainment. Perhaps most noteworthy was the 30 percent reduction in North Carolina

16. Stuart H. Kerachsky, "State of Health and the Utilization of Medical Care," in *Rural Income Maintenance Experiment*, vol. 5, chap. 5.

17. Rebecca Maynard and David L. Crawford, "School Performance," in ibid., vol. 6, pt. 2, chap. 12.

in absences for those in the second-to-eighth-grade sample. The 19 percent increase in achievement test scores is also noteworthy.

Finally, migration and mobility represent forms of human capital in their own right. As noted above, there are positive experimental effects in the sense that those on the experiment were more likely to move. Although the effect was significant only for those families with a wage earner at the beginning of the experiment, the results do suggest an increase in capital formation in this form.

In conclusion, there is considerable evidence that the program encouraged the accumulation of human capital by the family. Nutrition was improved by those nutritionally impoverished and there was some tendency for a general improvement in health status; school performance was improved, at least among the younger groups. At the same time, wives were able to give more attention to household activities, and many young people were enabled to withdraw from labor market activities and use this time for training and self-improvement. In summary, there may be a longer-run increase in the supply of labor services offered to the economy that more than offsets the short-run reduction.

Psychological Well-Being and Marital Dissolution

The income maintenance payments had little measurable effect on a wide variety of measures of psychological well-being.[18] Effects were generally small, scattered, and unstable over time, both for the groups as a whole and for major subgroups. Moreover, effects did not vary systematically with the level of guarantee or tax rate on earned income.

Two policy implications can be drawn from these results, and Middleton draws both of them. The first is that, although there was no evidence of an experimental effect on psychological well-being, there was also no evidence that the income maintenance program undermined self-respect or brought a reduction in self-esteem. There is a common belief, of course, that income maintenance programs would have such effects.

The second policy implication, also a negative one, is that moderate increases in income alone, with other elements of socioeconomic status remaining relatively constant, cannot be expected to have a major sociopsychological impact. Put somewhat differently but more to the point, a modest income maintenance program should not be regarded as a panacea for the social and personal ills of the poor in rural America.

18. Russell Middleton, "Psychological Well-Being," in *Rural Income Maintenance Experiment,* vol. 7, chap. 7.

An income maintenance program could be expected to have contradictory effects on marriage stability. On the positive side, it could be expected to raise levels of satisfaction with living standards, reduce marital strain, and lower rates of marital dissolution. However, a reduction in the financial dependence of partners in the marriage due to income maintenance payments could lessen the constraints on marital dissolution. Which of these is more important is an empirical question.

Middleton and Haas argue that there is a slight hint of a negative effect on marital dissolution in the data from the rural experiment.[19] But Hannan's fascinating disentangling of the results suggests that the nature of the relationship is much more complex, and one requiring further analysis.[20]

Hannan's important caveat aside, it seems unlikely that a modest income maintenance program is likely to have a major impact on either psychological well-being or on marriage as an institution. With respect to marriage per se, it is not likely that a short-term experiment can tell us very much in a definitive way in any case.

Political Behavior

The impact of the income maintenance program on political behavior is important from a policy standpoint, for it may shape the constraints on policymakers in the future. Experimental data were obtained on involvement in the 1970 statewide elections and the 1972 presidential election. The analysis suggests that there were positive experimental impacts on voting and more comprehensive measures of political participation for married men, married women, and female heads of families for both the 1970 and 1972 election.

The change in voting probabilities among the experimental group compared to the control group was on the order of 5–10 percent. Heffernan argues that these effects are either large or small, depending on individual perspective of changes that might be expected.[21] But Hannan speculates that increases of 5–10 percent in voting percentages that are localized in the population, for example, in the lower class, is sufficient to alter a good many election outcomes. His argument would appear to have

19. Russell Middleton and Linda Haas, "Marital Dissolution and Family Interaction," in ibid., chap. 8.

20. Michael T. Hannan, this volume.

21. Joseph Heffernan, "Political Behavior," in *Rural Income Maintenance Experiment*, vol. 6, chap. 13.

special force if a state or region, such as the Southeast, had a large proportion of the population made up of the poor.

Hannan also makes another point that has important implications. This is that the income maintenance experiments create a new and potentially strong link between the individual and the state. He argues that, just as participation in organizations linked to the state and used for political socialization (schools, for example) leads to increased political activity, so might participation in government programs.

In my view there are two other factors that may lead to a considerable understatement of the potential impact of the program on political behavior. In the first place, the stakes of the program were relatively modest. If the size of the income transfers were larger, there might be more substantial political participation to protect the income base, or to enlarge it.

Second, and perhaps more important, the experiment was indeed an experiment—and advertised as such—and it had a definite cutoff point after only three years. Much of the potential dynamics of the political process was probably neutralized as participants did not see the program as one they needed to defend or which had expansion potential. Equally important, there was less of a tendency for political entrepreneurs to emerge and to cultivate and mobilize political forces.

Given Hannan's two points about the results, and the "sterilization" of the political processes by the very nature of the experiment, the results appear to have rather important implications. A permanent income maintenance program that continued long enough to enable political leadership to emerge might have substantial political consequences.

Administrative Considerations

A number of administrative policy implications appear to be emerging from the combination of the urban and rural income maintenance experiments. A few of these are worth singling out, although a detailed analysis could lead to a substantial paper in its own right.

One implication is that there seems to be no overriding justification for differentiating income maintenance programs by geographic region or by ethnic groups. There clearly were differences in response between the Iowa and North Carolina samples in the case of the rural experiment, and there were similar differences among ethnic groups, some of which are rather anomalous. But for the most part these differences appear to be primarily due to differences in economic circumstances. The differentials in ethnic response, in particular, do not seem to be in directions that would be of any concern, and those differences that have occurred appear to be partly due to experimental and analytical problems.

On the other hand, there appear to be differences between wage earners and the self-employed that require administrative differentiation. The behavior of wage earners was broadly similar and independent of whether they were in urban or rural areas. But the self-employed faced a different opportunity set, and had different degrees of freedom, both in terms of their economic alternatives and the way in which they reported their income. Their household production made their income-reporting a great deal more complicated. Because of the possibility of evasion in reporting, and of errors of memory, the monitoring process was much more difficult. If an effective and efficient income maintenance program is to be established for the self-employed, a great deal more research will be required to devise an appropriate system.[22]

The rather discouraging failure of the participants to understand the nature of the program also has important administrative implications. This appeared to be a more serious problem in the rural than in the urban experiment, and may reflect the lower level of education of this group. It is also possible that the demands of the experiment itself were burdensome and created confusion. In a regular program that is less saddled with obtaining research data, participants might grasp the basic principles with more ease. In any case, there is a definite need for additional instruction and assistance in understanding the program.

Finally, much has been learned about the administration of an income maintenance program. For example, a carry-over provision was an innovation of the rural experiment, and this is now recognized as appropriate for all such programs. But solutions to other problems are yet to be worked out. For example, Primus points out that underreporting of farm assets and farm income among the rural self-employed was much more likely to increase program costs than any expected labor response among farmers.[23] This underlines the importance of the administrative dimensions of the problem.

22. Upper-income farmers also avoid taxes, with a substantial cost to the government treasury. My comments do not imply a double standard, but rather the recognition of a problem that arises in comparing the self-employed with wage earners.

23. Wendell E. Primus, "Impact of Data Errors upon Treatment Estimates of Farm Population," in *Rural Income Maintenance Experiment*, vol. 2, chap. 3.

General Equilibrium Effects

Most of the analysis of the data has been conducted in a partial equilibrium framework. Very little attention has been given to second-order effects of a universal income maintenance program, or to the more general effect on the economy. For the most part the wage rate has been assumed to be unaffected by labor withdrawal, the exception being the implicit wage of the self-employed. Other general equilibrium effects have been ignored as well.

These general equilibrium effects deserve more attention since in some cases they may not be inconsequential. Moreover, they constitute a mixed bag. In some respects they will tend to mitigate the negative consequences of the negative income tax, while in other respects they may create additional problems for policymakers. The potential importance of such effects is amply demonstrated by the medicare and medicaid programs. The increased demand for the services generated by these programs in the face of a relatively inelastic supply of such services, at least in the short run, has bid up the cost so much that recent data suggest the poor are paying more for medical care than they did prior to the programs. And it does not help to note that part of this consequence is an aberration due to the supply-restrictive power of the American Medical Association. The consequences are real, and to the best of my knowledge they were largely unexpected.

Perhaps the best way to start this analysis is with the labor supply response. Although the wage-hour reductions of husbands is very small, the overall family wage-hour reduction of 13 percent cannot be ignored. Most of the studies I have seen suggest that the demand for labor is inelastic in the short run. Hence, the reduction in labor supplied could result in a substantial increase in market wages, just as with the implicit wages of the self-employed. This increase in the wage rate would tend to offset the disincentive effects of the negative income tax, and make the net supply effect smaller than the measured results suggest.

The 13 percent reduction is not an estimate of the total reduction in labor supply in the economy, however, since the poor make up only a fraction of the total labor force. Two points are important in evaluating the overall impact. First, as previously noted, there is a regional or geographic concentration of the rural poor. Bawden estimates that the eight states he used for the aggregation of results represented 28 percent of the low-income, rural nonfarm population of the United States in 1970.[24] Similarly, the poor self-employed in agriculture are also concentrated in the Southeast. Hence, an observable and not insignificant increase in wage rates would be expected in the regions where the poor are concentrated—in this case, particularly in the Southeast.

Second, the low-income groups tend to be unskilled and concentrated in particular industries. In the Southeast, for example, they would tend to be concentrated in wage employment in agriculture. Hence, one could expect sizable wage increases in certain industries—primarily, the industries employing the unskilled. More generally, there would be a change in the wage structure in the economy, with wages for the unskilled rising relative to those for the skilled.

Thus, we could expect to see some narrowing of the regional disparities in wage rates, and a narrowing of the wage structure, as a result of a universal implementation of the program.[25] The rise in the wage rate would offset some part of the direct disincentive effect of the tax. And interestingly enough, the higher wage rate could, in principle, induce sufficient positive supply response on the part of those not covered by the program so that there need not be a net reduction in the aggregate labor supplied to the economy. To say anything sensible about this, however, would require much more empirical knowledge about the labor markets.

There are other general equilibrium effects to be considered if a full national program were to be implemented. First, the shift in wage structure would induce a shift in the product mix, with industries dependent on unskilled labor declining in importance. It is true that in the aggregate the poor farmer and rural wage earner produce only a small proportion of total agricultural output, and therefore program-induced changes in the quantity and cost of such output are expected to contribute little to the cost of a national program. But to the extent that these groups are asso-

24. D. Lee Bawden, "Work and Income Response of Rural Wage Earners" (University of Wisconsin–Madison, Institute for Research on Poverty, October 4, 1976; processed), pp. 29–30.

25. Butler and Heckman have noted a similar effect in the recent convergence in black-white wage ratios. They argue that an important (and neglected) part of this convergence is due to the voluntary withdrawal of low-skill workers from the labor force due to participation in income transfer programs. Richard Butler and James J. Heckman, "The Government's Impact on the Labor Market Status of Black Americans: A Critical Review," Working Paper 183 (National Bureau of Economic Research, Center for Economic Analysis of Human Behavior and Social Institutions, 1977; processed).

ciated with individual labor-intensive enterprises, there could be sizable impacts on individual commodities.

Whether these impacts would be large or not would depend on whether the increase in wage rate induces the adoption of labor-saving technology. While the adoption of such technology might protect our trade position in such products, the employment effects might be considerable. On balance, then, we could expect to see a shift away from industries that are intensive in unskilled labor, or a shift in the labor-intensity of those industries. In either case, the spillover effects of a generalized program could be sizable and negative. Moreover, there would tend to be an increase in the average skill-intensity of the economy, which would ultimately have an effect on the aggregate demand for education and training.

An example of an industry that might be affected by such a policy is that of tobacco. Until a way is found to mechanize the harvesting of the tobacco, it is likely to become noncompetitive on the export market if there is a substantial increase in the wage rate.

Another instance in which the general equilibrium aspects of the labor market might become important is what might best be described as the short-run dynamics of the market. Two aspects should be considered: (1) the problem of overtime for an individual industry, and (2) the situation of tightness in the aggregate labor market when there is full employment. The results suggest that groups that are permanently attached to the labor force tend not to withdraw totally from the labor force but to make small adjustments at the margin. Thus they may not be particularly responsive to overtime rates to induce them to supply additional labor when demand is strong. This problem is compounded by the substantial withdrawal rates of women and dependents as a result of the increased marginal tax rate. Since these tend to be the groups given employment in a period of tight demand, the firms may find themselves facing a rather inelastic labor supply in a period of strong demand, whether or not they want to increase their production activities by extending shifts or using additional workers.

Similarly, it is when the economy is approaching full employment that marginal workers are brought into the economy. With the protection of a negative income tax program, there may be less of a supply of women and young people to bring into the economy. Under both circumstances there may be more upward pressure on wages in periods of tightness in the labor market than there would be in the absence of the program. To the extent that wage rates lack flexibility on the down side, the net effect may be a tendency for wages to rise over time.

These general equilibrium effects in the labor market may give rise to political consequences different from those considered in the experiment. A private sector faced both with higher taxes to support an income transfer program, and higher wage rates as a consequence of the program, may become politically active against it.

As a final point, it should be noted that a consideration of the general equilibrium effects could make the issue of the tax rate more important. There was somewhat more evidence of a response to the tax rate in the rural experiment than there was in the urban experiment. To take one example: when the implicit tax rate was increased by five points (from 45 to 50 percent), Bawden found that the reduction in wage hours for the family as a whole increased from 13 to 15 percent.[26] If this reduction should be sharply higher for tax rates approaching 100 percent, it seems clear that the issue of the appropriate tax rate is not inconsequential.

Research Suggestions

Research begets more research, and the income maintenance experiments, and the analyses they have stimulated, are no exception to the rule. The many studies and analyses raise as many questions as they answer, and any attempt here to do justice to the rich research potential in the data already at hand would be pretentious.

Some questions that have been raised by the rural experiment could productively be explored in further research, however. The objective in the present section is the rather modest one of speaking to these questions.

My interpretation of the data that bear on the accumulation of human capital suggests that an income maintenance program may do more toward this end than many have believed possible. Moreover, it suggests that such programs might have long-run positive effects on the supply of labor that outweigh the negative effects occurring in the short run. If this interpretation is correct, it suggests the importance of further work with life cycle models and with the intergenerational transfer of assets and wealth. In fact, the intergenerational transmission of poverty status may be as important a question as any raised by the experiment. Aside from

26. D. Lee Bawden, "Income and Work Response of the Family," in *Rural Income Maintenance Experiment*, vol. 3, pt. 1, chap. 2, table 22.

234

G. Edward Schuh

Hannan's very valuable contribution to this conference, the issue has not received much attention. Whether people are indeed trapped in a culture of poverty has an important bearing on what program costs will be over the longer run. We need a great deal more research that can provide answers to this question.

The interpretation of the data bearing on the accumulation of human capital, as well as other problems, is prejudiced by the segmented nature in which the analyses have been conducted to date. Such specialization was probably imperative as a first step in the analysis of the mass of data bearing on such a broad spectrum of problems. But it can be quite misleading, and as Hannan's synthesis suggests, there may be more cohesion and substantive results in the data than is immediately obvious. A second round of analysis that approaches the data with more comprehensive models should have a high payoff.

The way time withdrawn from the labor market is used is a basic determinant of the welfare gains and losses to society. Questions such as the following arise: Do the wives give more attention to their children, thereby making them more productive in the future? Do they spend their increased household hours on self-improvement, or are they spent in consumptive leisure activities? Are the household work activities of the husband reduced, thereby enabling him to specialize in his market activities and possibly to be more productive? And do the young people use their increased leisure in consumption activities? Or do they use it for self-improvement as well?

We really do not know the answers to these questions. And until we do, we will be far from knowing what the net benefits of an income maintenance program are, either in the short or long run. Careful studies of the allocation of time in the household are required as a basis for understanding this critical sector of the economy and the ultimate consequences of an income maintenance program.

There were very few attempts to make cost/benefit analyses of the program or to calculate cost-effectiveness in attaining certain goals. Given the multiple goals that an income maintenance program can ultimately have, such calculations will be inherently complex. Moreover, to the extent that the program takes on the characteristics of an investment program, social rates of return become equally as important. Given the rather broad range of policy instruments that can be used to attain some of the relevant goals, the attempt to evaluate the cost-effectiveness, and the rates of return to society of the various programs, takes on added importance.

To do such research in an appropriate way, and to design more effective income maintenance programs, requires more research on policy goals. The useful interchange stimulated by the Mahoney-Mahoney paper at the Brookings conference on the urban experiment raised important questions about just what the goals of policy are. Do we want to make incomes in this country more equal? Or are we more concerned with the opportunity to earn income? If it is incomes, whose incomes are we talking about? Should our concern be for individuals? Or for families? Or for those actually earning the income? Without answers to such questions as these, we cannot proceed very far with a useful analysis of the data. Certainly we are limited in the valid policy implications we can draw. Social scientists should, in my view, give a great deal more attention to identifying the socioeconomic goals of society. Their analyses will become much more relevant if they do, and their contributions to policymaking more precise and specific.

Income maintenance programs have inherent disincentives associated with them, especially in the short run. Research designed to develop institutional means by which these disincentives could be offset or mitigated would appear to have a high payoff. Such research requires more institutional creativity than economists are prone to come up with, and it requires that we have a forward-looking stance rather than what has been our endemic concern with the past. Now that social experimentation has become acceptable, the possibility of evaluating institutional innovations has improved. The potential return from research that designs such institutions is now considerably higher than it was in the past.

The difficulties raised by the experiment with the self-employed suggests a whole range of research needs. New techniques should be sought for the correct valuation of farm assets and housing in the absence of a robust market-pricing system for such assets. Systems need to be designed for the accurate and timely reporting of income and expenses. And improved auditing systems are needed to spot missing or obviously inaccurate data. These are just a few of the many areas where additional research is needed to improve the administration of income maintenance programs for the self-employed.

Very little attention has been given to date to the general equilibrium effects of income maintenance programs, and this may be a major shortcoming of our research efforts. More attention needs to be focused in this area.

Similarly, not much attention has been given to the disincentive effects of higher taxes on upper income groups that might be required to support a universal income maintenance program. That is probably because we are only now beginning to grasp the nature, complexity, and relative magnitude of the costs that might be associated with the programs themselves. But sound policy will depend on knowledge of these other disincentive effects as well.

Many of the analyses of the program, including mine, have generally assumed that the underlying base for comparison is an economy without distortions. This is not the case, of course, and a large part of the justification for income maintenance programs is to replace the hodgepodge of income maintenance programs we now have, many of which have strong elements of a negative income tax. An analysis of the net costs and benefits of a universal program will have to take into account its displacement of existing programs and the distortions they have already introduced.

Some Concluding Thoughts

Income maintenance programs, as presently conceived and as tested in the urban and rural experiments, are fairly modest. Paradoxically, we may be in danger of expecting too much from them along certain lines, while at the same time underestimating their potential both for good and mischief along other lines. It seems clear that income transfers of a modest size can have only a marginal direct effect in alleviating the social and economic woes of the poor in our society. But at the same time they may have important long-run effects in some unexpected ways, such as in mitigating the intergenerational transmission of poverty.

Finally, descriptive data on the participants in the rural experiment point up the extent to which the rural poor are illiterate, undereducated, and unskilled. This serves to emphasize the continuing need for effective human resource development programs directed to these population groups. Although income maintenance programs may be an important means of helping these groups make the appropriate investments in themselves, more direct public support for such investments would be desirable.

Comment by James T. Bonnen

Since Edward Schuh does such a superb job of evaluating the policy-relevant outcomes of the rural income maintenance experiment, I shall place my emphasis on the interaction between welfare and farm policy, and between welfare and rural development policy, both of which depend on the unique economic characteristics of the agricultural sector. Schuh mentions these characteristics in a brief paragraph but their full implications might easily be missed. Let me spell them out more fully here:

1. A low price elasticity of demand at the farm level, which in the short run causes large fluctuations in price, and thus income, for relatively modest changes in output.

2. At the high levels of income now common in this society, a very low income elasticity of demand for total farm output. As a consequence, demand grows very slowly and is generally limited to population change.

3. Continuing rapid technological change, which tends to shift the supply function to the right far more rapidly than demand.

4. Given the highly atomistic or competitive structure of the industry, a short-run downward pressure on prices leading to a longer-run phenomenon that forces the entire industry toward lower equilibrium.

5. Resources, once committed to specialized uses (mistakenly in an ex post view), become fixed due to a subsequent divergence between acquisition and salvage prices of these assets. This means that once there is an overcommitment relative to future market needs, excess capacity persists. Given the nature of demand and supply, the competitive industrial structure, and persistent excess capacity, there is a continuing downward pressure on prices and income that is chronic.

The consequence of these characteristics is that over time, supply shifts to the right faster than demand, and the industry exists in a condition of chronic low returns. This situation was characteristic of the agricultural sector from the great depression until the early 1970s. Over this period labor resources were squeezed out of agriculture at an incredible rate, but without ever reaching equilibrium as expected by neoclassical theory. Because of the specialized, spatially isolated capital structure, assets once committed remained fixed in production despite adverse market conditions. One observes substantial divergence between the acquisition price and salvage values for most farm assets. These classic characteristics of an industrialized agriculture have led to a condition of chronic excess capacity in land, labor, and capital, and continuing or chronically depressed prices and incomes for farmers.

In the period from 1965 to 1973, the United States changed its high price support policies to allow agriculture to operate at world market prices. At the same time, the United States began to sell off its accumulated stocks of grains and other foods and some of the excess capacity of the sector began to be absorbed.[27] This was the consequence of a number of events, including a substantial increase in demand for food as successful economic development in the less developed countries increased per capita incomes. The period ended in disastrous weather, which reduced production dramatically in Russia, China, and other countries, reducing U.S. and world grain stocks to near zero in 1973–74.

When grain stocks in government hands were eliminated, prices went through the roof. Thus in the period since 1974, U.S. agriculture has appeared to be in an equilibrium with little or no excess capacity in land, labor, or capital invested in agriculture. Under these conditions, any increase in output would come at full opportunity cost. This is a situation that has not prevailed for more than fifty years and it has great implications for the cost of food to the consumer.

The Implications of a Negative Income Tax for Agriculture

Great uncertainty has returned to any predictions about the world or U.S. food situation. This is not made any less uncertain now in 1976–77 when there is some buildup again in grain stocks and wheat and corn prices have begun to fall. The impact of a negative income tax on agriculture depends heavily on the food situation the world will face over the next few decades. There is the possibility that chronic excess capacity and depressed prices will return. Others predict that severe shortages and excessively high food prices will continue. My own expectation is that there will be great uncertainty in agricultural markets, with periods of shortage alternating with periods of surplus supplies.

Schuh suggests that on balance a negative income tax would probably increase farm output. In most industries the impact would not be large, but given the low price and income elasticities in agriculture, substantial price changes could follow from quite small changes in output. If this occurred during periods of excess capacity and depressed prices, it would exacerbate an already chronically depressed price and income situation. If it occurred during a period of shortage and tight markets, it could make a contribution to restraining explosive prices.

More importantly, large fluctuations in entry to, or exit from, the negative income tax population could cause fluctuations in farm output, thus

27. For a detailed and lucid explanation of this transformation see Dale E. Hathaway, "Food Prices and Inflation," *Brookings Papers on Economic Activity, 1:1974*, pp. 63–109.

adding to the basic instability of agriculture. Any such increase in instability would be offset by income from the negative income tax only on the low end of the income distribution in farming. Also, given the highly skewed distribution of output and income in agriculture, any price effects would be distributed more toward the upper end of the scale in output and income, so that the major impact would probably be on those who are not eligible for the negative income tax.

Indeed, the distributional issues are significant. It is likely that the impact of a negative income tax would be very different for (1) larger commercial farms, (2) part-time farmers who have adequate nonfarm incomes, and on (3) low-income farmers or those eligible for the negative income tax. An extreme example of differential market impact of prior changes is to be found in the explosion in commodity prices in 1973–74. In this instance, more than 90 percent of the entire increase in income accrued to the 15 percent of farms with gross incomes greater than $40,000; about 70 percent of the increase accrued to the 5 percent of farms with gross farm incomes $100,000 and above.[28] The explanation appears to lie in the fact that the short-run excess capacity in agriculture in 1973 was found in the largest farm sector. Thus it was these larger farmers who were able to take advantage of the increase in prices.

In passing, I should like to warn against thinking about farmers who may be eligible for the negative income tax as if they were potential beneficiaries of farm policy. They are, in fact, the long-term casualties of the industrial development of U.S. agriculture and are only marginally assisted by farm policies. Despite the potentialities discussed above, I doubt that a negative income tax would have a major impact on farm policy or on commercial agriculture. Its greatest impact clearly would be on rural development policy and on rural development per se.

The Implications of a Negative Income Tax for Rural Development

First, let me make it clear that there is no rural development policy in this country. There are only uncoordinated and generally incoherent patterns of programs. A coherent policy is yet to become a reality for rural society.

Schuh clearly points out the impact of a negative income tax on rural development. A negative income tax appears to cause a decline in wage

28. U.S. Department of Agriculture, Economic Research Service, *Farm Income Statistics,* Statistical Bulletin 576 (USDA, July 1977), tables 1D, 2D, pp. 52–53.

work for rural nonfarm labor markets, creating a drag on development potential. It also increases the investment in human capital—in its many dimensions of health, education, nutrition, and the like. Schuh believes, as I do, that the centerpiece in any coherent rural development policy should be investment in human capital. The proposition that investments in land, physical capital, and other material things will trickle down to solve the welfare problems of human beings in the rural sector has been tested—and it has not happened. At least, the distribution of benefits from these investments has been quite inequitable.

Schuh also points out that the impact of a negative income tax on job mobility and migration could be significant. If the post-1970 return migration in rural areas continues, its importance could increase. Some of this reverse migration is to farms but I doubt that it will significantly affect agriculture. Rather, the impact will be on rural society generally.

A good argument can be made that over the past century the goal of economic development of the United States has been to facilitate the transfer of resources, especially land and labor, out of rural society and its economic processes. These policies and the institutions that they have created for rural society are now dysfunctional. There is a clear need to encourage institutions that increase the investment in human capital in rural society, rather than to discourage such investment or to transfer it out of rural society.

In fact, if a negative income tax were implemented, my guess is that the investment effect on human capital might be the single most significant impact. Schuh states that "in a longer-run context, a key question is whether participants in the program use the cash transfer to enhance their material well-being, or whether they use it to substitute for alternative means of support. An important question is whether they use the income to make investments in assets that increase their earning ability in the future, or whether they use it in direct consumption. The accumulation of assets, in the form of either human capital or conventional capital, is an important means of building income-producing capability." It seems clear to me that farmers receiving negative income tax payments would increase both material and human capital while nonfarm wage earners receiving such payments would increase their investment primarily in human capital.

In my judgment, the single most important effect of the farm programs over the last forty years has been the investment impact on successful commercial farmers. This has come both through the asset inflation effect of farm programs and through farm program impacts on the cash flow of farmers. Both have increased the capability of farmers to invest in and manage new technologies—the gains that have gone primarily to the consumer over the 1920–70 period.

The human capital investment effect increases the capacity of human beings to cope with economic, technological, and social pressures. Even the reductions of income uncertainty under a negative income tax would have an induced investment effect.

Conclusion

Finally, there is a major overlooked element in the research that has been done on negative income taxation. A saturation experiment is needed. The impact of a negative income tax on rural communities is likely to be very significant, especially in the Southeast. Anyone who is familiar with the southeastern United States where a high percent of rural poverty is concentrated, and with the small town, knows that a negative income tax would have a major impact on the macroeconomic and the macropolitical behavior of those communities. It would tend to free those in economic servitude, white and black. It thus would lead to much more independent political behavior. It would lead to demographic shifts of a most unpredictable nature.

I agree with Schuh that the saturation or general equilibrium effects of a national negative income tax program need study. In fact, if we have learned anything from the uncontrolled experiments of the "great society," it is that the unintended systemic consequences of social programs more often than not swamp the intended consequences.

MARVIN M. SMITH

Summary
of Conference Discussion

The preceding chapters provided the background for
a two-day conference on the evaluation of the rural income maintenance
experiment held at the Brookings Institution on January 13 and 14, 1977.
The conference afforded the opportunity not only to evaluate the results
of the rural experiment, but also to compare these results with those from
the New Jersey experiment[1] and to contrast the operational design of the
rural experiment with those of the ongoing Gary and Seattle-Denver experiments.

The conference was marked by a spirited debate on a wide range of
issues that encompassed the theoretical difficulties that inevitably beset
such a large-scale social experiment, as well as specific operational concerns
encountered in its implementation, and, of course, the policy implications.
This chapter presents the highlights of the conference discussion.[2]

Experimental Design: A Retrospective View

The paper by Harold W. Watts and D. Lee Bawden provided a review
and assessment of the consequences of the basic decisions and omissions
that shaped the design of both the rural and New Jersey negative income

1. See Joseph A. Pechman and P. Michael Timpane, eds., *Work Incentives and
Income Guarantees: The New Jersey Negative Income Tax Experiment* (Brookings
Institution, 1975).
2. Whenever the phrase "general (dis)agreement" is used in the summary, it
should be noted that: (1) this does not indicate unanimous (dis)agreement on the
part of the conferees, but merely suggests that a majority were in (dis)accord; and
(2) no formal consensus was solicited, rather the judgment is based on the author's
appraisal of the discussion.

243

tax experiments. The authors distinguished between two types of issues: those anticipated and dealt with given the best information available and those which they referred to as "surprises," and which might have led to different results had they been anticipated in advance. Included in the former category were the variety of experimental treatments, the sample selection strategy, and the time-horizon issue; while the latter issues concerned the scarcity of *very* poor families eligible for inclusion in the sample, and the altering of the New Jersey welfare program during the urban experiment.

The Guarantees and Tax Rates

In their discussion of the guarantee and tax rates employed in both the urban and rural experiments, Watts and Bawden raised a number of points concerning the variety and range of the experimental treatments. Rather than having one guarantee-tax rate scheme (and a control group) or limiting the treatment to variations of only one or the other of those parameters, the authors clearly endorsed the strategy of applying a variety of plans that varied both (as was done in the rural and urban experiments). There was no disagreement voiced on this point by any of the conference participants.

Conference discussion of the paper initially focused on the range of the experimental treatments. In their paper, Watts and Bawden pointed out that very few families were available for analysis in the 70 percent tax rate (the highest) in both the urban and rural experiments. As a consequence, the two experiments provided little evidence for assessing the possible labor supply response of families confronted with tax rates above 50 percent. They cited the confounding effects generated by the aid to families with dependent children–unemployed parents (AFDC-UP) program in New Jersey[3]—a welfare program initiated in the state after the urban experiment was under way that covered the same popu-

---

3. The welfare payments in the generous AFDC-UP plan tended to dominate the experimental payments in two of the least generous experimental plans—those with a 50 percent guarantee and a 50 percent tax rate (the 50-50 plan) and a 75 percent guarantee and a 70 percent tax rate (the 75-70 plan). Since families were given the opportunity to choose between payments from the welfare program or the experiment, many opted for the welfare payments. This attrition significantly reduced the overall sample size, particularly in the 70 percent tax rate cell.

For a detailed discussion of this point, see Pechman and Timpane, eds., *Work Incentives and Income Guarantees,* especially the formal discussion by Henry J. Aaron, "Cautionary Notes on the Experiment," pp. 88–110.

lation—as a factor in the urban experiment, and the low policy importance attached to the 70 percent tax rate as a contributing factor in the
rural experiment (the latter led to low policy weights and few observations assigned to the 70 percent tax rate cells in the sample allocation
process). They further noted that the low breakeven levels of income—
the income levels at which payments fall to zero—associated with such a
high tax rate resulted in some families being ineligible for payments during the experiment. Although it was generally agreed that these suggested
explanations had merit, several conferees sought to explore their implications and to offer alternative causes.

One of the formal discussants suggested that the design of the Conlisk-
Watts sample allocation model[4] may have led to the relatively small number of families allocated to the 70 percent tax rate cell. He felt that some
consideration should be given to the appropriateness of the model by
reassessing its underlying assumptions. While some participants acknowledged that the allocation model may have contributed to the shortfall of
families in the 70 percent tax rate cell, there were considerable differences of opinion over its relative importance—especially given the confounding effects of the AFDC-UP program on the urban experiment's
results.

In discussing the implications of the breakeven levels of income, some
participants argued that the truncation of the sample (there was a requirement that families have incomes in the year prior to the experiment
of 150 percent or less of the official poverty line in order to be eligible for
inclusion in the sample) excluded most families with multiple earners,
thus precluding valuable information on their behavioral and attitudinal
responses. One conferee added that the fact that the marginal tax rate
changes abruptly at the breakeven point, when coupled with the truncation problems, makes the generalization to a national program very difficult. He felt this to be a potentially crucial problem because a national

4. For a description of this model, see John Conlisk and Harold Watts, "A Model
for Optimizing Experimental Designs for Estimating Response Surfaces," in American Statistical Association, *Proceedings of the Social Statistics Section* (1969), pp.
150–56. Further discussion of the model can be found in Charles E. Metcalf, "Sample
Design and the Use of Experimental Data," in Harold W. Watts and Albert Rees,
eds., *Final Report of the New Jersey Graduated Work Incentive Experiment* (University of Wisconsin–Madison, Institute for Research on Poverty, and Mathematica,
1974), vol. 2, pt. C, chap. 5. The use of the model enabled the experimenters to
make more precise estimates of experimental effects given the budgetary constraints
and the desired stratification by age and sex of household head.

negative income tax program, if instituted, would have to be merged in some continuous manner with the positive income tax.

On the same subject, another formal discussant cautioned that the sample truncation in the rural experiment may not only have yielded fewer secondary workers in the sample, but may also have caused additional estimation problems. He pointed out that recent methodological research by Hausman and Wise[5] indicates that even when considering only single-earner families, the act of sample truncation creates numerous statistical problems for nonexperimental uses of the data. While this point was noted by the participants, it was not pursued any further.

Sample Selection

In both the urban and rural experiments, a few experimental sites were carefully selected in a nonrandom manner. This type of strategy involved the studying of households "in specific localities that were thought representative of major and possibly distinct types of labor markets." An alternative option would have been to utilize the "national sample" strategy—which entails a highly dispersed but randomly selected sample "that could be readily and routinely generalized to all geographic areas or a wider range of household categories." Further, the scattered sample approach employed in the two experiments might be contrasted with the "saturation" approach—in which "all families in one or several areas are eligible for an experimental treatment."[6] After reviewing the objectives of the two experiments, as well as considering the administrative feasibility and budgetary implications of the aforementioned strategies, Bawden and Watts maintained that the scattered sample approach of predetermined sites remained the most appropriate choice. While most conferees agreed with the wisdom of this decision, a number of points were raised concerning the relative merits of the various sample strategies.

One participant thought a strong case could be made for pursuing the "saturation" approach. He argued that when only a small percentage of the people in a given locality are involved in an experiment, the results obtained might differ considerably from those resulting from a national program which would affect *all* the low-income people in the area. These

5. Jerry A. Hausman and David A. Wise, "The Evaluation of Results From Truncated Samples: The New Jersey Income Maintenance Experiment," *Annals of Economic and Social Measurement,* vol. 5 (Fall 1976), pp. 421–45.

6. The quotations are from Harold W. Watts and D. Lee Bawden, this volume, p. 58.

possible "community effects" on the tastes, attitudes, and behaviors of the people as well as employers, he contended, may not be inconsequential. While recognizing the desire to have a more representative national sample, he felt that the potential worth of saturation strategies should be reconsidered.[7]

Another conferee, concerned with the large outlay and effort expended on income maintenance experimentation covering four separate experiments, suggested that, in retrospect, a national sample could have been designed that led to well-structured site-specific experiments. These experiments, he argued, would have yielded a more representative distribution of the nation's population. In responding to this point, Watts concurred that the notion of planning and administering one large experiment in lieu of several smaller ones seemed quite appealing. However, he felt that the planning for such an endeavor—had that option been chosen—would be so time-consuming that the experiment might still be in the design stage.

Duration of the Experiment

The rural and urban (New Jersey) experiments were each conducted for a three-year period. The significance of the duration of the experiments becomes quite clear when one considers whether the behavior exhibited on the part of the experimental groups (for example, the labor supply response) simulates the long-run effects that would prevail under a permanent negative income tax or merely represents temporary responses to a short-term program. The conference participants expressed divergent viewpoints on the appropriateness of a three-year time span for the experiments. One group supported the basic arguments presented in the conference paper, namely, that extending the duration of the experiments, while desirable on some grounds, would have served to (1) postpone the availability of the final results, and (2) increase costs, which, in turn, would have reduced sample sizes (given a fixed budget).

Another group argued that the continued uncertainty about the validity of the results from a short-term experiment for a permanent program suggests that either the time span of the experiments should be increased or the duration made an explicit experimental variable. In particular, one

7. For a discussion of saturation experiments and the possible problems involved in carrying them out, see Larry L. Orr, Robinson G. Hollister, and Myron J. Lefcowitz, eds., *Income Maintenance: Interdisciplinary Approaches to Research* (Markham, 1971).

of the formal discussants found the argument of "an increased waiting time for results" to be somewhat questionable. He pointed out that a multiple duration experiment generates behavioral results in the early stages as well so that during the first three years of the experiment, families on five- or twenty-year plans, for example, should be exhibiting differential behavior.

Commenting on the budgetary concerns of a variable duration experiment, one conferee suggested that the problem may not be with the level of the budget, but rather with its allocation among different periods of treatment. He contended that the same budget would buy approximately an equivalent number of family years of information if allocated over three-, five-, or twenty-year payments. The most noteworthy difference would be that the information would be coming from different families.

After much discussion, the conference participants remained divided on the time-horizon issue. It was pointed out, however, that the design of the Seattle-Denver experiment does in fact introduce the duration of experimental treatments as a variable—with most families receiving payments for three years, some for five, and a few for twenty. The hope was expressed that the results from this experiment would provide more definitive information on this score.

Where Are the Poor?

What would a study of poor people be like without an abundance of poor people? One of the unexpected surprises in the urban experiment and the Iowa site of the rural experiment, according to Watts and Bawden, was the scarcity of families meeting the income eligibility criteria for inclusion in the samples. In the urban experiment, the authors noted that "using the income criterion of 150 percent of poverty, we found a lower density of eligible families in designated poverty areas than census data suggested; more than two-thirds were above the poverty threshold, and virtually none were below 75 percent." As far as the rural experiment was concerned, they were equally surprised to find "farmers with low incomes and low equity in their business assets, but with large gross incomes, in control of sizable business assets, and living in a style comparable to middle class families."[8] Given such experiences, the authors were prompted to ask whether the poor really existed in the numbers that the Bureau of the Census figures suggested.

8. The quotations are from Watts and Bawden, pp. 63, 64.

This inquiry drew quick responses from some of the conference participants. Most of the comments focused on the nature of Census data. One conferee thought the Census income figures used in identifying the poor are themselves suspect. According to him, there are differential underreporting effects in the Census tabulations by source of income. He further noted that a close examination of the amount of transfer payments reported in the Bureau's field surveys indicates that public assistance, for example, is underreported by nearly one-fourth to one-third.[9] As a consequence, a large amount of income in the lower 10 to 20 percent of the population simply goes unreported. In addition, he argued that any reasonable attempt to adjust the Census figures may result in merely placing individuals into higher income brackets so that "the alleged poor simply are not there."

Another participant observed that the Census projections contain very few able-bodied, prime-age male heads of households—the prime target group of the experiment—who have poverty incomes that are substantially below the poverty level. Most of them, he noted, have incomes close to the poverty line. So the fact of not finding a large number from this group, at least, is not so surprising.

Those conferees who commented on the whereabouts of the poor seemed to agree that much more accurate information is needed about the so-called poor population in order to obtain better estimates of the number of families that might be eligible for a negative income tax; but they were confident that the poor were there.

Farmers' Labor Supply Response

In his paper assessing the labor supply responses of farmers in the rural experiment, Finis Welch did not present a critique of the estimates of farmer labor supply obtained by the rural experiment's analysts, but opted instead to "spell out why we should have little interest in these estimates."[10]

Using data from the rural experiment, Welch performed some calculations of his own. In one such set of calculations, he employed a three-way split of the combined data from Iowa and North Carolina—namely,

9. For a study documenting this occurrence, see Joseph J. Minarik, "New Evidence on the Poverty Count," in American Statistical Association, *Proceedings of the Social Statistics Section* (1975), pp. 554–59.

10. This volume, p. 99.

females, males who worked off the farm in 1969, and males who did not work off the farm in 1969—to obtain "averages" of hours worked on and off farms for experimental and control farmers along with net farm income for the three years of the experiment. After cautioning that the "averages" obtained in his analysis should not be construed as accurate estimates of program effects, but instead viewed as indicative of general response patterns, Welch showed that total hours of work by the various groups changed very little. The composition of hours worked, however, changed dramatically. There was significant substitution from off-farm work to farm work. Coincidentally with this compositional change, reported farm income decreased noticeably. The author suggested as a possible explanation that only reported and not actual farm income fell for these groups, stating that "the overwhelming evidence of the analysis file is that farmers underreport income." Welch pointed out that there was a marked difference between the stated and actual tax rates faced by the treatment group —for example, a dollar of net farm income added 9 cents to taxable income in the range of taxes that included 70 percent of the participants; thus, there existed approximately a 3 to 6 percent tax rate on farm income.[11]

As a result of what he believed to be shortcomings in the experimental design (some of which are discussed below), Welch viewed the quality of the data with suspicion and thus was not inclined to place much faith in any of the results reported. During the discussion, he reaffirmed his skeptical view by noting that even though one might agree that complicating factors and unforeseen events would no doubt accompany a real world negative income tax program, it is questionable that we can simulate an average amount of such distortions in a three-year experimental program. Therefore, even though the experimental results may indicate little labor supply effect, it is debatable to conclude that there is likely to be little effect in a permanent income maintenance program. As far as he was concerned, the experimental program implemented in Iowa and North Carolina was not a textbook negative income tax but something quite different.

Welch's views provoked spirited and wide-ranging responses from the conference participants. These are discussed below under four categories: (1) estimation and related problems, (2) accounting procedures, (3) underreporting of income, and (4) general problems.

11. These estimates are based on analysis of benefits in relation to the experimenter's best estimate of "true" farm income.

Estimation

It was generally agreed that the small sample size for farmers weakened the power of the statistical tests of significance. However, some conferees questioned the wisdom of Welch's decision to aggregate experimental groups across plans and states in carrying out his analysis. Although it was done presumably to ensure the reliability of the results, some thought that the procedure combined reactions in two sites that were structurally different and thus precluded the analysis of site-specific differences in the employment and earnings of those in experimental groups.

One of the formal discussants noted that the sample size problem might have been circumvented had the author taken into consideration that a pooled analysis could have been undertaken with the appropriate use of dummy variables to identify the two sites—which, in addition, would preclude the performing of separate analysis for each state.

There was also some concern expressed that experimental families with incomes either negative or above the breakeven level might have faced different real tax rates from those confronting other experimental families assigned to the same plan. The apprehension was that since experimental families with earnings above breakeven levels were confronted with tax rates similar to those faced by control families, their behavior might be more like that of the controls. Although many of the conference participants joined Welch in acknowledging the problematic nature of this situation, some of the participants not only viewed the problem as a tractable one, but also felt the issue was somewhat exaggerated in the paper. While there was no consensus on a solution to this "breakeven issue," one conferee suggested that the problem could be handled by simply having higher guarantees or having only families with lower incomes, thereby ensuring that none of the experimental families was above the breakeven level.

Accounting Procedures

A number of problematic accounting features were addressed in the paper and debated at the conference. One problem noted in the discussion was the use of cash basis accounting in the computation of income for determining benefit payments. Under this method, costs incurred and revenues received are accounted for only when they are realized and not as they accrue. Further, the income upon which payments were made was computed on the basis of a three-month moving average, with a twelve-month carry-over of excess income or expenses to be counted in the three-month average. According to Welch, this procedure probably led to questionable behavior by some farmers, thus confounding the interpretation of the results obtained. He illustrated his point with the following example. Consider a farmer who produces durable products (corn in the case of Iowa and tobacco in North Carolina) that have rather low storage costs and who is confronted with an experimental tax rate of 70 percent. There is a real question as to whether any of the products would be sold during the period of the experiment. As long as the rural experiment was willing to subsidize 70 percent of the expenditures incurred in raising the crop, the product would be held off the market until after the experiment ended so that the revenues from the sale of the crop would be taxed at the IRS norm and not at the 70 percent rate. One conferee, however, was very skeptical that such a distortion was of major consequence. He noted that on the basis of postexperimental data, there was no evidence that goods were in fact withheld from the market until after the termination of the experiment. It was pointed out that farmers currently employ cash accounting in income tax computation, and no doubt "would press to have the privilege extended in a negative income tax."

Another feature of the rural experiment's accounting system involved the double taxation of farm assets. Welch pointed out that under the "rules of operation" as set forth in the experiment, net equity in farm-owned assets (such as farmland, buildings, machines, livestock, and grain inventories) above $20,000 was taxed directly and the revenue generated from these assets was later taxed. One of the formal discussants stated that "society does not favor income transfers to households with massive wealth, even if that wealth was accumulated out of past earnings that were taxed," and therefore felt that double taxation would probably continue. While the author was sympathetic to the idea of not paying an individual welfare "if he is sitting on $100,000 worth of land," he had some reservations as to whether double taxation of farm income would attend a national negative income tax program.

The third and, according to Welch, "the most interesting, most subtle, and most important wrinkle of the rural experiment's accounting" concerned the "carry-over" provision.[12] In his paper he demonstrated that,

12. The carry-over provision was an experimental design feature to take account of the uneven flows of farm income throughout the year. Earned income in excess of the breakeven level was carried forward for a maximum of one year and added to income in any period in which it fell below the breakeven level. Benefit payments were calculated on the basis of the sum of current income and the carry-over assigned to that period.

with the aid of the carry-over provision and the appropriate sequencing of family income, it is possible for two families with identical incomes assigned to the same experimental treatment plan to end up three years later with different benefits received.

In response to this demonstration of the gains from sequencing under the rules of the experiment, several participants felt that even if sequencing were not available, farmers were likely to seek other legal avenues to circumvent their tax liabilities. Welch acknowledged that if a national negative income tax program were put in operation for many years, most of the problems associated with the accounting system would go away. However, he maintained that his major concern was that in an experiment of short duration the incentive structure is *very* different; therefore, it is debatable whether the near zero labor supply response under this structure would prevail in a national income maintenance program.[13]

Underreporting

Perhaps the most debated issue was the underreporting of farm income for payment purposes. There was much discussion about its origin and significance with most conferees agreeing that underreporting could have compromised the quality of responses obtained during the quarterly interviews.[14]

One participant suggested that the short-term nature of the rural experiment may have generated behavioral responses such as the sequencing of income, which altered the pattern of income flows and, in turn, resulted in the actual levels of reported income to be lower than expected by the experimenters.

However, to the extent that there was some underreporting, others argued that the misreporting of income by farmers is a problem that the Internal Revenue Service has and will continue to have, and one that any national income maintenance program will have; therefore, one should not lay the underreporting issue at the doorstep of the experiment. If anything, it was contended, the rural experiment simply replicated what should be expected in an actual program.

13. It was pointed out, however, that since preenrollment income entered the calculation for the first two payments, Welch's example of what might happen may be somewhat exaggerated. It was further noted that even in his extreme example, equilibrium payments would be reached before the end of the experiment.

14. In fact, the quarterly interviews on which analyses of behavioral responses were based were first edited to remove a substantial portion of the underreporting.

There was considerable disagreement among the conference participants on the extent of the underreporting that took place. One conferee,
citing a study he had completed on the subject, indicated that in terms of
cash income and expenses, farmers on the average reported only 60 percent of what the experimenters thought their real yearly income to be—
excluding capital gains and depreciation. Further, underreporting seemed
to be concentrated in gross omissions of gross income—as opposed to
padding expenses. In addition, farmers underreported their assets—principally farm machinery and land—by between 15 and 25 percent (see
the paper by Bawden and Harrar in this volume). Some participants questioned the validity of the information since it hinged upon knowing what
the farmers' true incomes were. This point, as well as the general issue of
underreporting, was debated at length but there was no resolution of the
issue.

General Problems

The finding of a small overall change in the labor supply response of
farmers—and its use as an indicator of the relevant response in a national program—not only bothered Welch but concerned other conference participants as well. One conferee stated that since there are so many
potential biases in the data, he was unwilling to conjecture whether there
would be a large or small labor response in a national program. He added
that, in all probability, any experiment of short duration would grossly
underestimate the true income effect on labor supply and no doubt overestimate the true substitution effect.[15]

One curious finding noted in the conference paper was that farmers
tended to decrease their wage work and increase their farm work while
their farm profits decreased. Some participants suggested that this may
have resulted from an increase in the consumption value of farming (via
income in-kind). In short, the true labor supply function should not depend upon net wages and net income only but should also take into consideration the price of other commodities.

In view of the many objections concerning the origin and interpretation of the labor supply responses of farmers, some conferees suggested

15. This observation was in fact verified in the New Jersey experiment. For a discussion, see Charles E. Metcalf, "Predicting the Effects of Permanent Programs from
a Limited Duration Experiment," in Watts and Rees, eds., *Final Report of the New
Jersey Graduated Work Incentive Experiment*, vol. 2, pt. C, chap. 3.

that labor supply, as measured in hours, may not be the proper issue. In-stead, it was argued that the appropriate issue should be the "work ef-fort," as measured in output, expended by farmers. As one participant suggested, more attention should be focused on the output from farms—which, incidentally, declined very slightly. Still others felt that more con-cern should be given to the income of farmers rather than their hours of work, as an indicator of the well-being of farm families.

Perhaps one of the overriding issues in the discussion was the extent to which the rural experiment demonstrated how a negative income tax pro-gram would actually operate in the real world. Unlike the author, many conferees felt that it was a real world demonstration despite the con-founding design features and the unforeseen behavioral responses on the part of farmers. The significance of the experiment in their viewpoint was perhaps best summed up by Luther Tweeten who stated in his formal comments that, "If the experiment is in fact a demonstration of what we might expect from a negative income tax scheme actually implemented, it is important to examine the results for what they can tell us about the real world."

Wage Earners' Labor Supply Response

According to Orley Ashenfelter, the author of the conference paper on the labor supply responses of rural nonfarm wage earners, "The results of the rural negative income tax experiment show an unambiguous average decline in the work effort of all family members in the experimental group of wage earners." He arrived at this conclusion after reviewing the results obtained by the rural experiment's analysts as well as his own estimates derived from the experimental data. Ashenfelter's calculations showed that the wage income of husbands declined by 8 percent and that of wives by 27 percent, while family wage income (the weighted sum of the results for husbands and wives) averaged a 12 percent decline. These estimates, as noted by the author, are quite close to the regression estimates com-puted by the experiment's analysts, except for a discrepancy in the ex-perimental effect on total family wage income—which can be attributed, at least in part, to the presence of additional wage earners in the analysts' family estimates. In addition, these results from the rural experiment, though somewhat smaller, closely resemble the estimates calculated by

Robert Hall of the urban experiment's effect.[16] However, Ashenfelter points out that since there are differing estimates of the effect of the urban experiment on labor supply,[17] the comparability of the results between the two experiments depends on whose urban estimates are used.

Nonetheless, the results of the rural experiment drew mixed responses from the conference participants—some tending to accept them as reasonable estimates, with others placing less faith in them. During the course of the debate concerning these results, two topics tended to dominate the discussion: (1) the experimental treatments, and (2) the ramifications of program costs.

Experimental Treatments

A number of conferees voiced concern about the proposition that the implicit tax rate in most welfare programs (including the rural experiment) is not in fact the statutory tax rate. Ashenfelter suggested that this possibility might be illustrated within the context of a pure tax avoidance model. He proceeded by noting that, on a pure tax avoidance basis, one would expect people in a negative income tax program to report less earned income simply because that would raise their payments—as indeed occurred in the rural experiment. An interesting question then becomes whether a change in reported income reflects an actual reduction in earnings or simply less accurate reporting of the same level of earnings. According to Ashenfelter, one way to approach this issue is to consider whether tax avoidance varies with the guarantee or tax rate. He argued that tax avoidance probably does not vary with changes in the guarantees because, once they are fixed, those with higher guarantees have no more incentive to avoid additional taxes than those with lower guarantees. The tax rate, on the other hand, fosters tax avoidance since the extra amount received from a change in reported income varies directly with the tax rate. Since the experimental data showed no effect for the guarantee and large effects for the tax rate, Ashenfelter suggested that a plausible interpretation might be that there was no actual change in labor supply or earnings but simply a change in the amount of earnings reported.

16. See Robert F. Hall, "Effects of the Experimental Negative Income Tax on Labor Supply," in Pechman and Timpane, eds., *Work Incentives and Income Guarantees,* pp. 115–47.

17. See Aaron, "Cautionary Notes on the Experiment," and Albert Rees and Harold W. Watts, "An Overview of the Labor Supply Results," in Pechman and Timpane, eds., *Work Incentives and Income Guarantees.*

There was no disagreement among the conferees on the validity of the author's reasoning concerning tax avoidance; however, some participants doubted that this was the appropriate interpretation of the results—and therefore did not accept the conclusion that the labor supply response was necessarily small.

A closely related issue involved the appropriate statistical representation of the experimental treatments. Some participants argued that the use of a dummy variable—in addition to tax and guarantee variables—to indicate whether a family was in the experiment or not may have been an unwise decision. They felt that much more work was needed on the proper representation of treatments so that more confidence could be placed in the behavioral effects of the tax rates as well as guarantees.[18]

Speaking in defense of the treatment dummy, one participant pointed out that if being in the experiment itself had some independent effect on behavior—and the subsequent significant coefficient on the treatment dummy seems to indicate as much—a major concern should be the marginal effects that the guarantee and the tax rate had beyond the effect of being in the program. Thus, he argued, the planners were correct in thinking that it would be better to use a treatment dummy to capture this independent effect than to leave it out and force all of the response through the tax rate and guarantee.

The author of the conference paper expressed some disappointment that the rural experiment, like its urban predecessor, failed to show—with any degree of statistical significance—differences in response among guarantee levels. He felt that the seemingly large coefficients for the tax rate and the rather small guarantee coefficients were indicative of the failure to capture these effects appropriately. He suspected this might have been due to the inclusion of the treatment dummy, or to not having used some other representation of the experimental treatments that would have captured the "right" (or at least a more "reasonable") response. As a result, Ashenfelter and several other conference participants questioned the validity and usefulness of the responses obtained in the rural experiment.

A number of conferees, however, took exception to this viewpoint. Their view was best summed up by one of the participants who felt that although being able to separate out income and substitution effects would

---

18. One conferee did note, however, that the analysts experimented with a number of different specifications of the treatment but reported only the results yielded by the one they believed best.

undoubtedly increase the usefulness of the results,[19] the labor supply results as a whole were of considerable value.

Program Costs

Another topic that received much discussion was the potential cost of a national program. Since one of the primary purposes of the rural experiment was to gain insight into the comparative costs for various types of negative income taxes, the conference participants attempted to focus on this objective in light of the results obtained from the experiment.

In discussing possible program costs, Ashenfelter pointed out that the labor supply figure in his analysis pertained to a program involving only families who were below the breakeven level. He noted that the inclusion of families both above and below breakeven would increase the total dollar cost of the program. This point is particularly instructive since it is possible that with a national program some families with earnings just above the breakeven point might reduce their labor supply and thus become eligible for the program, thereby increasing total program costs.

Following up this point, another participant noted that even the small labor supply responses found in the rural experiment may have significant cost implications for a national program because of the shape of the U.S. income distribution. The U.S. population has a high concentration of families near the breakeven point; these families receive relatively small transfer payments and even a very modest change in their earnings would result in a substantial percentage increase in their benefits and total program costs. This type of sensitivity of program costs to small changes in labor supply has been found in national simulations of the preliminary Seattle-Denver results and in some cross-sectional analyses.

A third participant thought the preoccupation of all the experiments with variations in the tax rate and guarantee might have been at the expense of other important variables in the design of a negative income tax program (for example, the definition of income, the income accounting period, the definition of the filing unit). Minor changes in these variables might exert a greater impact on total program costs. Further, he expressed concern that the narrow focus on these particular experimental treatments

19. According to the conferee, the separating out of income and substitution effects could be important for (1) distinguishing between transfer costs and real resource costs, (2) simulating the costs of programs that were not tested, and (3) simulating the costs of programs for populations other than the sample populations.

may have caused the Congress to be unresponsive to a thorough consideration of all of the elements involved in designing a national program.

In contrast, another conferee argued that it was precisely because of these experiments that so many individuals are now sensitized to the confounding nature of such design features. It was pointed out that the experiments have been extremely helpful in reducing the uncertainty of the expected labor supply response, thus enabling the policy analysts and policymakers to look to other issues. It was noted that the experiments did in fact yield considerable information on some of the other design features in question, which previously had been neglected.

Other Behavioral Responses

Although the primary focus of the rural experiment was on the labor supply response to the experimental treatments, it was thought that other information on consumption behavior (for example, purchases of housing, clothing, and medical care) and noneconomic outcomes (such as impacts on marital dissolution, migration, political participation, and psychological well-being) would provide added dimension to our understanding of the total impact of a negative income tax program. This additional information might aid in the overall planning of a national program as well as illuminate other costs and benefits of such a program.

The Consumption Studies

Robert Michael, the author of the conference paper evaluating the studies on consumption behavior, summarized the findings of these papers as follows: "The additional income and the income guarantee provided by the experiment improved average nutritional intake in the North Carolina sample (but not in Iowa where the levels were initially more nearly adequate), increased consumption of clothing (somewhat less for male than for female clothing), slightly increased household inventories of durable goods and cars (except for cars for farm households), and reduced short-term farm debt and increased farm liquid assets somewhat." Although some of the preceding results closely resemble those obtained in the New Jersey experiment[20] while others reveal more consistent patterns

20. Except those results pertaining to nutrition and clothing, which were not analyzed in the New Jersey experiment.

than in New Jersey, one important caveat is in order. The implications of
these observed consumption effects for a long-term income maintenance
program of similar structure depend, to a large extent, on whether the
experimental families regarded the payments they received as transitory
income or as a permanent component of their income stream—that is, if
the experimental payments were treated as permanent additions to family
income, the resulting changes in consumption patterns might serve as an
indication of the consumption behavior in a permanent national program.

Even though the studies on consumption behavior reported many interesting effects, Michael was somewhat disappointed in the papers' preoccupation with estimating the response to the experimental treatments
—the guarantee and payment. He suggested that more descriptive studies
were needed to gain insight into the expenditure behavior and mobility
patterns of those "in poverty." One conference participant cautioned that
in view of possible truncation of the sample, use of truncated data might
lead to biased results—studies purporting to describe the expenditure
patterns and poverty status of the low-income population might be grossly
misleading.

At various points during the conference, participants touched on specific technical (or estimation) problems and experimental design features
(such as small sample size, short duration, and availability of quality
data) that plagued a number of the consumption studies. Nonetheless, the
possible implications stemming from the results of the two studies concerning health effects and indebtedness received considerable attention.

Michael and several other conference participants were concerned that
the lack of positive effects on the health variables—the conference paper
reported *no* experimental effects—might be misconstrued. They feared
the inference might be drawn that giving money to poor people does not
improve their health and the further implication that the money was, instead, inappropriately spent by the treatment group. Pointing to such considerations as the relatively small sample size and the self-reporting problems, the concerned participants urged that the health results should be
interpreted with great care.

Another thorny issue concerned the appropriate interpretation of the
results on indebtedness. It was pointed out at the conference that three
sources (the overview paper by Larry Orr in this volume, the original
paper on this subject prepared by the rural experiment's analysts, and the
summary report by the U.S. Department of Health, Education, and Welfare) all report somewhat different results. For example, one suggests

loan debt substantially decreased while another indicates a substantial increase. After some discussion it was pointed out that these diverse findings could be reconciled since one source reports the long-run effect, another the short-run effect, and the third both effects. This still left unanswered the question of which results should be reported to the public at large. There was no consensus among the conference participants on this point.

One conferee observed that in spite of the many qualifications associated with the debt data from the urban, rural, and Gary experiments, one response seemed common to all three, namely, an increase in indebtedness on the part of the experimental families that was found to be tied quite explicitly to the acquisition of durable goods.

Noneconomic Outcomes

Michael Hannan's paper, which reviewed and evaluated the findings of the noneconomic outcomes of the rural experiment, reports the following results: higher overall incidence of marital dissolution among the treatment group as compared to the control group (though not statistically significant), with those on the most generous plan having lower rates (than the control group) and those on least generous plans having higher rates; a positive impact on geographic mobility (primarily in the North Carolina sample); improved performance for students in North Carolina with respect to absenteeism, comportment, academic grades, and standardized achievement test scores (with statistical significance for primary grade students); no significant overall effect on delinquency; positive treatment effect on voting and political participation (with significance only for married women); a small (and insignificant) overall treatment-control differential in the assessment of psychological well-being; and a narrowing of the occupational aspirations and expectations gap of teenagers.

To Hannan's and other conferees' surprise, many of the noneconomic outcomes in the rural experiment had positive treatment effects. However, most participants seemed to regard them as tenuous. They cited as their source of skepticism the various confounding features such as small sample size, too short a time span, low reliability of sociological and psychological variables, sample attrition, low understanding on the part of the treatment group, and the lack of well-defined theory governing the social and psychological effects studied. In fact, Hannan suggested that the studies might be best viewed as "exploratory." One conferee, on the other hand, aptly summed up the sentiments of many participants by stating that the rural experiment was poorly designed for the comprehensive study of sociological effects of a negative income tax.

One topic that received some attention and on which there were differing perceptions, concerned the culture of poverty theory—and what the experimental evidence suggested about poverty cycles. As Hannan pointed out, "whether or not the culture of poverty is an important causal factor in the persistence of poverty depends on whether or not individuals can shift living styles once the culture becomes maladaptive." He further noted that "if adults are indeed trapped by their origins, they cannot respond to environmental changes such as that afforded by income maintenance." Since the rural experiment allowed the income environments of families to be manipulated, Hannan felt the experiment offered a unique opportunity to "separate effects of culture and class from those of current variations in employment or income." During the conference discussion, Hannan indicated that a strong reading of the culture of poverty argument suggests that no experimental effects would occur on any of the noneconomic outcomes either singularly or collectively. Whether or not the results of the experiment were inconsistent with that view depends upon how one reads the evidence. On this score, the participants were unable to reach an accord.

Hannan's reading of the results—although considered overly optimistic by some—led him to believe that there was evidence of a mild rebuff to the culture of poverty thesis. Aage Sørensen—a sociologist as is Hannan—took an opposing viewpoint. He emphasized the need to observe possible changes in the relevant noneconomic variables over several generations before assessing whether the culture of poverty thesis still holds.

Overview and Policy Implications

With the papers by Larry L. Orr, G. Edward Schuh, and D. Lee Bawden and William S. Harrar as background, the conference participants were charged with the task of making a critical assessment of the overall significance of the rural experiment and to suggest possible policy implications.

By and large, the conferees tended to fall into one of two camps as far as their general impressions of the experiment were concerned. One group viewed the experiment as providing valuable information on the labor supply response of rural families to a negative income tax and pinpointing some of the difficulties involved in administering such a program to the self-employed.

Members of the other group, while acknowledging the insight gained in administrative issues and the implications of the experiment for future social experimentation, nonetheless took a more cautious approach. Their major sources of skepticism stemmed from the problematic experimental design features and the statistical techniques used in some of the analyses.

In spite of the methodological and empirical difficulties encountered in the rural experiment, some participants thought a number of noteworthy outcomes were obtained that had immediate policy relevance. Apart from the obvious interest in the work response of welfare recipients to governmental transfer schemes, a growing concern among policymakers is the denigrating effects associated with most public assistance programs. On this score, it was suggested in the paper by Schuh that one policy implication that might be drawn from the rural experiment results was that although "there was no evidence of an experimental effect on psychological well-being, there was also no evidence that the income maintenance program undermined self-respect or brought a reduction in self-esteem."

Another outcome that was regarded as having possible far-reaching effects from a policy standpoint was the experimental impact on political behavior. While the findings of the rural experiments indicated only a modest increase—5 to 10 percent—in the voting probabilities of those in experimental groups, Schuh suggests that this effect may considerably understate the potential impact since "the stakes of the program were relatively modest." He contends that "if the size of the income transfers were larger, there might be more substantial political participation to protect the income base, or to enlarge it." One conferee speculated that the possible fear among incumbent politicians of a *large* political impact might partially account for the difficulties being experienced by the negative income tax concept in the Congress.

A closely related issue involved the overall impact of a national program on rural towns and communities. Several participants expressed concern that the macro impact of a universal program on the social, economic, and political structure of small towns—especially in the Southeast —is very likely to generate unpredictable behavioral and structural changes that could significantly affect, inter alia, (local) labor markets, political awareness, and demographic shifts.

Commenting on the possible impact on labor markets, one conferee noted that the observed reduction in labor supply in a dispersed experiment may not be translated into an equal reduction in aggregate output. This might occur—given less than full employment—when marginal workers, responding to a negative income tax, reduce their labor supply (either partially or totally) and are replaced by others (on a part-time or full-time basis) who were nonrecipients. Since the total number of workhours might remain approximately the same, aggregate output might show little change. Consequently, the impact might simply result in a reshuffling of unemployment with virtually no change in aggregate output.

Some participants thought that a universal program might improve the functioning of labor markets by providing recipients with the opportunity of increased job search and occupational mobility. They felt that the support payments might serve as an income cushion that could be used to defray the opportunity costs incurred when making beneficial job changes or engaging in more productive job searches. While the results from the rural experiment varied from one treatment plan to another, a standard experimental plan (50 percent tax rate and guarantee of 75 percent of poverty level) did result in members of experimental groups locating jobs with higher wages, presumably through longer job search. In addition to possible improvements from job search, Schuh points out that "another possible outcome is that income transfers may be viewed as earning subsidies, increasing the job stability of some workers or supplementing income from jobs with good earnings prospects but low initial wages." Thus, it was concluded that although an income maintenance program, such as a negative income tax, might generate some adverse labor market effects, there are some positive outcomes affecting the job environment through more rewarding search methods that should not be overlooked.

After some discussion of the uncertainties surrounding the nature and extent of the impact of a national program on rural communities, a number of conferees were prompted to suggest that a saturation experiment— preferably in a small southeastern town—might be one possible strategy for gaining insight into the potential outcomes.

At one point in the discussion there was some concern over whether a 10–12 percent reduction in family labor supply should be regarded as large or small. Some participants argued that the labor supply response should be considered small in light of popular concern over a large-scale withdrawal from the labor force by recipients. Other conferees were much less inclined to look upon the labor supply numbers as small. Their view was best summed up by one participant who remarked that he did not regard 10–12 percent as zero. According to him, zero is a very significant political number. It was further noted by this group that the long-term effects as yet are unknown. Thus, the long-term response might be larger than the 10–12 percent obtained from the short-term experiments.

It was noted, however, that although the farm labor supply response was of central importance in the rural experiment, there are relatively few low-income, nonaged farmers in the United States. Thus, their labor supply responses—whether very large or very small—would make little difference in either the national costs of a negative income tax program or in the agricultural sector of the economy. The rural nonfarm work responses, on the other hand, were considered far more important from the standpoint of a national program and were roughly consistent with the results of the New Jersey experiment.

The two days of discussion indicated that there was disagreement over the usefulness of the farm work and income responses for estimating the effects in a national program, but that the work and income responses of rural nonfarmers were viewed as useful additions to the New Jersey and cross-sectional findings for the estimation of the possible effects of a universal program. In addition most conferees generally agreed that much was learned about the administration of an income maintenance program to the rural self-employed. Some participants, in fact, argued that the rural experiment was most instructive in pinpointing and assessing the nature as well as the relative magnitude of some of the problematic areas—such as the definition of income, and the administrative and reporting procedures governing the potential underreporting and misreporting of income and assets by the self-employed—that could be expected to accompany a universal program. As Welch concludes in his paper, "when dealing with social experiments or longer-run welfare programs, it really matters how these programs are administered—more so than many of us would have suspected."

Even though the conference participants differed in their perceptions of the validity of the findings in the rural experiment, there was widespread agreement that any results reported to the public should be done with the appropriate qualifications and without bias.

Conference Participants

with their affiliations at the time of the conference

Orley Ashenfelter *Princeton University*

Michael C. Barth *U.S. Department of Health, Education, and Welfare*

D. Lee Bawden *Urban Institute*

James T. Bonnen *Michigan State University*

Michael J. Boskin *Stanford University*

W. Keith Bryant *Cornell University*

Irwin Garfinkel *University of Wisconsin*

Michael T. Hannan *Stanford University*

William S. Harrar *Mincome Manitoba*

James J. Heckman *University of Chicago*

Robinson G. Hollister *Swarthmore College*

Kenneth Kehrer *Mathematica Policy Research, Inc.*

Stuart H. Kerachsky *Mathematica Policy Research, Inc.*

David N. Kershaw *Mathematica Policy Research, Inc.*

Mordecai Kurz *Stanford University*

Robert J. Lampman *University of Wisconsin*

Stanley H. Masters *University of Wisconsin*

Charles E. Metcalf *Mathematica Policy Research, Inc.*

Robert T. Michael *National Bureau of Economic Research (Stanford)*

Russell Middleton *University of Wisconsin*

Larry L. Orr *U.S. Department of Health, Education, and Welfare*

John L. Palmer *Brookings Institution*

Joseph A. Pechman *Brookings Institution*

John H. Pencavel *Stanford University*

G. Edward Schuh *Purdue University*

Aage B. Sørensen *University of Wisconsin*

Robert G. Spiegelman *Stanford Research Institute*

Marvin M. Smith *Brookings Institution*

Ernst W. Stromsdorfer *U.S. Department of Labor*

Luther G. Tweeten *Oklahoma State University*

Harold W. Watts *Columbia University*

Finis Welch *RAND Corporation*

Index

Aaron, Henry J., 6n, 57n, 120n, 244n, 256n

Accounting, 20, 108; accrual, 42–43, 77, 89; for assets, 44–45, 252; cash, 42–43, 77, 87, 92, 106, 251; period, 45; problems of, 251–53

Administration of income maintenance programs, 100; accounting rules, 20, 36, 42–45, 47–49; importance, 265; income defined for, 35–36, 40, 42, 50–51; policy implications, 228–29; reporting requirements, 36, 38–41, 49–50

Age, 4; behavioral responses by, 10; of sample family heads, 32

Agriculture: economic characteristics, 237–38; employment stability, 215; and income maintenance, 238–39; poverty, 211–12. *See also* Farm income

Agriculture, Department of, 77, 150n, 158n, 239n

Aid to families with dependent children–unemployed parents (AFDC-UP), 6, 57; and urban experiment, 66, 244, 245

Alexander, Donald C., 49n

Allen, Jodie T., 46n, 47n

Allen, Vernon L., 201n

Allingham, Michael G., 137

Amemiya, Takeshi, 175

Ashenfelter, Orley, 52, 101, 109, 119n, 126n, 256

Assets: accumulation, 221–22; double taxation, 87–88, 91, 106; and income maintenance, 14–15, 159–62, 164, 170–71, 179–82, 259; misreporting, 20, 21, 39, 229; of self-employed, 44–45

Banfield, Edward C., 185

Barr, N. A., 115

Bawden, D. Lee, 6n, 7n, 23, 47n, 53, 78n, 87n, 94n, 109n, 114, 120, 149n, 175n, 184n, 213n, 230, 233, 243, 246, 254, 262

Becker, Gary S., 191n

Beebout, Harold, 46n

Behavioral responses, 6–19; methods of measuring, 130–31; tax rates and, 96–97, 104, 107–08

Benefits, income maintenance, 36; based on preenrollment income, 112–13, 126, 132; boundary, 82–83, 97; computation, 80–83; and labor supply, 112, 114–15; regulations governing, 37–41

Blacks: assets and debts of, 160–61; marital dissolution, 163; net worth, 222; in samples, 31, 65

Bonner, James T., 236

Boskin, Michael J., 100, 147

Boundary benefits, 82–83, 97

Bryant, W. Keith, 14n, 149n, 158n, 161, 162n, 169, 175n, 181, 222n

Bureau of Labor Statistics, 150n

Bureau of the Census, 248–49

Butler, Richard, 213n

Cain, Glen G., 6n, 119n, 127n, 134n

Capital: conventional, 221–23, 240; human, 223–26, 233, 234, 240, 241

Capital gains, 43, 64

Chamberlain, G., 145n

Clothing expenditures, 159–60, 169–70, 259

Cogan, John, 81

Conlisk, John, 28n, 245n

Conlisk-Watts allocation model, 28–29, 52, 245

Consumer durables, 14; accumulation, 222; household holdings, 159–62, 164, 170–71; marginal propensity to consume, 161–62, 181; in New Jersey

269

experiment, 179–80; ownership, 150–51

Consumption responses, 13–15; evaluation, 162–64, 171, 173–74, 259–61; explanation, 149–50; and future programs, 172–73; to price changes, 154–55, 156; from raising income, 153–54, 156; from reducing income variance, 155, 156; by source of income, 152

Coppedge, Robert O., 212n

Cost-benefit analysis, 234–35

Costs: of income maintenance programs, 70, 112–14, 207, 258; of social experimentation, 67, 76; transfer, 130, 133

Crawford, David L., 18n, 195, 225n

Cross-section studies, 117–19, 124, 265

Davis, Carlton G., 212n

Debts: household, 159–62, 164, 170–71; and income maintenance, 14–15, 150, 259, 261; in New Jersey experiment, 179–80

Delinquency, 18, 188, 197–99, 261

Dennis, Barbara D., 52n

Depreciation, 20, 43–44

Double taxation, 87–88, 106

Duncan, Otis Dudley, 186

Durables. *See* Consumer durables

Education, 4, 175; family heads, 32, 39; and income maintenance, 225–26; and labor supply, 143–44

Employment. *See* Work effort

Ethnic responses, 65, 69, 227

Evans, Lewis T., 10n, 13n

Fair, Jerilyn, 50n

Family: income responses, 9–10, 119–20, 130; marital stability, 17–18, 34, 83, 163; multiple jobs, 214, 217–18; net worth, 222; participating in program, 111–12, 134, 135; preenrollment income, 110–11, 122–23; program eligibility, 57, 248–49; questionnaires, 38–41; rural versus urban, 3, 59–61; size, 4, 20, 39, 65; unit for income payments, 36, 49–50; utility function, 131–33; work response, 9–10, 129, 255

Farmers: assets and debts, 15, 44, 88, 171, 221, 229; hours worked, 12–13, 78–79, 105; income response, 10–13; labor supply response, 78–79, 84–85, 249–53, 254–55; multiple jobs, 214; work response, 10–13, 21, 214, 255

Farm income, 10–11; accounting methods, 42–44; alternative ways of measuring, 92–93; fluctuations, 88–90; underreporting, 11, 20, 39–41, 80, 93, 94, 99, 106, 116–17, 229, 253–54

Fender, Lynne, 10n

Food and Nutrition Board, National Research Council, 193

Food stamps, 164, 174

Friedman, Milton, 152n

Garber, Steve G., 6n

Garfinkel, Irwin, 68, 71

Gary experiment, 26, 50n, 182

Geographic mobility, 7, 17, 188, 194, 218–19, 226, 240, 259, 261

Goldman, Fred, 168n

Greenberg, David H., 134

Groeneveld, Lyle P., 190n, 191n

Grossman, Michael, 168n

Guaranteed income levels, 7, 9, 16–17, 29–30; behavioral response, 107, 110–12, 125–29; employment disincentives and, 220–21; explanation, 3; proposed alternatives, 56, 57, 71, 244; range, 3, 57

Haas, Ain, 18n, 197, 198, 199, 203

Haas, Linda, 17n, 18n, 163, 189, 192, 203, 227

Hager, Christine J., 14n, 149n, 158n, 161, 162n, 169, 175n, 181, 222n

Hall, Robert E., 62n, 115, 124, 134, 147

Hannan, Michael T., 183, 190n, 191, 207, 208, 210, 227, 228, 261, 262

Harper, Wilmer, 105

Harrar, William S., 6n, 10n, 20n, 23, 53, 78n, 87n, 94, 95, 109n, 149n, 175n, 184n, 213n, 254, 262

Hathaway, Dale E., 238n

Hauseman, Jerry A., 72, 175n, 246

Heads of household, 2, 3; education, 32; nonaged female, 28, 30, 59, 60, 65; nonaged male, 28, 29, 59; occupation, 32; older, 28, 30, 59

Health care: and income maintenance, 166–68, 174, 179, 224–25, 226, 260; and nutrition, 207

Health, Education, and Welfare, Department of, 8n, 27, 49, 77, 150n, 165n, 223n, 260

Heckman, James J., 126n, 127n, 138, 143n, 147, 231n

Heffernan, Joseph, 19n, 200, 227

Hershey, Alan M., 49n

Hollister, Robinson G., 47n, 173, 247n

Hours of work: farm versus wage, 85, 105; and income maintenance, 11–12, 21, 78–79

Housing: and income maintenance, 14, 168–69, 178–79, 223; in-kind program for, 174; rent-free, 20, 44, 64

Houthakker, H. S., 152n

Husbands: income response, 9, 10, 21, 123–24, 128, 130; labor supply elasticity, 118–19; work response, 9, 10, 21, 213, 216

Income: and labor supply, 84, 101, 112, 114, 118; preenrollment, 110–11; reducing variance, 155, 156; response to experiments, 10–13, 21, 96–98, 121–24, 130; self-employed, 42–44, 66–67; temporary versus permanent sources, 131, 152, 153, 154. *See also* Farm income; Guaranteed income levels; Wage income

Income maintenance experiment. *See* Rural experiment; Urban experiment

Income maintenance payments. *See* Benefits, income maintenance

Income maintenance program: alternatives to, 210, 220; cost, 70, 112–14, 130, 133, 207, 258; general equilibrium effects, 230–33, 235; national, 246, 253, 263; purpose, 70; temporary versus permanent, 135–37. *See also* Rural experiment; Urban experiment

Internal Revenue Service, 20, 42–44, 64, 96, 253

Interviews (rural experiment), 4, 30–31, 38, 74

Inventory: farm, 91, 93–94; household, 259

Job search and turnover, 7, 16, 17, 210, 219–20, 240, 264

Johnson, Aaron C., Jr., 14n, 17n, 149n, 168, 194, 218, 219n, 223n

Johnston, Bruce F., 212n

Kastman, Brian, 10n

Keeley, Michael C., 54n, 145n

Kerachsky, Stuart H., 11n, 14n, 78, 79n, 105, 149n, 166, 179, 225

Kershaw, David N., 46, 47n, 50n

Killingsworth, Mark R., 133n

Knudsen, Jon Helge, 190n

Kosters, Marvin, 134

Labor supply, 147–48; elasticity, 111; farmers' response, 78–79, 84–85, 87,

99, 254–55; general equilibrium, 230–33; heterogeneity of behavior, 65; income effects, 84, 101, 112, 114, 117–18; and income maintenance, 87, 90–91, 99, 100, 101–04, 106, 131; intersectoral adjustments, 217–18; life cycle model, 139–43; response by demographic groups, 143–45; in rural experiment, 121–22, 124, 125, 143; schedules, 70, 71; in urban experiment, 119–20, 143; wage effects, 84, 101, 102, 110–12, 117–18, 121, 130–33, 255–56

Lampman, Robert, 46, 206

Lefcowitz, Myron J., 47n, 247n

Levy, Frank, 151n

Lewis, Oscar, 185, 186

Life cycle theory, 139–43

Lillard, Lee A., 151n

McCall, John J., 151n

Madden, J. Patrick, 13n, 149n, 165, 184n, 192, 224

Mahoney, Bette S., 216, 235

Mahoney, W. Michael, 216, 235

MAR. *See* Mean adequacy ratio

Marginal propensity to consume: clothing, 158; durables, 160–62; long-run, 181; nonmarket time, 126

Marital stability: experimental effects on, 17–18, 34, 83, 163, 187, 189–92, 204, 205, 206, 227, 261; and school performance, 207

Masters, Stanley H., 171

Maynard, Rebecca, 18n, 195, 225n

Mean adequacy ratio (MAR), 13, 158n, 165–66

Medical care. *See* Health care

Medicare and medicaid programs, 230

Metcalf, Charles E., 28n, 71, 101, 136n, 140, 143n, 156n, 171, 176, 177, 180n, 181, 245n, 254n

Michael, Robert T., 149, 153n, 259, 260

Middleton, Russell, 17n, 18n, 163, 187, 189, 192, 197, 198, 199, 201, 202, 203, 204, 226, 227

Migration. *See* Geographic mobility

Miller, Robert E., 219n

Minarik, Joseph J., 249n

Mobility. *See* Geographic mobility

Morris, J. Jeffrey, 49n

Moynihan, Daniel P., 185n

Negative income tax. *See* Income maintenance program

New Jersey experiment, 1, 2, 6, 23, 50n,

81, 110, 119, 150n, 265; analysis of
durables, 179–80, 182; analysis of
housing, 179; consumption effects,
259–60; duration, 177; guaranteed income levels, 57; interviews, 74; and
labor supply, 101, 176; and marital
stability, 190n; sample size, 26, 29,
73–74; and welfare programs, 66, 245
Newman, Edwin, 71
Nicholson, Walter, 178n, 180n
Nutrient adequacy ratios, 165
Nutrition: experimental effects on, 13–
14, 21, 157–58, 164, 165–66, 174, 178,
187, 192–94, 204, 209, 224, 226, 259;
health care and, 207; poverty and, 151

Occupation. *See* Job search and turnover
O'Connor, J. Frank, 13n, 149n, 165,
184n, 192, 193, 224
Office of Economic Opportunity, 2, 27,
28, 55, 59, 60
Orr, Larry L., 1, 47n, 52n, 247n, 260,
262

Pechman, Joseph A., 1n, 6n, 57n, 62n,
110n, 213n, 243n, 244n, 256n
Pennsylvania experiment, 110, 119
Political behavior: experimental effects
on, 19, 188, 199–201, 207, 227–28,
261; social experimentation and, 67
Population: density, 24; rural poverty, 5
Poverty: culture of, 185–86, 204, 210,
262; cycle, 184; definition, 151; ex-
periments' criteria for, 63–64, 69; ex-
tent, 26; rural, 5, 211–12
Prais, S. J., 152n
Price effects of income maintenance,
154–55
Price efficiency, 13
Primus, Wendell E., 12n, 78, 95, 96,
214n, 229
Prindle, Allen M., 13n, 149n, 165, 184n,
192, 224
Psychological well-being, 7, 21, 188–89,
201–02, 207, 226, 261, 263
Public employment program, 210, 220
Puerto Ricans, 64, 69, 74

Race: asset and debt holdings, 15; site
selection and, 24; work responses, 8,
10
Rees, Albert, 28n, 101n, 120, 176n,
178n, 190n, 201n, 245n, 254n, 256n
Regional variations, 53–54
Rowlatt, J. Donald, 115
Rural development, 39–41

Rural experiment, 3–5; accounting
period, 45, 47–49; alternative plans,
56–57, 68, 71–72; budget, 99; compared with urban experiment, 100–03;
data, 91–92; definition of income, 35–
36, 42–44, 50–51, 64, 66, 74, 79–80;
duration, 72–73, 247–48; eligibility,
32, 63–64, 69, 248–49; extrapolation
of results, 54; family unit, 36, 49–50;
income response, 10–13, 21, 96–98,
121–24, 130; purpose, 23; sites, 5, 24–
26; substitution effects, 78, 100, 101,
102, 112, 177. *See also* Administration of income maintenance programs;
Benefits, income maintenance; Samples

Samples: censoring, 175–76; demographic characteristics, 59–61; heterogeneity, 53, 65–66, 73; merging,
53–54; national approach, 58–59, 68;
saturation, 57–58, 73; scattered, 56,
57, 246; selection, 28–31, 73, 246–47;
size, 26–28, 52, 75, 101, 147, 209;
truncation, 65, 148, 245, 246; variations, 31–32, 34
Sandmo, Agnar, 137
Saupe, William E., 12n
Schiller, Bradley R., 151n
School performance: experimental effects on, 18–19, 21, 188, 195–97, 209,
225; marital stability and, 207
Schreier, Jeanette, 87n
Schuh, G. Edward, 207, 211, 212n, 262,
264
Scott, Robert A., 190n
Seattle-Denver experiment: consumption data, 176, 182; cost, 258; duration, 6, 72, 248; and marital stability,
190n, 209; sample, 27, 53
SED factors. *See* Socioeconomic-demo-
graphic factors
Self-employed, 2; compared with wage
earners, 229; income, 42–44, 66–67;
labor supply response, 213, 214; rules
for defining, 20; in Southeast, 231;
underreporting of income, 100, 229
Shore, Arnold R., 190n
Shultz, George P., 49n
Sites, experiment, 3, 5, 24–26
Smith, Marvin M., 243
Social experimentation, 55, 235; cost, 67;
evaluation, 76; model formulation,
146–47; political influence, 67
Socioeconomic-demographic   factors
(SED), 24–26

Socioeconomic status, 186; and marital stability, 189; and political behavior, 199; and school performance, 195
Sørenson, Aage B., 208, 262
Spiegelman, Robert G., 52
Stern, James L., 52n
Subsidy. *See* Benefits, income maintenance
Substitution effects, 78, 100, 101, 102, 112, 117–18

Tax evasion, 116, 137–38, 256–57
Tax rate for income maintenance, 7, 9–10, 16–17; accounting period, 47–49; alternative treatments, 56, 57, 71, 244; behavioral responses, 96–98, 107–08, 125–29, 233; employment disincentives and, 220–21; explanation, 3; marginal, 80, 89, 103, 232; policy weights assigned to, 29, 57; range, 3, 57; versus effective tax rate, 115
Technical efficiency, 13
Timpane, P. Michael, 1n, 6n, 57n, 62n, 110n, 213n, 243n, 244n, 256n
Transfer costs, 130, 133
Transfers-in-kind, 164, 174
Tuma, Nancy B., 190n, 191n
Tweeten, Luther G., 16n, 104, 219n, 220n, 255

Unemployment, effects of experiment on, 16, 264
United States Employment Service, 17
Urban experiment: compared with rural experiment, 100–03; duration, 72–73, 247–48; eligibility, 63, 69, 248; family characteristics, 59, 60, 65; income definition, 66, 74–75; and labor supply, 119–20, 124, 143, 256; tax rate, 216, 233; transfer cost, 130. *See also* Gary experiment; New Jersey experiment; Pennsylvania experiment; Seattle-Denver experiment

Wage earners: assets and debts, 15; compared with self-employed, 229; hours worked, 12–13; income response, 7–10, 21, 122–23, 126–29, 130; labor supply response, 131–37, 255–56; rural versus urban, 213–14; work response, 7–10, 129, 139, 213
Wage income: experimental effects on, 110, 117, 123–24; labor saving technology and, 232; labor supply response, 121–24; regional differences, 231; reported, 95, 117; urban experiment, 119–20
Watts, Harold W., 28n, 101n, 119, 120, 127n, 134n, 176n, 178n, 190n, 201n, 243, 245n, 246, 254n, 256n
Welch, Finis, 46, 48, 144n, 148, 249–53, 265
Williams, Robert G., 49n, 115
Willis, Robert J., 151n
Wise, David A., 72, 175n, 246
Wives: income response, 9, 10, 21, 123–24, 128–29, 136; labor supply elasticity, 118–19; work response, 9, 10, 21, 213–14, 216
Wooldridge, Judith, 178n
Work effort: disincentives, 213–14, 220–21, 235–36; experimental effects on, 7–13, 21, 23, 110–12, 129, 139

ABSOLUTE NOTHINGNESS

Foundations for a Buddhist-Christian Dialogue

by
Hans Waldenfels

translated by
J. W. Heisig

PAULIST PRESS
New York/Ramsey

Library of Congress
Catalog Card Number: 80-81442

ISBN: 0-8091-2316-9

Published by Paulist Press
*Editorial Office:*1865 Broadway, New York, N.Y. 10023
Business Office: 545 Island Road, Ramsey, N.J. 07446

Printed and bound in the
United States of America